Dyslexia, the self and higher education:
learning life histories of students
identified as dyslexic

Dyslexia, the self and higher education:
learning life histories of students identified as dyslexic

David Pollak

Trentham Books

Stoke on Trent, UK and Sterling, USA

Trentham Books Limited

Westview House	22883 Quicksilver Drive
734 London Road	Sterling
Oakhill	VA 20166-2012
Stoke on Trent	USA
Staffordshire	
England ST4 5NP	

First published 2005

British Library Cataloguing-in-Publication Data
A catalogue record for this book is available from the British Library

Cover illustration by Mercedes Arijón-Barazal who was assessed as
dyslexic in her second year at Manchester Metropolitan University, and
went on to obtain a First.

ISBN-13: 978-1-85856-360-2
ISBN-10: 1-85856-360-7

Designed and typeset by Trentham Print Design Ltd, Chester and printed
in Great Britain by Bemrose Press Ltd, Chester.

To my parents, Olwen and Tony Pollak, who have always
supported my endeavours

Contents

Tables

Figures

Vignettes

Acknowledgements

My first acknowledgement must go to the informants of the research set out in this book, who spoke so frankly during their interviews and in subsequent telephone conversations, letters and emails. I hope I have given a true picture of what they told me and that I have not offended anyone.

Particular acknowledgement of course goes to my research supervisors, Professor Mary Hamilton of Lancaster University, UK, and Dr John Kearsey, late of De Montfort University, UK, for their expert guidance, direction and encouragement. Without their support, this work would never have been completed.

I would like to thank John McKeown, Chartered Psychologist of Brighton, who not only stimulated me to begin research at the time of my MA but was also indirectly responsible for my move into Higher Education. Gratitude is also due to Dr Roz Ivanic (University of Lancaster), who introduced me to dyslexia 30 years ago and has been an inspiring friend and colleague, and to Professor Barry Cooper (University of Durham), who was my original supervisor when he was at the University of Sussex.

These acknowledgements must also include Michael Flijanis, a psychotherapist and colleague; my good friend Dr Robert Young, late of the University of Sussex, who cast a journal editor's eye over some of my writing; and Frank Swift, Head of Student Learning Advisory Service at De Montfort University Leicester UK, who has supported my work over the last seven years.

Abbreviations

ADA	Americans with Disabilities Act
APA	Accreditation of prior achievement
APEL	Accreditation of prior experiential learning
APL	Accreditation of prior learning
BDA	British Dyslexia Association
BMA	British Medical Association
BMJ	British Medical Journal
BPS	British Psychological Society
BTEC	Business and Technology Education Council (now a 'brand name' only)
CLA	critical language awareness
CSE	Certificate of Secondary Education
DI	Dyslexia Institute
DDA	Disability Discrimination Act
DES	Department of Education and Science
DfE	Department for Education
DfEE	Department for Education and Employment
DfES	Department for Education and Science
DSA	Disabled Students' Allowance
EP	Educational Psychologist
FE	Further Education
GCE	General Certificate of Education
GCSE	General Certificate of Secondary Education
GUT	grand unifying theory
HE	Higher Education
HEFCE	Higher Education Funding Council for England

HEI	Higher Education Institution
HMSO	Her Majesty's Stationery Office
HNC	Higher National Certificate
HND	Higher National Diploma
IDA	International Dyslexia Association
ICT	Information and Communication technology
IQ	Intelligence Quotient
LCC	London County Council
LEA	Local Education Authority
MRI	magnetic resonance imaging
NUD.IST	non-numerical unstructured data indexing searching and theorising
NWP	National Working Party on Dyslexia in Higher Education
OHT	overhead transparency
ONC	Ordinary National Certificate
OND	Ordinary National Diploma
PC	personal computer
PCAS	Polytechnics' Central Admissions Service
PET	positron emission tomography
PGCE	Postgraduate Certificate in Education
REHAB	British Council for the Rehabilitation of the Disabled
SAT	(USA) Scholastic Aptitude Test
SENDA	Special Educational Needs and Disability Act
SpLD	specific learning difficulties
STM	short-term memory
TOE	theory of everything
UCCA	Universities' Central Council for Admissions
UCAS	Universities and Colleges Admissions Service
UK	United Kingdom
US	United States of America
WAIS	Wechsler Adult Intelligence Scale
WFN	World Federation of Neurology
WISC	Wechsler Intelligence Scale for Children
WRAT	Wide Range Achievement Test

Preface

This Preface has been set out with the text aligned to the left only. Although the tradition for academic books is justified text, this causes the words to be slightly unevenly spaced; for that reason, many dyslexic people prefer left-alignment. This book has also been set in a sans serif font, as most dyslexic people find that easier to read. Meares-Irlen Syndrome, which causes a range of visual disturbances when the text is black and the page white, is also experienced by many dyslexic people; hence the cream paper used in this book.

I discovered the existence of dyslexia in 1973. Arriving, unqualified, at a rural residential girls' school to teach French and Latin, I found that many of the students had particular difficulties with English. It was explained to me that they had been diagnosed as having a condition known as dyslexia. Reading the current literature on the subject (Critchley, 1970; Miles, 1970; Naidoo, 1972; Newton and Thomson, 1974), I viewed dyslexia as 'a disability which requires special understanding' (Miles, 1970:vi).

The special study I completed at the end of my Postgraduate Certificate in Education (PGCE) (Pollak, 1975) concluded with the words of Critchley, who held that dyslexic children should be

> ... diagnosed at an early age, and ... granted without delay the services of special remedial teaching at the hands of sympathetic experts (Critchley, 1970:121).

This view was not without its critics (see Chapter 1), but as a modern languages graduate with an interest in social work, I was drawn to what was then known as remedial teaching, which combined a focus on language with a group described as disadvantaged and potentially the victim of prejudice.

In the 1980s, having set up my metaphorical brass plate and become a private tutor of dyslexic children, I took a Diploma at the Hornsby Dyslexia Centre in London and continued to believe that 'dyslexics' brain cells may be arranged differently from those who have no difficulty with reading and writing' (sic) (Hornsby, 1984:15). Much of the dyslexia literature of the 1980s tended to confirm this view (Wales, 1982; Snowling, 1985; Pavlidis, 1986; Seymour, 1986; Congdon, 1989; Galaburda, 1989). It was not until the 1990s that British literature paid any significant attention to the affective and social aspects of life in educational institutions for students labelled dyslexic; in the USA, the earlier versions of Rawson's (1995) unique 55 year study had appeared in 1968 and 1978.

In the UK, a lead in that direction was provided by Pumfrey and Reason (1991), who reported on a national inquiry initiated by the Division of Educational and Child Psychology of the British Psychological Society, covering 'educational, psychological and medical aspects of specific learning difficulties' (the latter term having meanwhile become prominent). They included a chapter on social and emotional aspects, and made the following statements:

> Recent British cognitive research into SpLD (dyslexia) seems remarkably devoid of mention of social and emotional factors.

> (...) A clearer understanding of these social and emotional influences and ways in which their effects can be alleviated, or turned to advantage, is needed (Pumfrey and Reason, 1991:66).

My subsequent Master's work (Pollak, 1993) was in part a response to Pumfrey and Reason's recommendation. I was by then working at a small residential special school for dyslexic teenagers. Once they were so labelled they became weekly boarders – residential students – outside their Local Education Authorities' areas. The school saw its primary tasks as overcoming students' feelings of helplessness in the face of their difficulties, and counteracting the effect of previous negative experiences of schooling. The value of the dyslexia concept and the negative impact of being labelled as in some way defective were not questioned; on the other hand, the school took the affective and social aspects of dyslexia into account as well as the cognitive ones.

Using a self-esteem inventory (Coopersmith, 1981) and personal construct psychology (Kelly, 1955), I investigated changes in the students' self-esteem, the constructs of staff about the students, and students' constructs about their learning difficulties. This project showed (by repeating the inventory) that students' self-esteem improved markedly by the end of their first year at the school, as their attitudes to dyslexia changed. By tape recording staff development work (in which colleagues' attitudes to students were compared, and contrasted with those students' self-images), and by recording their feedback on the sessions, it was shown that the research had been valuable both in deepening awareness of inter-personal factors and in challenging perceptions staff had of some students (Pollak, 1993).

The study reported in this book continues and expands on those themes. I moved into learning support work in higher education at a time, 1995, when the number of students in UK higher education (HE) was increasing (Singleton, 1999), and more and more of them were being identified as dyslexic (Gilroy, 1995). It may seem obvious that undergraduates' self-concept is likely to have a direct effect on their academic and social success, but at the time I began my research, there was little literature on this (Miles and Gilroy, 1986; Pumfrey and Reason, 1991; Hetherington, 1996; Goodwin, 1996). I did however take with me into higher education work the conviction that in one-to-one teaching or learning support, the quality of the relationship with the student is as important as the academic content (Miles and Miles, 1975; Edwards, 1994). It was partly with this in mind that I undertook counselling training in the 1990s.

The 1990s brought new approaches to dyslexia (West, 1991; Davis, 1995). As adults, HE students tend to be articulate about the way they cope with the demands of University study, and I began to learn from those I was supporting. Although I still believed in the existence of dyslexia, I began to see the validity of the 'difference' as opposed to the 'disability' model (Cairns and Moss, 1995). While she holds that, in respect of dyslexia, 'the diagnosis is clinical', Rawson (1988:5) also states that 'the differences are personal'. She adds:

> The student will progress faster and more securely if he understands his own nature and the relationship between his makeup and the way he is being taught. (*ibid*, 217)

It became increasingly clear to me not only that this was true, but also that the ways in which students understood their 'own nature' varied widely and were worthy of investigation.

Through email discussion forums, I then became aware of the social model of disability (Oliver, 1988; Oliver, 1996), which in turn led me to the concept of the social construction of special educational needs (Barton and Tomlinson, 1981; Tomlinson, 1982; Barton, 1988). Reading about adult education (Fieldhouse, 1996) I came upon an alternative view of special education, emanating from the perspective of Adult Basic Education (Hamilton, 1996). Hamilton writes of 'the medical disability model of dyslexia' (*ibid*, 161). I also discovered the concept of situated literacies and the social nature of literacy practices (Barton and Ivanic, 1991; Barton, 1994) (see Chapter 9). My earlier certainties as to the nature of dyslexia began to disappear. Reading and writing are culturally esteemed skills; if a person's ability to draw is extremely poor, why do we not label this 'dyspictoria'? (Edwards, 1993).

In the 1990s, dyslexia's prominence as an issue for HE grew (Gilroy, 1991; Goodwin and Thomson, 1991; Cairns and Moss, 1995; Stephens, 1996). It has been asserted (Corbett, 1998) that dyslexic children receive disproportionate amounts of resources in compulsory education; British dyslexic undergraduates certainly claim the lion's share of funding under the Disabled Students' Allowance (Hurst, 1996). The UK's National Working Party on Dyslexia in Higher Education (NWP) (Singleton, 1999) was formed in 1994. In 1995, I began individual learning support work with undergraduates, and became aware both of the personal issues for the students and of the institutional tensions connected with the subject of dyslexia (Stephens, 1996). Such issues extend far beyond funding. If there is more than one form of intelligence (Gardner, 1987), there is also a range of cognitive styles (Dunn and Dunn, 1978; Given and Reid, 1999), not all of which lend themselves to the kind of linear thought which is required if one is to write an essay or manage one's time. It may be that the academy – the HE establishment – esteems linear thought, for example the conventional structure of an essay, above other forms, and this may disadvantage those who do not naturally think that way. Learning support issues are admirably summed up by Peelo (1994) when she avers that successful support must address cognitive, affective and social aspects.

While entry into HE is challenging for all students in terms of their sense of identity, it is particularly so for those who are labelled dyslexic. Ivanic (1998:10) describes identity as 'the everyday word for people's sense of who they are'. Like Ivanic, I take a social constructionist view of identity: that it is not generated by an individual's sole efforts, but the self is continually shaped and reshaped through interactions with others and involvement in social and cultural activities (Denzin, 1989; Stevens, 1996a). Individuals' identity is the result of affiliation to particular beliefs and possibilities which are available to them in their social context. The first year of a degree course is difficult for many students, and if university precipitates an identity crisis in some students, how will it affect a dyslexic person facing the prospect of three years of reading and writing? This may be toughest for mature students, for whom entry to University may mean a mismatch between the social contexts which have constructed their identities in the past and the new social context they are entering.

Many authors and trainers in the dyslexia field have relatives, usually children, who have been identified as dyslexic. I have no dyslexic relatives, nor do I see myself as dyslexic. As a non-disabled researcher investigating 'disabled' people, I have 'responsibilities aris(ing) from the privileges I have as a result of my social position' (Barton, quoted in Hurst, 1996, page 123). Although Hurst refers to dyslexia because it is legally recognised as a disability, he implicitly separates it from vision, hearing, mobility and mental health issues, as do I. Nevertheless, I acknowledge that as a researcher and tutor working with students who struggle with academic procedures, I have privileges in terms of facility with reading and writing and status within the academy.

Hurst (1996) quotes Barton again, referring to the privileged researcher using his/her knowledge and skills 'to challenge the forms of oppression disabled people experience and thereby help to empower them' (page 124). Leaving aside the potentially patronising word 'empower', I am indeed motivated by a desire to challenge the way dyslexic students are perceived, in a manner which may be beneficial to them. But although that was my primary motivation when I began the research reported in this book, the process of examining the data and the literature I have studied since have led me to widen my view.

Mason (1996) urges researchers to ponder the answers to five key questions before starting work. Here are mine.

What is the nature of the phenomenon I wish to investigate?

Dyslexia clearly exists, and is believed in by a great many researchers, educators and students. However, most of the literature about dyslexia is not only focused on children (Doyle, 1996; Broomfield and Combley, 1997; Thomson, 2001), but it also tends to take a neuropsychological stance (Galaburda, 1999; Snowling, 2000; Fawcett and Reid, 2004) and to use a discourse of disability (HEFCE, 1995; Singleton, 1999; Lloyd, 2005). There is very little literature which sets out the dyslexic person's point of view (Gilroy and Miles, 1996: appendices; Riddick, Farmer et al, 1997), certainly not a great deal about adults and even less about HE. Insight into the socio-emotional aspects might help the academy to come to terms with these students; that is therefore the aspect of dyslexia I wish to investigate.

What might represent evidence or knowledge of this phenomenon?

The best way is to ask the students, but also to look at documentary evidence of 'expert' opinions about them, the educational psychologists (EPs), because of their role in officially identifying students as dyslexic. The discursive interview, tracing an informant's learning life history, has the potential to bring out the way an individual's view of him or herself as dyslexic has developed. The term 'informant' is preferable to 'respondent' or 'subject,' as it conveys the collaborative nature of the enterprise.

What is the focus of this book?

Rawson (1995: xviii) points out that 'personal history' is a potentially valuable source of 'insights and understanding'. Undergraduates labelled dyslexic may be mature – over 25 – or recent school leavers; they may have been identified as dyslexic in childhood, or since admission to University. Whichever category they fall into, they have an educational history. Life history literature (Plummer, 1983; Thomson, 1994; West, 1994; Yow, 1994) demonstrates that the fields of psychology, anthropology and sociology can gain from the exploration of people's life stories. It is widely held that screening or assessment for dyslexia should begin with an educational history (Klein, 1993; McLoughlin *et al*, 1994; Cairns and Moss, 1995). In the case of University students, what I call a learning life history needs to include the present day in order to seek insights into on-course issues. So the book focuses on the sense of self of students labelled dyslexic, as revealed in their learning life histories.

What is the intellectual puzzle?

This may be summed up as an interest in the meaning of dyslexia in HE today, specifically curiosity as to whether the learning life histories of students can throw light on it. Subsidiary parts of the puzzle include finding out whether students see dyslexia in the same way, and whether there are any patterns in their learning life histories. Bearing in mind that student life raises affective and social issues as well as cognitive ones (Peelo,1994; Rickinson, 1998; Peelo, 2000a), and also that academic writing can raise major identity issues (Ivanic and Simpson, 1992; Ivanic, 1998), I examine how the various influences which have been brought to bear on dyslexic students impact on their identity and self-concept, and how this in turn affects their university careers.

What is the purpose of this book?

I wish to add to dyslexia research in two particular ways: by investigating personal experiences, and by focusing on Higher Education. I hope to increase understanding of dyslexia, to produce insights which may help universities to work with dyslexic students, and to contribute to the debate about academic literacy (Street and Street, 1991; Lea and Street, 2000) and reductionist views of special educational needs (Tomlinson, 1982; Corbett, 1998). In a study sub-titled *Growing up with a specific learning difficulty* (Riddick *et al*, 1997:viii), the authors are concerned with 'how a diverse range of students with dyslexia can best be identified and supported at (...) university'. I prefer to widen this by replacing the words 'with dyslexia' with 'who regard themselves as dyslexic'. However, like Riddick *et al*, I hope that my work may be of help to both students and university staff. Ultimately, the HE sector has to accommodate 'a diverse range of students,' a range widened by the introduction of Access courses in the UK (DfES, 2002). The Disability Discrimination Act 1995 (HMSO, 1995) and its extension, the Special Educational Needs and

Disability Act 2001 (HMSO, 2001) – now known as the Disability Discrimination Act Part 4 – make it unlawful for educational institutions to discriminate against disabled students. Dyslexic people are included in this category.

In sum, the concept of dyslexia has been defined and described in many ways since the term was coined in 1887, and today there exists a range of discourses which influence the views and attitudes of dyslexic students and of significant people in their lives. Dyslexia is not a unitary phenomenon, and for that reason many have been and are sceptical of its existence (Plowden, 1967; Tizard, 1972; Kerr, 2001). Whether or not it exists, there are large numbers of students who accept the label, and many struggle to succeed in HE (Singleton, 1999; Kurnoff, 2000; Rodis *et al,* 2001). If we are to provide an inclusive experience for these students who, I know, usually work very hard and are interested and committed, we must support them (Gilroy and Miles, 1996) in new ways.

Chapters 4 to 8 will set out the results of a research project designed to explore the meaning of dyslexia for students in higher education. But first, three chapters which set the scene by reviewing a little history and investigating the nature of identity and the self-concept.

Chapter 1

The concept of dyslexia and the educational response

Introduction: early milestones

The contribution of luminaries such as Kussmaul, Berlin, Hinshelwood, Pringle Morgan and Orton to the history of the dyslexia concept has been well documented (Critchley, 1970; Hynd, 1983; Pumfrey and Reason, 1991; Ott, 1997; Miles and Miles, 1999). Notably, they were all medical professionals of one kind or another; the 'milestones in knowledge about dyslexia' (Doyle, 1996:169) between Kussmaul (1878) and Orton (1925) all came from medical men. Pringle Morgan's 1896 paper about a 14 year-old English boy encapsulates three images of dyslexia which still prevail: the dyslexic person as a medical case; the view that dyslexia involves a discrepancy between underlying ability and academic achievement; and the suggestion that heredity might be a factor. Pringle Morgan, however, introduces the notion of an alternative mode of learning and teaching, when he comments that the boy's teacher believed that he 'would be the smartest lad in the school if the instruction were entirely oral' (Morgan 1896:1378).

Before the word 'dyslexia' was coined, individuals had been seen to experience diminution or loss of the ability to read, write or speak following strokes or blows to the head. The long history of the dyslexia concept began with medical practitioners noting similar indicators to those for acquired dyslexia in people who were not suffering from disease or accident. For over a century, the notion of dyslexia has also included an element of 'unexpectedness' (Miles and Miles, 1999). Orton (1925, 1928) took the view that dyslexia was fundamentally a visual issue, and his work widened the use of the term 'word blind'. He also introduced another factor: 'cerebral dominance', or one hemisphere of the brain as 'leading'. Orton had studied neurology so had a different perspective from those who had published about dyslexia before him. The notion of cerebral hemispheric differences (Springer and Deutsch, 1998) has continued to contribute to awareness about dyslexia.

The early pioneers believed that the difficulties are unexpected, may be hereditary, involve speech and spelling as well as reading, and may lead to unfair labelling as a dunce. The explanation for these difficulties was said to be primarily medical, specifically neurological. However, there are 'vagaries and antagonisms surrounding definition' (Kavale and Forness, 2000: 239) which are worthy of comment.

Exclusion and discrepancy

The description of Pringle Morgan's boy patient may have influenced the formal definition of dyslexia drawn up by the World Federation of Neurology in 1968 and still being quoted today:

> A disorder manifested by difficulty in learning to read despite conventional instruction, adequate intelligence, and socio-cultural opportunity. It depends on fundamental cognitive disabilities which are frequently of constitutional origin (Critchley, 1970:11).

This definition formalised the notion of exclusion – stating what dyslexia is not – and such exclusion was until recently found in the definitions used by Dyslexia Associations and Societies (for example, the Orton Dyslexia Society, see Reid Lyon, 1995). Another significant feature of the World Federation definition is its focus on reading, which has been used in research studies of children over the past 50 years. Such a focus has allowed the concept of dyslexia to be challenged, notably by Stanovich over a long period (1982, 1991, 1997).

Stanovich's central thesis is that those labelled dyslexic do not differ significantly from poor readers who do not have a reading/IQ discrepancy. This book shows that people identified as dyslexic have a great deal more to contend with than reading. But attainment/IQ discrepancy remains a live issue in justifying special examination arrangements, as we will see. Is there not another way of looking at discrepancy in students: to ask whether the problem lies not within the student but within the institution (Lea and Stierer, 2000)? As Turner (1997:18) puts it: 'school and teaching arrangements ... may have contributed largely to the predicament in the first place'.

If not focused on reading, published definitions of dyslexia often centre around literacy in a broader sense. For example, The British Dyslexia Association's 1997 version used the phrase 'a specific difficulty in reading, spelling and written language', and Reid (1996b) referred to 'restrictions in literacy development and discrepancies in performance within the curriculum'.

Disorder

The American Psychiatric Association publishes a *Diagnostic and Statistical Manual of Mental Disorders* or DSM (DSM IV: American Psychiatric Association, 1994), influential as a classificatory system and periodically updated. This used to include dyslexia under 'academic skills disorders', but the fourth edition changed this to 'learning disorders' and listed under these 'reading disorder' and 'disorder of written expression,' among others, without using the term dyslexia. The definitions given for the terms in the fourth edition are firmly based on IQ/attainment discrepancy.

The word 'disorder' and cognate terms such as 'deficit' and 'dysfunction' have been used by many authors and researchers in connection with dyslexia. A common viewpoint is that identification of dyslexia requires evidence of a cognitive processing deficit (Seymour, 1986; Coltheart *et al*, 1987; Nicolson and Fawcett, 1994; Snowling, 2000). Frith places this at the centre of a three-level model (Frith, 1997, 1999), according to which biological factors produce effects at the cognitive level, which then result in behavioural manifestations. Frith, Snowling and others hold that the cognitive level is essential to a clear definition of dyslexia; the term means 'difficulty with words', and dealing with words, whether spoken, heard, read and written, is by definition a cognitive process. As an example of the kind of 'specific deficit' in the centre of her model, Frith posits a phonological deficit, believing that 'the underlying cognitive deficit appears to be circumscribed, specific, persistent and universal' (Frith, 1997:17).

Syndrome

Few people working in the dyslexia field have been as consequential as Professor Tim Miles, who began publishing on the subject more than forty years ago. In 1994 he summed up his position, that dyslexia was best defined as a taxonomy which makes it possible 'to pick out those individuals in whom the balance of skills is unusual' (Miles, 1994a:209). This is consistent with his statement almost twenty years earlier, that dyslexia is 'a family or cluster of disabilities rather than ... a single condition' (Miles and Miles, 1975:5), and with the title of his book *Dyslexia – the pattern of difficulties* (Miles, 1993). Miles seems to have long avoided the word 'syndrome'; etymologically, this means 'running together' and thus might seem apposite, although as the *Shorter Oxford Dictionary* tells us, its primary meaning is 'a concurrence of several symptoms in a disease'. However, in 1999 the UK National Working Party on Dyslexia in Higher Education (NWP) stated:

> Dyslexia is properly described as a syndrome: a collection of associated characteristics that vary in degree and from person to person. (Singleton, 1999:25)

In the same year, in the concluding pages of the second edition of their survey 'Dyslexia: a hundred years on', Miles and Miles express support for 'a taxonomy that lumps together the manifestations of the syndrome, specific dyslexia' (Miles and Miles, 1999:170).

The syndrome concept seems to be simultaneously strong and weak: strong because there are so many people who clearly demonstrate Miles' pattern of difficulties, and large numbers of what Turner (1997) calls the 'practitioners' who recognise it, and weak precisely because there are so many 'indicators' on the list (Vinegrad, 1994).

The brain and its hemispheres

Stein (2000) points out that if the 'deficit' he posits in the visual neuro-logical pathways did not confer any advantages, it would not have remained in the genetic system. To that extent, he concurs with West's (1997) argument that some prominent intellectual and creative people, such as Einstein and many successful exploiters of information and design technology today, are or were identifiable as dyslexic. West (1997) pro-poses that such people use a basically holistic, three-dimensional mode of thought. His list of examples goes back to Michael Faraday, born in 1791.

West has something in common with Miles and others when he sets out 'constellations of traits' associated with dyslexia. He also seems to support the 'wiring of the brain' approach which was popular in the 1970s and 80s (Franklin and Naidoo, 1970; Wales, 1982; Hornsby, 1984), but rephrases this as 'a different wiring diagram, a way around' (West, 1997:97), and quotes Galaburda in support of the idea of 'solving problems' differently, rather than 'having' a problem. Whereas Miles, Frith, Stein and others have long held the view that dyslexia involves much more than reading difficulties, West goes further, claiming that there is an association between verbal difficulties and visual talents, and that the twenty-first century will see such talents in the ascendancy. The NWP's definition of dyslexia includes the sentence: 'These characteristics encompass not only distinctive clusters of *problems* but sometimes also distinctive *talents*' (Singleton, 1999:25, original emphasis).

West (1997) refers to a 'different' wiring diagram; Stein (2000) speaks of the dyslexic brain as 'different' and having many strengths. Krupska and Klein (1995) say that dyslexia is 'not a defect, but an individual difference in cognitive style' (Krupska and Klein, 1995:14). And Pollock and Waller's practical book for classroom teachers opens by stating that 'dyslexia should be seen as a different learning ability rather than as a disability' (Pollock and Waller, 1994: xiii).

So Orton's ideas about the roles of the two hemispheres of the brain have clearly been taken a great deal further. Springer and Deutsch (1998) describe a combination of split-brain experimentation and neuroimaging techniques which demonstrate conclusively that each cerebral hemisphere specialises in certain functions. Though they warn against over-simplification along the lines of 'left brain = linear thought, right brain = holistic' (*op. cit.* page 299), Springer and Deutsch present evidence of considerable right-hemisphere involvement in the complex manoeuvring of objects in the mind's eye. West's 1997 catalogue of 'visual thinkers' and 'gifted people with learning difficulties' presents such people as having remarkable gifts; Edwards (1993) and Williams (1983) prefer to see such abilities as part of everyone's potential, given the right teaching.

These theories all combine three strands of thinking about dyslexia: it is a neurological matter; the kind of brain under discussion fits with the normal range of human brain development; this in turn gives rise to a continuum of ability and to a distinctive cognitive style.

Deficit, difference and literacy

Tomlinson (1982) catalogues the development over a century of terminology referring to children considered unsuitable for mainstream education, ranging from 'idiot' through 'retarded' to 'with special educational needs'. The language of dyslexia has also changed, and use of the word 'difference' is currently on the increase. Writing about the HE sector, Singleton *et al* state:

> The *deficit model of dyslexia* is now steadily giving way to one in which dyslexia is increasingly recognised as *a difference in cognition and learning.* (Singleton, 1999:27 – original emphasis)

The report of the NWP nevertheless presents a model of dyslexia which seeks to make the point that 'the surface manifestations (derived from the 'literacy framework')' (Singleton, 1999:28) are not the only 'issues that are fundamental to educational success' (same page) in connection with dyslexia. The Report goes on to propose that numeracy, oral skills, attention span, personal organisation and socio-emotional factors are all involved. This is consistent with its fundamental view of dyslexia as a syndrome. The Chair's preface refers to 'fireworks' over 'the process of reaching agreement between fourteen very experienced individuals [in the working party] each with their different professional and personal perspectives' (Singleton, 1999:13), and this inevitably shows through.

In a lecture the following year, Singleton summed up his personal view as follows:

> Developmental dyslexia is a constitutional condition which results in differences in some aspects of information processing by the brain, and which causes difficulties in specific areas of learning, particularly literacy skills. It may confer advantages in other skill areas, such as visual or practical thinking. (Singleton, 2000)

This definition again uses the word 'literacy'. What does this really mean? Its definition might appear to be common sense – a person can either read and write at a socially acceptable or personally practical level, or s/he cannot. But it is not as simple as that; literacy takes place in a cultural context. Language development, although clearly profoundly cultural, is broadly similar across societies (Crystal, 1997), but literacy development varies greatly across cultures (Hannon, 2000).

Some authors (Barton, 1991; Street and Street, 1991; Hamilton *et al*, 1994) posit a model of literacy as a social practice. According to this model, the literacy practices required at school or University simply constitute one set of behaviours among a range of possibilities, albeit an intensely privileged one.

Lea and Street (2000:34) set out three models of student writing, the second two subsuming the ones above them:

- The 'study skills' model – a potential student deficit in atomised skills; student writing as a technical skill

- The 'academic socialisation' model – acculturation of students into academic discourse; student writing as a transparent medium of representation

- The 'academic literacies' model – different literacies seen as social practices; students' negotiation of contrasting literacy practices; student writing as constitutive of identity; meaning-making as contested.

The act of writing is more challenging for most dyslexic HE students than any other aspect of academic life (Gilroy and Miles, 1996); there is a potential parallel between the deficit aspect of the 'study skills' model and the deficit model of dyslexia. Furthermore, documents such as the UK Higher Education Quality Council's 1996 paper on 'the attributes of graduateness', which proposes 'the ability to write in grammatically acceptable and correctly spelt English' (HEQC, 1996:para. 14) as an essential 'ancillary quality', lays down a marker which is difficult for dyslexic students to reach.

If Frith and her colleagues (1999) are right about the range of factors involved, then activities which cover much more than academic study will be affected by a person's cognitive processes. Given and Reid (1999) remind us that most effective problem solvers exercise both analysing and synthesising skills, but they accept that the majority of learners have a preference for either 'sequential' (left-brain) or 'global' (right-brain) approaches (*ibid*, 59). Another word for 'sequential' might be 'linear', as a sequence leads from point A to point B to point C and so on. A link between the areas of difficulty experienced by dyslexic students becomes clear when we consider that these areas involve linear thought: essay planning, sentence structuring, time management, memory for instructions and common sequences. The Report of the NWP refers to 'a lack of prioritising skills' (*op. cit.* 36), which themselves must by definition be a matter of linear thinking. The British Arts Dyslexia Trust includes the following in its definition of dyslexia :

> It is now recognised that the talents of those who learn best by using their visual-spatial skills (as dyslexics do), are not adequately met by linear, reductionist strategies. (Arts Dyslexia Trust, 2005)

In the context of education, there is another way of conceiving the whole question of students who have 'difficulties': is it the academy which is disabling them, rather than they who are disabled? Disabilities may not just be socially constructed but socially *created*. Disability is not synonymous with special educational need, but accounts of the former can throw light on thinking about the latter. Oliver (1988:17) sums up three possible ways of conceptualising disability:

■ Disabilities are an individual problem – the essentialist view, most popular in education

■ Disabilities are socially constructed – some people define others as disabled and therefore treat them differently

■ Disabilities are socially created – society disables people with impairments by the way it treats those people.

Being a student involves compliance with the literacy practices of the institution and, in HE, of the Faculty. In order to further understanding of its view of non-linear thought, the Arts Dyslexia Trust describes itself as 'working to create more appropriate learning environments' and 'developing ways to encourage educators and employers to recognise and inspire visual-spatial skills' (Arts Dyslexia Trust, 2005).

Models of disability

Some physically disabled researchers and campaigners seek to question the cultural representation of disabled people in terms of tragedy, the impaired body and 'otherness' (Oliver, 1996; Barnes, 1996). They point to the sociological analysis of disablement which links it to deviance, illness and stigma, with the focus on the individual with a problem. The social model proposed locates disablement primarily within the structure of society: its values, political economy, physical environment and welfare system. Albert, a disability awareness trainer, suggests an image of a person in a wheelchair at the bottom of a flight of stairs:

> Why can't this person get into the library? Most people, assuming the medical model, will reply 'Because he or she is in a wheelchair'. That is where the problem is located. If you then ask them to look again and say that it is the stairs that are causing the problem ...it is as if you have given

them a new set of cultural lenses through which to see and understand the world (Albert, 1995).

Using this analogy, a social model of dyslexia might picture a dyslexic student inside the same library. S/he is not suffering from a 'chronic neurological disorder', but has a cognitive style which does not easily cope with the academy as it has traditionally been organised. Is s/he as entitled to access to the academy as someone who uses a wheelchair?

In the US, where dyslexic people are usually labelled 'learning disabled', Gerber *et al* propose a new way of construing the self, for which they use the term 'reframing':

> Reframing refers to the set of decisions relating to reinterpreting the learning disability experience in a more positive or productive manner. (Gerber *et al,* 1992:481)

This involves self-recognition followed by acceptance, leading to understanding and finally action towards one's goals. Gerber *et al* also recommend seeking what they call 'goodness of fit', or finding an environment where one's skills and abilities can be optimised.

Gerber *et al* made these comments about employment, but Gergen proposes that social constructionism applies to the world of education. Pointing out that graduates are expected to 'write well', he comments:

> ... there is a certain colonialist attitude inhering in the presumption that all intelligent writing should conform to certain standards – namely the standards popular among the educational elite. (Gergen, 1999:183)

In calling for 'reflexivity, collaboration and polyvocality' in education (*op. cit.* 184), and particularly for acceptance of what he calls 'the performative' as a mode of expression by students (*op. cit.* 188), Gergen has moved well away from the DSM IV definition of dyslexia.

Educational responses to dyslexia: the early twentieth century
The steadily increasing number of HE students who identify themselves as dyslexic, and the legal status of dyslexia as a disability, constitute a challenge to the sector (Singleton, 1999). Before I examine this, it is useful briefly to survey responses by the education profession to the phenomenon of dyslexia.

Pumfrey and Reason (1991) suggest that the responses of individual professionals depend on their training. Theirs is one of several extensive historical surveys of the growth in knowledge about, and response to, dyslexia (Ott, 1997; Miles and Miles, 1999; Anderson and Meier-Hedde, 2001). Rather than repeat this here, we take a fresh look at responses to dyslexia in the twentieth century, in terms of the images revealed by those responses.

In Britain, the earliest educational responses to dyslexia took place in a medical context; in the 1940s, neurologists held specialist clinics at two London hospitals (Scott, 1991). In 1964, Critchley wrote the first British attempt to sum up current knowledge, *Developmental Dyslexia*, later revised (Critchley, 1970). The Preface to the revised edition shows that he saw his readers as consisting of 'doctors, parents, teachers or psychologists' (Critchley, 1970:ix); he regarded the nature of dyslexia as medical, but the effects as purely educational.

More influential on teaching methods in the US was the private publication in 1956 of Gillingham and Stillman's systematic teaching kit. This strongly influenced approaches and many are still in use today (Ott, 1997), such as Hornsby and Shear's *Alpha to Omega* (1975). As Hornsby (2000) wrote: 'We are all really building on what they espoused then'. A key aspect of this structured, phonic-based approach is that it is individualised; the assumption is that dyslexia is an educational disability – the 'word blind' being helped to 'see' words by building them up from their component parts – and that the student will be taught individually (Hornsby and Miles, 1980).

In the 1960s and 1970s in Britain, dyslexia initiatives continued to come from private institutions. The Invalid Children's Aid Association (ICAA) held a conference at a hospital in 1962 entitled Word Blindness or Specific Developmental Dyslexia? The conference proceedings (Miles, 1962) were published by a medical imprint. That conference led to the establishment in 1963 of the Word Blind Centre in London, which continued for nine years. This was not an original idea: the first Wordblind Institute was opened in Denmark in 1936. The London centre inspired the founding of voluntary local dyslexia associations, eight of which were set up between 1965 and 1972, the year of the formal founding of the British Dyslexia Association. 'Here at last was a political ginger group to help bring the matter before both Parliament and the public', wrote Radnor (2000).

In 1969, a Bill entitled 'Children with Learning Disability' was introduced in the US Senate. The label of learning disability, and the teaching programmes devised for the children, did not necessarily save such students from 'serious academic and social problems' later in life (Zigmond and Thornton, 1988:199). Learning disability experts, although divided into 'schools and factions' (Strydom and du Plessis, 2000:4), seemed united in assuring children and parents that learning disability meant a lifetime of difficulties (Cohen, 1986). The 1969 Act led to the promotion of drugs for the learning disabled (Coles, 1987). Burka (1983:289), writing about the emotional aspects of learning disability, focused on the effect of such factors on children's capacity to 'compensate for the disability'.

The 1970s

Helen Arkell, herself dyslexic, opened her Centre in Surrey in 1972. A report on research by the Helen Arkell Dyslexia Centre into how children learn to spell was published in June 1999, and was available from the UK government DfES Publications Centre (Brooks and Weeks, 1999), indicating how it had penetrated the educational establishment. This had begun in 1973, when BDA representatives had their first meetings with officials at the Department of Education.

The BDA was formed in 1972, and in the same year the Dyslexia Institute (DI) was founded near London for the assessment and teaching of dyslexic people and teacher training. It opened its first outposts in 1976 and rapidly obtained charitable status. 'Another important episode in the whole history of dyslexia took place when Mrs Wendy Fisher formed the Dyslexia Institute' (Radnor, 2000). It has grown to 27 local branches, employing some 250 teachers and is often regarded as the principal source of infor- mation on dyslexia in towns where its branches are found. The DI's influence is thus out of proportion to its size; like the BDA, it had access to the House of Lords, as Lord Radnor was for a time both Chairman of the BDA and President of the DI.

In 1967, a British government report on primary education (Plowden, 1967:214) had denied the existence of 'specific dyslexia', but by 1970 it appeared in UK legislation. The Chronically Sick and Disabled Persons Act required LEAs to provide 'special educational treatment ... for children suffering from acute dyslexia' (HMSO, 1970: Section 27). Placing this requirement in such an Act indicates the view of dyslexia as a medical matter. Lord Radnor believes this Act to have been a 'most important moment'. 'It was then at last on the Statute Book, but unfortunately was described there as a disease and not as a disability' (Radnor, 2000).

This legislation led to a further governmental response, as the Secretary of State sought clarification of the dyslexia issue. He turned to the Advisory Committee on Handicapped Children, this being seen as the right forum for consideration of dyslexia, as it was a handicap. The result was the Tizard Report: *Children with specific reading difficulties* (Tizard, 1972). This report echoed Plowden in rejecting the existence of specific developmental dyslexia, and proposed the expression 'specific reading difficulties' in- stead. It also expressed the view that there was 'a continuum spanning the whole range of reading abilities from those of the most fluent readers to those with the most severe difficulties' (*ibid,* para. 8). Unfortunately for educational provision, Tizard failed to make progress in relation to the Chronically Sick and Disabled Persons Act, in that the report did not explain precisely the characteristics of those with specific reading difficulties. However, the proposal of the new terminology may be said to indicate a slight shift towards a scholastic as opposed to a medical view of dyslexia, since Tizard did refer to writing, spelling and number difficulties as had the WFN definition of dyslexia in 1968.

A Professor of Sociology at the University of Surrey (Tropp, 1974) stated that Tizard offered a striking programme for educational reform which would, if fully implemented, give the dyslexia lobby everything it could ask of the government. He commented:

> The controversy over 'dyslexia' is not ... one between firmly established scientific knowledge on the one hand and a group of axe-grinders and neurotic middle-class parents on the other. (*op. cit.* 5)

This tension was widespread in the 1970s. *Dyslexia Review,* Issue 12 (winter 1974) quoted a newspaper article which referred to

> ... the overzealousness of middle class parents who are suspected of pre-ferring to label their dull children dyslexic rather than 'backward'. (*The Times*, December 9 1974)

A British government report on English language teaching (Bullock ,1975) raised the profile of dyslexia as an issue for mainstream schools to con-sider. *Dyslexia Review* noted that

> the report does state that dyslexic children should be given special diag-nosis and treatment at reading clinics, 'a facility which should be available in every authority'! (Vernon, 1975:9)

In spite of this medical language, the debate had moved out of the paediatric consulting clinic and into the classroom.

It seems that the first publication by any official body to look at dyslexic adults in the UK was a British Council for the Rehabilitation of the Disabled (REHAB) report entitled *People with dyslexia* (Kershaw, 1974). It included recommendations for further and higher education, and some brief case studies to illustrate 'specific problems at university level'. This was almost certainly the first UK publication to include material on dyslexia in higher education. The image of dyslexia conveyed by this report is of the exclu-sionary school: 'we would also wish to exclude such other causes as social and cultural deprivation and emotional disturbance' (*ibid,* 5), but basically sees dyslexia as an academic issue, pointing to difficulties with mathe-matics and music as well as reading and spelling.

The report recommends the provision of an amanuensis for examinations, a practice which is now wide-spread. It also comments on the amount of time a dyslexic student takes to study books and to write, and suggests staying on for an extra academic year, a proposal which has not found favour. The REHAB report, in calling for further research, refers to 'various areas such as visual, auditory and kinaesthetic perception, integration or central processing, genetic and emotional factors' (*ibid,* 147), and uses the term 'syndrome' to indicate that it sees dyslexia as a 'pattern of difficulties', to use Miles' phrase, although the first edition of his book of that title only appeared in 1983.

Meanwhile, dyslexia had been featuring in the UK media. In August 1975, BBC2 broadcast a documentary called 'If you knew Susie', featuring the British actress Susan Hampshire. The producer later wrote:

> Susan ... could say 'Some experts believe it exists, some don't. But I believe it exists, I believe I am dyslexic, so come and look at it through my eyes. This is my world of dyslexia'. (Dale, 1976:13)

What sort of world was presented? After consulting what he termed 'a list of experts in the field', the producer was convinced that 'in a 'normal' person the one dominant hemisphere controls and inter-switches all the functions concerned with reading and writing', but in a dyslexic person 'the direct connectors between the hemispheres are so few in number that they're of very little use' (*op. cit.*14-15). The continuing prevalence of the cerebral dominance approach is shown by the fact that nine years after the BBC documentary, an authority like Hornsby (1984:129) was still describing 'a confusing traffic jam of nerve signals ... in the corpus callosum between the language areas in the opposite sides of the brain'.

The 1980s

Early in the 1980s came the publication of several books about personal experiences of dyslexia. 1981 saw the British edition of the American psychotherapist Eileen Simpson's Reversals (Simpson, 1981), sub-titled *a personal account of victory over dyslexia.* Simpson broadly takes the view that dyslexia is a syndrome. She refers not only to reading difficulties but also to spelling, speech, sense of direction, map-reading, use of numbers and memory for names. However, she also uses other medical language, writing of seeing herself 'cured' of her 'symptoms' (*ibid,* 217).

In the same year, Susan Hampshire published *Susan's Story, an autobio-graphical account of my struggle with words* (Hampshire, 1981).The publisher's text on the back cover stated:

> dyslexia is word blindness, the learning difficulty that turns ordinary sentences into meaningless tangles of jumbled letters.

Hampshire's own text is somewhat less alarmist. It takes a neurological view: 'the section of the brain governing language does not function properly' (*ibid,* 3). Because of Hampshire's fame, her book received wide publicity, and the coverage in the media must have reached many dyslexic adults.

1981 also saw the original publication of a different kind of personal memoir: Jean Augur's story of bringing up her three dyslexic sons (Augur, 1995). Like Hampshire, Augur presents dyslexia in a neurological manner:

'one or more of the pathways to his brain necessary for reading and spelling has not fully matured' (*ibid,* 2). Such celebrity cases have the effect of popularising the concept of dyslexia and may have influenced the views of dyslexic students, their families and their teachers. Dyslexia thus becomes part of what Barton and Hamilton (1998:20) call a 'public narrative'.

In the US, public awareness of the legal status of learning disabilities led to a huge increase in the numbers identified in the 1980s. Edgar and Hayden (1984) reported that between 1976 and 1982, the number classified as learning disabled increased by 119 percent. Franklin (1987) collected a range of questioning voices in his '*Learning Disability: Dissenting Essays,*' including the proposal that the expression 'learning disabilities' be replaced by 'teaching disabilities,' on the basis that the problem lay in the education system and not within the student.

Thus the first seventy years of the twentieth century saw the simultaneous flourishing of these strands of response to dyslexia:

- It was seen as a 'disorder' and a 'disability'

- The key to it was seen as a discrepancy between 'ability' or 'IQ' and educational attainment; it was thus often regarded as having purely educational implications, mainly involving reading

- There remained a substantial body of opinion among both psychologists and teachers, that there was no such thing as dyslexia

- There were increasing numbers of campaigners who sought publicity and increased provision for dyslexic people.

The Warnock Report

In UK educational terms, a major event of 1981 was the Education Act arising from the Warnock Report (Warnock, 1978). This was the work of a Committee of Inquiry into 'the education of handicapped children and young people'. Baroness Warnock wrote recently:

> We were specifically told that dyslexia did not count among officially recognised 'handicaps'. It was still thought to be a middle-class invention, to cover the tracks of stupid middle-class children. I was sure at the time that this was not true, but there was a study to be done. But when we re-invented the ground rules – thinking not of what was wrong with children, but of what they needed – the concept of dyslexia re-introduced itself, inevitably. (Warnock, 2000)

A major outcome of the Warnock Report was the adoption of the concept of 'children with special educational needs', to cover the previous range of labels such as 'educationally subnormal'. The temptation to add some terminology was not resisted, however; we owe the wide acceptance of the expression 'specific learning difficulties', which is still current, to

Warnock also (Warnock, 1978: para 3.26). This time however, it may be that the new term was of some use (if only because it was not associated with what were seen as middle-class pressure groups). Pumfrey and Reason (1991:213) surveyed 882 EPs, of whom 87 per cent found the term 'specific learning difficulties' useful, compared with 30 per cent who liked the term dyslexia.

A further outcome was the official recognition of a discrepancy definition of what is in effect a coded reference to dyslexia:

> ... there are ... children whose disabilities are marked but whose general ability is at least average and for whom distinctive arrangements are necessary (Warnock, 1978: para 11.48)

Here is a government-sponsored report, published ten years after the WFN (1968) definition of dyslexia with its often paraphrased words 'despite conventional instruction, adequate intelligence and socio-cultural opportunity', which effectively accepts that such a discrepancy can be the key to identification.

Before Warnock, special education was focused on individual assessment, with remediation usually taking place by withdrawal from the classroom or special school placement (Bines, 1988). Warnock rejected the system of statutory categorisation of children, substituting the concept of a continuum of 'needs'.

The subsequent Education Act in 1981 enshrined Warnock's recommendations in law. It contains the term 'learning difficulty', which Pumfrey and Reason (1991:24) call 'disastrously ill-defined'. The parliamentary debate which led to this Act was aware of the question of attaching legal status to dyslexia. The Minister of Education hoped that the removal of categories of handicap which the Bill contained, and the new arrangements for the assessment of special educational needs, would 'end the arguments which have taken place over what is dyslexia' (Hansard, 14th January 1981).

Unfortunately, the eventual Education Act (HMSO, 1981) failed clearly to identify children with special educational needs. It stated in Clause 1 that:

> For the purposes of this Act a child has 'special educational needs' if he has a learning difficulty which calls for special educational provision to be made for him.

Subsection (a) of that Clause states that:

> A child has a 'learning difficulty' if he has a significantly greater difficulty in learning than the majority of children of his age.

There then began a period of case law creation, during which many parents took legal action in the attempt to force their LEAs to issue a Statement of Special Educational Need for their children. Some cases (such as Regina v. Hampshire County Council in 1985) achieved considerable publicity.

A working party of the Division of Educational and Child Psychology of the BPS (Cornwall *et al,* 1983) reported that the 1981 Education Act had encouraged groups such as the BDA to press for resources. The report stated:

> The medical model with its disorder/disease-treatment orientation and the psychological model with its emphasis on learning process and products almost inevitably lead to contrasting interpretations of certain ... reading difficulties. (*ibid,* 9)

It added:

> Parents and professional workers will no doubt continue to use the term dyslexia and EPs should accept that this is so, though they may wish to view the term only as a descriptive label, having no aetiological implications. (*ibid,* 19)

In 1987, the House of Commons Select Committee for Education invited the BDA to submit a memorandum on the implementation of the 1981 Education Act, and the Under Secretary of State for Education said in Parliament on 13th July 1987:

> The Government recognise dyslexia ... The important thing is to be sure that something is being done about the problem. (quoted in Scott, 1991: 17)

In that same year, a Wiltshire student became the first candidate to be allowed to use a word processor in public examinations because he was dyslexic (*ibid,* 18).

After more than ten years of delays and inconsistencies, and further prominent cases (*e.g.* Regina v. Secretary of State for Education and Science ex parte Davis in 1988), the DfEE published its own research in 1992 which concluded that specific learning difficulties cause undue anxiety to parents and, in the worst cases, damage to a child's education at a critical stage of development. One result of this was the Education Act 1993, which the government hoped would eradicate delays over issuing Statements and inconsistency between LEAs. The Act included a Code of Practice, setting out a five-stage model for identifying, assessing and supporting children with special needs. It reproduced almost verbatim the definitions of special educational needs given in the Act of 1981. The BDA nevertheless welcomed the Code of Practice, noting however that LEAs and school governors were required to 'have regard' to it: 'What is 'regard'? That remains to be seen' (Orton, 1994:8). The Code set a time limit for LEAs to produce a Statement of Special Educational Need, required every school to have a special educational needs co-ordinator, and set up a Tribunal and Appeals Committees to adjudicate on disputes.

The UK Education Acts of 1981, 1993 and 1996 refer to learning difficulties, but there remains the question of the way in which such difficulties are construed. A member of the Warnock committee wrote:

> The degree to which situations are handicapping is determined by the community, and its attitudes and its provision for individuals who form part of it. (Fish, 1985:5)

Schools
It thus appears that at the time, there was a degree of shift towards a conception of special needs as socially created. Yet as Tomlinson (1982:162) reminds us:

> ... when challenged, the education system will defend itself by reverting to innate, individualistic explanations stressing the pupils' deficiencies.

This approach has been given added impetus in the UK in recent years by such factors as financial delegation to schools, and league tables. Riddell (1996) maintains that managerial issues, such as pressure for school and teacher accountability, are bringing about a return to the search for within-child deficits. This coincides with the demands of pressure groups such as the dyslexia lobby, which wishes to present dyslexic people as a separate group with congenital difficulties. Where it was once frowned upon, the word dyslexia has begun to appear in British government publications (DfE, 1994; HEFCE, 1995; DfES, 1999; DfES, 2004).

Meanwhile, private schools which cater for dyslexic children continue to flourish. The website of one (Ewart, 2001) pays lip-service to LEAs' efforts to teach 'moderately dyslexic' children in mainstream schools, but adds that the special school's concern 'is with the severely dyslexic minority who need a more intensive and holistic approach' (*ibid*). However, there is still a debate about the best setting in which to educate such children (Anderson and Meier-Hedde, 2001).

Further and Higher Education
The UK Education Acts of the 1980s and 1990s did not cover Further or Higher education. The 1992 Further and Higher Education Act (HMSO 1992), which set up the 'new Universities' and was focused on funding and administration, instructed (in respect of Further Education) that 'each council shall have regard to the requirements of persons having learning difficulties' (section 4.2) but made no parallel observation in respect of Universities.

The Dearing Report, *Higher Education in the Learning Society* (Dearing, 1997) did not refer to dyslexia. It did however propose widening the participation in Higher Education of members of ethnic minorities, the socio-economically disadvantaged and the disabled, and wider availability of the

Disabled Students' Allowance (DSA). The latter was already being claimed by dyslexic students, and many professionals interpreted Dearing's references to the disabled as including the dyslexic (Waterfield, 1996 – which did not appear until 1998; Singleton, 1999). Between 1992 and 1997, numbers of students claiming the DSA for equipment such as computers tripled (Laycock, 1999). There was also a quadrupling of the numbers claiming the allowance for 'non-medical help', under which fees are paid for dyslexic students' individual learning support sessions.

Reference to the DSA brings us to the construction of dyslexia in HE. In terms of legislation, Dearing had been preceded in the UK by the Disability Discrimination Act (DDA) (HMSO, 1995). This was focused on employment issues, but did allocate responsibility for disabled students to the Funding Councils for Higher Education. The guidance notes to the Act referred to 'severe dyslexia' as falling within its definition of a disability (which identifies a substantial adverse effect on a person's ability to carry out normal day-to-day activities). The Disability Discrimination Act has been extended more specifically to education in the UK by the Special Educational Needs and Disability Act (SENDA) (HMSO, 2001), of which the Code of Practice gives many examples of ways in which discriminatory practices involving dyslexic students may be illegal under its terms.

In the US, a process is taking place whereby the principles of the No Child Left Behind Act of 2001 are aligned with the Individuals with Disabilities in Education Act (Fletcher *et al*, 2004). This allows states to move away from an IQ/attainment discrepancy model of learning disability, and to include response to instruction criteria in identification. The thrust of this legislation is to move beyond the fact that dyslexic students (and those with other learning disabilities) can simply attend mainstream schools; their achievements must be improved. The US Americans with Disabilities Act (ADA) of 1990 is the example which the UK's DDA followed. For example, it specifies that 'reasonable accommodations' must be made for students with 'learning disabilities', and the DDA refers to 'reasonable adjustments'.

The report of the NWP (Singleton, 1999) stated that the major dyslexia-related controversy in HE was focused not on the existence of dyslexia but on the right of dyslexic students to be in HE at all, and ways in which they should be identified and supported. In an article on developments since the Report was published (Singleton *et al*, 2001), the authors state that the sector is continuing to struggle with issues connected with overall institutional and national policy, staff development and institutional awareness, admissions, identification and assessment, evaluation of needs and provision of support, counselling, examinations and careers. They conclude:

> Dyslexia support is an equal opportunities issue. Dyslexic students need
> the right opportunities to learn the necessary skills for higher education

and to demonstrate the skills and knowledge they have acquired. They need access to the learning methods that will enable them to use un-orthodox learning approaches and they need provisions that will minimise the effects of their dyslexia. A level playing field should be provided. It is likely to be bumpy, but then so it is for most people in different ways at some time. (*ibid,* 5)

Singleton and his colleagues adopt a medical model of dyslexia, focusing on defining it as a disability and placing the 'problem' within the student (see the word 'unorthodox' in the above extract). However as this chapter has shown, there are other models of dyslexia.

Summary

This chapter has explored some historical models of dyslexia, none of which has been entirely abandoned or superseded, and the tensions the various models engender in the educational world. There are people who have a recognisable pattern of strong and weak areas which often occur to-gether. Some authors see this as a syndrome or condition i.e. an essen-tialist view. Another view is that the disability discourse constructs the condition. A third view is that if the academy were less insistent on its autonomous model of literacy practice, there would be no problem.

The twentieth century saw campaigns by groups and individuals, publica-tion of personal stories and the gradual insertion of dyslexia into public policy and legislation. The debate in the new century is moving on to the equal opportunities and widening participation agendas.

Chapter 2
Self-image and identity

Introduction

This book focuses on the personal experiences and self-image of dyslexic students. The terms 'identity' and 'self' are central. This chapter looks at how they are defined and Chapter 3 links them with the socio-emotional aspects of dyslexia.

One dictionary of psychological terms (Reber, 1985:341) defines identity as 'a person's essential, continuous self, the internal, subjective concept of oneself as an individual'. Reber defines self as 'the compelling sense of one's unique existence, what philosophers have traditionally called the issue of personal identity' (*ibid,* 675). Ivanic is more down to earth:

> The word 'identity' is useful, because it is the everyday word for people's sense of who they are (Ivanic, 1998:10).

This sense inevitably involves the body; 'the pulsating organs which I inhabit are a constant part of my feeling and thinking' (Craib, 1998:10). Chief among them is the brain: conscious awareness consists of cognition, which includes memory and beliefs (Temple, 1993; Stevens, 1996a; Pinker, 1997). But we also have a sense of agency, of our ability to act and influence events, and this involves responsibility. With this comes a sense of reflexive awareness, the ability to stand back and reflect on experience. There can be a sense of fear, because 'I' am both subject and object, so have freedom to choose the meaning my life will have. However, reflexivity involves other people. We have both personal identity and social identity, and the kind of person we are is influenced by our social setting, particularly how other people categorise us and assign roles to us (Stevens, 1996a: 21 and 22).

In addition there are emotions, both conscious and unconscious. According to transactional analysis theory, influenced by Freud, we begin unconsciously writing the script for our life pattern early in infancy (Berne,

1972; Stewart and Joines, 1987). Each way of conceiving of identity, the biological, the cognitive-experimentalist, the experiential, the Freudian and social constructionism, has consequences for dyslexia. These are explored in Chapters 5 to 8.

Furthermore, each aspect of the self is interwoven with the others. They are now considered and their connection with the concept of dyslexia explored.

The biological view

It is possible to adopt an entirely biological view of the self; indeed much of the literature on dyslexia cited in Chapter 1 is biological in emphasis. Genes and hormones do influence our behaviour, and the brain is the seat of consciousness and emotion (Pinker, 1997; Temple, 1993). It is also the seat of memory, without which we have no sense of continuity.

A biological view of consciousness holds that conscious experience is a property of the physical brain, and depends upon the integration of its various parts and their functions; furthermore, chemical substances can be identified in the brain, the role of which can be analysed on a causal level in terms of emotions (Toates, 1996). Toates refers to Singer's work on the relationship between affective states and discrepancies between a person's self-belief categories, such as 'actual self', 'ideal self' and 'ought self'. People with big discrepancies between actual self and ideal self were found to be prone to depression, associated with a lack of serotonin (Singer, 1993). EPs with a biological view of dyslexia tend to write reports which not only ascribe dyslexia to brain deficits, but also spell out discrepancies between intellectual potential and academic attainments such as reading and spelling ages, thus creating an 'ought self'. This practice exemplifies the complex interaction between biological and social processes (Stevens, 1996a; Toates, 1996).

In his provocative book *The Learning Mystique*, Coles (1989) inveighs against the concept of learning disabilities and minimal neurological dysfunction. He rejects the search for biological variables:

> Put succinctly, the alternative perspective suggests that learning difficulties ... develop not from within the individual but from the individual's interaction within social relationships. (*ibid*, 369)

Coles believes that the development of an individual's learning problems and neurological make-up can be explained as part of the totality of social interactions with parents, teachers and so-called experts. Sigmon (1989) supports this view. Seeking to connect the social foundations of education to 'special education', he proposes that before a person is classified as 'learning disabled' under the assumption that s/he is suffering from a neurological dysfunction, other possibilities must be explored, such as motivation, knowledge of learning strategies, and amount as well as quality of previous instruction.

Knowledge of learning strategies involves metacognition (Hunter-Carsch, 2001), which is difficult to carry out without awareness of one's cognitive style. 'It appears very likely that cognitive style is the missing piece in the jigsaw of understanding the self', since it 'has been shown to affect learning, feeling, decision making and social behaviour' (Riding and Rayner, 1998:190). Chapters 7 and 8 address this link between cognitive, affective and social factors.

The cognitive experimentalist view

Cognitive style links with looking at the self from a cognitive experimentalist perspective, examining intrapersonal processes such as attribution, as is involved in the concept of 'learned helplessness' (Butkowsky and Willows, 1980) and motivation. Such explanations, too, cannot be understood without reference to social processes such as cultural influences (Lalljee, 1996).

Bryan (1986) sheds further light on this when she raises the issue of 'learned helplessness':

> Individuals who hold learned helpless attributions believe that events are the result of uncontrollable factors (*ibid,* 218).

Butkowsky and Willows (*op. cit.*) also looked at learned helplessness, in a study of children with varied degrees of reading ability. They list the indicators of 'this perceived independence of response and outcome' as including 'passivity, lack of persistence in the face of failure, negative self-attitudes about intellectual performance and competence, and lower self-esteem' (*ibid,* 410). As Bryan points out, the significance of learned helplessness includes the fact that there is not always a direct cause and effect relationship between reading success and positive self-esteem, since some students feel unable to take personal credit for their success. She adds:

> The parallels between descriptions of learned helpless attitudes and behaviours and descriptions of the learning disabled are striking. (Bryan, 1986:218)

Dyslexic students often believe that success is more likely to occur because tasks are easy than that failure is likely to occur because tasks are difficult (Bryan, 1986:219). Often they do not take personal credit for success. Yet responses to coping with failure are critical in determining willingness to persevere when learning is difficult. This implies that affective and motivational variables are as vital as cognitive ones, and also calls into question the special education dogma that it is essential for success experiences to be arranged (Hornsby, 1984; Pumfrey and Reason, 1991).

To feel nervous about giving a presentation or speaking in a seminar, undergraduates do not have to be dyslexic. But when surrounded by those whom they perceive as higher achieving, dyslexic people may judge themselves more harshly, and this may undermine their performance (Bryan, 1986:220). On the other hand, success may be attributed to the ease of the task, and failure either to lack of ability or task difficulty. In other words, the locus of control and evaluation is external. The expectation of success felt by children who are poor readers declines rapidly after they experience failure; their academic self-esteem is easily damaged, and those with low self-esteem generally expect to fail (Butkowski and Willows, 1980).

The experiential perspective

A third way of viewing the self is what Stevens (1996a) calls an experiential perspective, involving elements of phenomenological, existential and humanistic viewpoints. As McLeod (1998:88) puts it, 'the image of the person in humanistic psychology is of a self striving to find meaning and fulfilment in the world'. This image owes much to the European tradition of existential and phenomenological philosophy (Blackburn, 1996). The focus is on subjective experience, asking questions about how it may be conceptualised and analysed, and emphasising what is experientially real rather than abstract (McLeod, 1998). Rogers (1951) adopted this perspective when he developed humanistic psychology; he focused on the 'here and now' in therapy, the current experiencing of the client.

Existentialist psychology also starts from the perspective of individual, subjective experience (Sartre, 1948); it is only by our thoughts and actions that we create who we are and give meaning to our lives (Deurzen-Smith, 1988), since existentialist philosophy sees human beings as suffering the anxiety of choice in the face of an indifferent universe (Blackburn, 1996).

The model of the person or self according to existential, phenomenological and humanistic perspectives focuses on the study of subjective experience, in particular the search for meaningfulness (Stevens, 1996a). We are able to reflect on the act of experiencing; this concept of the self includes the ability to examine potential sources of meaningfulness and to evaluate possible courses of action – in other words, we are aware of agency and choice. Kelly (1955) described people as 'scientists' in this respect, making discriminations about the world in terms of bi-polar constructs. For a person labelled dyslexic, such constructs might include 'good at reading/poor at reading' or 'academically successful/ academically unsuccessful' (Pollak, 1993).

In addition to choice and meaningfulness, there is a third existential concern: time. The personal world can be seen as 'a narrative of events', and involves 'memories of past experiences and anticipation of future ones' (Stevens, 1996a:185). This is relevant to the discussion of a dyslexic student's learning history in two ways: people are asked to review their lives in educational terms, and dyslexic people often have difficulty dealing with the concept of time because it is significantly linear (Herrington, 2001(b)).

The end of the line is death. Time cannot be turned back, and all animals live for a finite period. Awareness of that fact has generated a wide variety of defences, found in every human society, most notably doctrines of life after death. The psychological perspective which focuses on defences is the psychodynamic, of which more below. As in the case of the biological and cognitive perspectives, the experiential viewpoint overlaps with other perspectives in certain ways. Two examples illustrate this. Firstly, there are cultural variations in awareness of existential needs to find meaning-fulness, deal with choice and cope with time. Secondly, an Eriksonian perspective would reveal that different existential needs become salient at different developmental stages (Erikson, 1950, 1968). This is relevant to the 18 year-old undergraduate, separating himself from home, who is con-fronted with fitting 'dyslexic' into his identity picture.

The psychodynamic viewpoint

Reference to Erikson brings us to the psychodynamic perspective on the self, which assumes that human behaviour is fundamentally determined by the 'unconscious' (Thomas, 1996). Although Freud (who originated the psychodynamic concept), Melanie Klein and the British 'object relations' school differed in their views as to the nature of the self (Thomas, 1996), they agreed on the centrality of psychological defences against anxiety, and all believed that conscious awareness is only the tip of an iceberg that is mostly unconscious. Thomas explains:

> Psychodynamic theories assume that much of the self is hidden and our subjective experience of selfhood is partial. What we can experience directly is not only the 'tip of an iceberg' but may be disguised by uncon-scious motives and defences. The closest we can get to an overall picture of ourselves is through the eyes and ears of another person. (*ibid,* 312)

Freud assumed that that 'other person' would be a psychoanalyst. He pre-sented his ideas as a universal theory, yet they were based on a circum-scribed, patriarchal, culture-specific family structure. Nevertheless, the antecedent of the social constructionist and indeed other contemporary views of the self and identity can be said to lie in the work of Freud, whose influence continues to this day although he is under attack (Webster, 1995). One example of this influence is the theory of Erikson. Freud believed that the development of the self was completed by the end of childhood (Freud, 1953-74); Erikson (1950) devised a model of what he called the epigenesis of personality, referring to his hypothesis that each stage develops from the previous one through eight psychosocial stages. The first four stages of Erikson's model are close to Freud's description of childhood, but Erikson's best-known work, in which his independent voice emerges (Erikson, 1950), involves the analysis of human development from adolescence onwards. He was one of the first life-span psychologists, adding the concept of the psychosocial to Freud's theory of the psychosexual (Erikson, 1968).

Erikson defined what he called a psychosocial 'crisis', effectively a developmental task, for each stage of his model. For the fifth stage, at which 18 to 21 year-old undergraduates would find themselves, he identified the 'crisis' as deciding on an identity focus and repudiating alternatives. Identity for Erikson is 'an evolving configuration', and this evolution involves a gradual synthesis of awareness of personal capabilities, identification with others and tastes, but also defences and sublimations, showing the influence of Freud (Erikson, 1968:89).

The task of adolescence, Erikson proposes, is to integrate various identifications from childhood together with one's biological endowment, ego defences and the roles offered by society into a more complex identity than one's pre-pubertal configuration. He describes this stage as a time of rituals, both spontaneous, as in adolescents' ritualised relationships with each other, and formal, as in taking a degree. The question young people face at this stage is whether to be, or not to be, oneself.

The completion of the 'tasks' associated with each stage is held by Erikson to be essential if the individual is to move on to the next phase; as in the theory of the stages of grieving (Parkes, 1972; Bowlby, 1980), failure to complete each task means that they will re-emerge later in life. However, Erikson is fundamentally more optimistic than Freud. He believes that as human development continues throughout the life-span, the ego continually develops and adjusts. This view, combined with the notion that the sequence of stages is universal across all human cultures, and that the problem of identity is central for all individuals, constitutes Erikson's original contribution to psychology.

Erikson's ideas are relevant to the learning life histories of dyslexic students. He offers twin concepts: the young undergraduate who is still involved with the 'who am I?' decision, and the mature student potentially revisiting fundamental issues from previous stages.

Heinz Kohut also built on the ideas of Freud. He developed what Wolf calls the 'psychoanalytic psychology of the self' (Wolf, 1987:259). As Kahn explains, Kohut proposed that there were two parallel lines of human development, one of which was

> the development of the self, which, in the healthy individual, goes on throughout a life-time. In Kohut's view, there are three strong needs that

must be fulfilled if the self is to develop fully: the need to be 'mirrored,' the need to idealise, and the need to be like others. (Kahn, 1991:84)

All these needs are relevant to the issues faced by a dyslexic child. Firstly, the parental 'mirror' may not tell the child s/he is wonderful often or effusively enough if s/he is perceived as having a problem. Secondly, the child may be unable to idealise a parent who also has dyslexic difficulties or who appears to favour a non-dyslexic sibling. Thirdly, and most obviously, children need to feel that they share important characteristics with their parents and with other children – in other words, that they are not too 'different:'

> If these three needs are adequately met, the child develops a healthy self, which entails high self-esteem, a guidance system of ideals and values, and the self-confidence to develop one's competence. (Kahn, 1991:88)

Self-esteem will be considered below. At this point, it is important to note that Kohut's perspective clearly involves a central role for other people, which leads us to the social constructionist view of the self and identity.

Social constructionism
Ivanic (1998) sums this up well when she states that identity is not generated by the individual's sole efforts, but that the self is continually shaped and reshaped through interactions with others and involvement in social and cultural activities. This is what Giddens (1991) calls the 'reflexive project' of the self. (See also Denzin, 1989; Stevens, 1996a.)

From a social constructionist perspective, a person's identity is thus 'the result of affiliation to particular beliefs and possibilities which are available to them in their social context' (Ivanic, 1998:12) and an adult student's adoption of the label 'dyslexic' is a cultural and political act. Furthermore, as Thomas puts it:

> The social constructionist view of the self is that we will each be a product of our historical time, culture and subculture. We will create and re-create ourselves. (Thomas, 1996:323)

The social and cultural context is thus much more than an influence on identity. Social processes and practices play a key role in forming a person's experience and behaviour, and language and discourse are central to those practices.

The relationship between the perspectives
For any one view of identity to predominate depends in part on the complex philosophical issue of the nature of reality. Does reality exist independently of the person who is thinking about it or perceiving it? The biological and experimentalist perspectives tend to hold that reality can indeed be defined scientifically (Stevens, 1996a). Yet the biological view

necessarily includes interactive aspects: the body is studied in interaction both with 'the environment' and 'the social matrix' (Toates, 1996:82). Similarly, the experimental perspective involves more than intrapersonal processes: cognitive factors are salient, but these operate in a context of interactional and cultural processes (Lalljee, 1996).

Applied to the learning life histories of students, the experiential perspective offers insights into the interview process. It emphasises sub-jective experience and personal constructs. People experience contrasting settings such as the worlds of home, work and leisure, and as students they have to come to terms with different literacy practices in those settings. But most importantly, the experiential perspective is concerned with the search for meaningfulness and autonomy, issues which are crucial for all students, but particularly so for those who are labelled 'disabled'. This perspective makes certain assumptions: that subjective experience has the capacity not only to represent reality but also though reflexiveness to generate the kind of person we become, and furthermore that these concepts are not unaffected by social and cultural factors (Stevens, 1996a).

The psychodynamic view of the self, with its basic assumption that 'the structure, content and dynamics of the psyche are not necessarily available to consciousness' (Thomas, 1996:359), may be more valuable in a psycho-therapy context than as a tool for social psychology. This casts doubt on the wisdom of using as research data the reported experiences and beliefs of respondents. However, the core of psychodynamic interaction is the interpretation of such material. This is relevant to the learning history work, as is the psychodynamic perspective's emphasis on what Thomas calls the 'residues of emotional experiences of childhood' (Thomas, 1996:360):

> Some kind of interpretive approach is essential because to understand the person in a social world requires getting to grips in some way with the web of meanings that constitutes personal life and social worlds. (Thomas, 1996:361)

So researchers need to be cautious in interpreting material which may in-clude 'unconscious' meanings and 'defensive' processes.

The social constructionist view is that language and discourse construct social and individual realities. Whereas other perspectives assume the existence of a consistent, self-contained individual, social constructionism posits a 'distributed self which regards a person as made up by all the different kinds of interactions he or she engages in' (Stevens, 1996a:358). Perhaps more importantly still, this perspective questions whether true knowledge can be independent of a person's socio-cultural context. And people who are labelled dyslexic have inevitably been influenced about dyslexia by such contexts. They may construct themselves as dyslexic people in their interactions with the interviewer.

To sum up: the perspectives on the self described above all throw some light on the concept of dyslexia. The biological viewpoint is strongly represented in the literature on dyslexia (as seen in Chapter 1), with its emphasis on the neurological aspects of reading, writing and memory. In contrast with this reductionism, the experimental perspective sees dyslexia in terms of cognitive processes, as applied both to literacy practices and to the attribution of success or failure. The experiential viewpoint would examine a person's constructs about learning and literacy, and might reframe the experience of being labelled. The psychodynamic perspective would relate a student's history of associations and attachments to their relationships with teachers, and look for defensive behaviour and also transference. While all the perspectives explored here offer valuable insights, the social constructionist approach is particularly useful for investigating students' learning life histories. It examines the total context of their experience, looking for ways in which their internal narratives have been produced. It also suspends the weight of assumptions about dyslexia which have built up over the last hundred years. So what are the sources of these internal narratives?

Identity and discourse

Social and cultural interaction is inevitably mediated by language. Vygotsky (1962) believed that thought consists of internal dialogues, and that these reflect the cultural values and beliefs of the social world. Teachers impress these values upon children. 'The very learning activities which form the basis for children's cognitive and conceptual development are those which induct them into particular cultural values and beliefs' (Stevens, 1996a:252). This process involves exposure to what Mead (1934) calls the 'generalised other', what she described in terms of morality – that children shouldn't do such-and-such – but which might as easily be construed in terms of educational performance – 'children of my age should be able to spell accurately' – and descriptions of 'different' children – as in 'if you can't read yet, you're probably dyslexic'.

This kind of language has enormous power. Foucault (1976) holds that the world of health care, particularly mental health, is influenced by scientific discourse. Thus special needs education is influenced by psychological 'experts'. Such figures, Giddens (1991) suggests, form part of the 'abstract expert systems', such as psychotherapists, which we call upon in order to define ourselves. Parents and teachers call upon abstract expert systems such as Schools' Psychological Services to define children – and in the UK, LEAs continue to demand EPs' reports before they award the DSA to dyslexic University students.

Identity, then, may be seen as a discursive product. Summerfield (1998) maintains that when people give personal testimony, for example in interviews, they are inevitably deploying cultural constructions, and quotes Scott: 'no one's personal testimony represents a truth which is independent of discourse' (*ibid*, 11). The social constructionist perspective is that people are not self-contained and separate but that the self is intertwined with the social context:

> Children are, right from the start, negotiating power relations through the dialogues in which they are involved, and which position them in particular ways. This positioning is an important aspect of the emerging social person. (Stevens, 1996a:264)

Children – and adults – are constantly assessing other people's evaluations of them. As they are also learning through the medium of language practices, 'learning a language, learning through language and becoming a particular person are all closely related' (*ibid*, 264). This process may include the internalisation of language about dyslexia.

Identity and self-hood: ontological security

Giddens (1991:53) defines self-identity as 'the self as reflexively understood by the person in terms of her or his biography'. The self as a 'reflexive project' involves, for Giddens, a process of continuous interpretation of one's life history. Ivanic (1998:16) suggests that for students, academic writing plays a significant role in this process. The entire experience of being a higher education student involves, for someone who accepts the dyslexic label, continuous confrontation of experiences which challenge self-concept and self-esteem, not least academic writing.

Without ontological security, students may suffer free-floating anxiety, asserts Giddens (1991). The task associated with adolescence is to decide whether or not to be oneself (Erikson, 1968). In adolescence one moves on from the early existential problem of coming to terms with external reality to another existential question: what sort of person am I? This 'I' is embodied as well as mental, and Giddens (1991:57) describes 'routine control of the body' as essential if we are to be 'accepted by others as competent'. Dyslexic people who are clumsy or who confuse left and right, often feel that they have failed this test. Giddens defines shame as 'essentially anxiety about the adequacy of the narrative by means of which the individual sustains a coherent biography' (*ibid*, 65), and maintains that shame depends on feelings of personal insufficiency. The narratives of dyslexic people are full of such feelings (Burka, 1983).

Dyslexic or not, we are all living in 'the late modern age' (Giddens, 1991:3), which offers a potentially confusing range of socially available options for the self. Embarking upon higher education involves moving into a new context which necessitates renegotiating one's identity (Ivanic, 1998). The negotiation for a person who accepts a discourse of dyslexia is complicated by the problem of seeing him or herself as a competent student.

Identity and self-hood: self as a range of associated elements

Craib (1998) sees the self as incorporating a range of associated elements or processes, among them identity, all underlaid with 'experience'. He looks at what he calls 'the sociological notion of identity' (*ibid,* 3) as opposed to the psychological or philosophical, and proposes that conventional sociology has concentrated on 'sameness' whereas recent sociology has focused on difference. People associate themselves with some social groups, and not with others. The process of self-categorisation involves not only identifying with similar others but also distinguishing oneself from a range of groups of 'others' – it is the boundary-setting and contrast which is important, rather than 'sameness'. As Hall puts it:

> Identities are ... representations, [and] that representation is always constructed across ... a division from the place of the Other (Hall and du Gay, 1996:6).

Hall also describes identity as a meeting point with 'discourses and practices which ... hail us into place as the social subjects of particular discourses' (*op. cit.* 5). Like Ivanic, Craib also refers to the social construction of identity: identity as 'something constructed through various disciplines and discourses' (Craib, 1998:7); however, while Hall believes that 'identities can function as points of identification and attachment only because of their capacity to exclude', (Hall and du Gay, 1996:8), Craib disagrees:

> Identities can only function to exclude and leave out because of their capacity to include and enclose. (Craib, 1998:8)

Some students identified as dyslexic actively embrace the label and seek out others through activities such as support groups (Gilroy and Miles, 1996). Similarly, some parents of dyslexic children become involved in Dyslexia associations (Barton and Hamilton, 1998).

Summary

This chapter has explored a variety of ways of construing the self, all of them potentially relevant to the developing sense of identity of a person labelled as having difficulties at school or university. From the social constructionist perspective, language and discourse construct individual and social realities. The next chapter makes further links between these ideas and the conception of dyslexia.

Chapter 3
The self-concept and dyslexia

Introduction

This chapter examines the constituent parts of the self-concept and relates them to dyslexia. It explores the socio-emotional aspects of dyslexia and discusses emotional support in higher education. First, some thoughts about discourse.

The concept of discourse in the context of dyslexia

The tensions between identity and self-hood discussed in Chapter 2 may be resolved by examining the term 'discourse' in the context of dyslexia and identity. Ivanic (1998:17) has examined 'discourse' in relation to identity and literacy, defining it as 'producing and receiving culturally recognised, ideologically shaped representations of reality'. She holds that people take on particular identities through discourse – this is the social construction of identity. Ivanic is analysing the discoursal construction of writer identity, specifically the identity of HE students as academic writers. Her work is pertinent to the present theme, because the concept of dyslexia may be said to be a 'culturally recognised, ideologically shaped representation of reality', and also because, like Ivanic's co-researchers, students labelled dyslexic are expected to express themselves through academic writing, which they usually find it hard to master (Benson *et al*, 1994; Clark and Ivanic, 1997; Singleton, 1999).

Fairclough (1989) points to a relationship between language and power. He also writes (Fairclough, 1992b) about discourse and identity, proposing that discourse contributes to the construction of three elements: social identities and types of self, social relationships between people, and systems of knowledge and belief. As Ivanic (1998:44) points out, Fairclough 'places the construction of identity in the context of fluctuating cultural and institutional values'. In the context of the present study, examining as it does the discourse of dyslexia in the context of higher education, this statement by Fairclough, even though it refers to spoken discourse, is apposite:

> ... discourse contributes to processes of cultural change, in which the social identities or 'selves' associated with specific domains and institutions are redefined and reconstituted. (Fairclough, 1992b:137)

He adds:

> Most if not all analytically separable dimensions of discourse have some implications, direct or indirect, for the construction of the self. (*ibid,* 167)

This is supported by Gee (1990:143), who defines a discourse as

> ....a socially accepted association among ways of using language, of thinking, feeling, believing, valuing, and of acting that can be used to identify oneself as a member of a socially meaningful group.

Wilson (1999) claims that life span stories are the narrative sites of identity production. Linde (1993:3) makes a similar point when she states that 'an individual needs to have a coherent, acceptable and constantly revised life story'. In order to achieve this, a 'coherence system' is required; Linde names Freudian psychology and astrology as examples of such coherence systems. Students identified as dyslexic may use discourses of dyslexia as coherence systems.

How can people conceptualise their identity? When we focus on self-knowledge in relation to a person's goals (Gerber *et al,* 1992; Gerber *et al,* 1996), we are adopting a cognitive approach to the self. As Markus and Nurius (1987:158) put it, 'the self-concept is not a unitary or monolithic entity, but rather a system of salient identities or self-schemas that lend structure and meaning to one's self-relevant experiences'. Craib (1998) asserts that while identity is a process rather than a 'thing', the process also involves 'internal negotiation': we have a variety of social identities which may change over time, but membership of these – such as uncle, Councillor, nurse – takes place within our overall identity. Such a process is operating when students talk about whether or not to join a group for dyslexic people; they may be a daughter, a student, an ice hockey player, but are they 'a dyslexic' in the sense of belonging to a club? Craib links this dilemma with anxiety:

> One of the ways in which we try to protect ourselves from the anxiety of living is by trying to identify ourselves with something, by trying to make our social identity into our identity. (*op cit* 170)

This 'narcissistic' process may offer 'reassurance and relief' from social isolation. Markus and Nurius (1987) hold that the self-concept is not constant or static. Rather, there exists a 'working self-concept' (*op cit* 162): 'that set of self-conceptions that are presently accessible in thought and memory'. They point to the variability of the self-concept: one can feel mature and confident in a work setting, very young in a family setting when being compared with a favoured sibling, and very old when in the company of much younger people. Once again, identity is located in contrasts with others, rather than 'sameness'.

Self-concept

Markus and Nurius (1987:163) refer to a 'total repertoire of self-conceptions', some of which may be 'domain-specific'. Coopersmith (1967), whose self-esteem inventory is useful in work with school students (Pollak, 1993), believes that self-esteem is developmental: early in life it is relatively undifferentiated, but it gradually becomes more complex and hierarchical. This view is confirmed by Battle (1990), a more recent inventory deviser. Marsh (1992) gives the following outline of such a hierarchical model:

Fig 3.1 : Marsh's hierarchical model of the self-concept

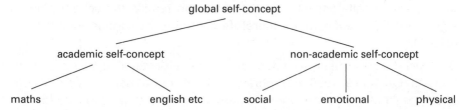

Here the items in the lowest row are specific to the domains in which they become salient (see also Schunk, 1990). According to this hierarchical view, whether or not poor self-esteem leads to poor academic performance or *vice versa* becomes irrelevant: it is seen as an interactional process, with separate components.

Self-esteem

Coopersmith (1967) adopted a similar theoretical approach to devise his self-esteem inventory. He allowed for the estimation of self-esteem in relation to social life (self/peers), home/parents and school/academic aspects, as well as what he called the 'general self' and the 'total self'. If self-concept is the umbrella term involving cognitive, affective and behavioural evaluation of the self (Burns, 1979; Riddick, 1996), then self-esteem is a measure of how far self-image matches the ideal self (Lawrence, 1996). This is Lawrence's diagram of the relationships between them:

Fig 3.2 : Lawrence's model of the self-concept

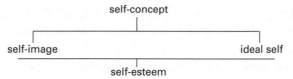

Lawrence comments on the central role of reading and writing at primary school in this regard, adding that it may not be failure to achieve which produces low self-esteem, but the way significant others react to it.

The notion of an 'ideal self' often develops from the remarks of such significant others; for example, parents and teachers often express expectations of 'good' behaviour, and young children often compare themselves with peers. Kelly usually included 'myself-as-I-would-like-to-be' as an 'element' in his repertory grid work, eliciting constructs by including this figure in triads with other elements such as 'best friend' and 'older sibling' (Kelly, 1955; Winter, 1992).

Among the 'core conditions' for successful psychotherapy Rogers (1951) includes empathy and positive regard, adding that these principles apply equally to education (Kirschenbaum and Henderson, 1990). Riddick (1996: 34) adds that 'a sense of acceptance, competence and worth' is necessary for a positive self-concept, and that after the family, the school plays a significant role. Teachers are therefore central to developing pupils' self-esteem.

But teachers are as likely to reduce children's self-esteem as they are to enhance it (Lawrence, 1996; Humphrey, 2002). I brought Kelly's personal construct psychology to my investigation of teachers' perceptions of the students at a special school for dyslexic teenagers, and the students' perceptions of themselves (Pollak, 1993). The project confirmed Lawrence's view, which I summarised as the social construction of self-esteem. As one teacher told me, 'we are always looking at pupils, but we don't always get the time to reflect on our own part in this dynamic' (Pollak, 1993). Lawrence added a chapter on 'The teacher's self-esteem' to the second edition of his book on self-esteem in the classroom (Lawrence, 1996); and in my study, another teacher commented that 'teachers have self-esteem needs too' (Pollak, 1993). About the labelling of children with special needs, Salzberger-Wittenberg (1983) *et al* point out:

> One way of easing everybody's distress has been by labelling the child as ESN, dyslexic, retarded or maladjusted and so on ... Such labels can be used to write children off, as well as, more appropriately, to relieve a self-critical teacher. (Salzberger-Wittenberg *et al,* 1983:132)

This view is contradicted by Humphrey (2002), who holds that identification as dyslexic should be carried out as early as possible, so as to enhance children's self-esteem.

There has long been a pecking order in education in the UK. Primary school teaching is seen as of lower status than secondary, FE lower than HE and so on. In the 1970s it was difficult to find a PGCE course focusing on primary education, as it was assumed that graduates would wish to teach their subjects, ideally to A Level. Similarly, Adult Basic Education is regarded as low status work, like what was known as 'remedial' teaching in compulsory education. This is where the desire of some parents to achieve special status for their children as dyslexic may coincide with the wishes of special needs teachers to be regarded as specialists. Much early literature on teaching dyslexic children emphasised this distinction between 'remedial' work and 'dyslexia specialist' teaching (Franklin and Naidoo, 1970; Naidoo, 1972; Newton and Thomson, 1974; Hickey, 1977).

Teachers and the self-concept

Teacher and tutor comments and reports are seen by students as sources of information about the self. Andersen (1987) notes that what others actually say in this 'social feedback' is less important than how these opinions are perceived. For example students identified as dyslexic commonly contest the marks they have been given (Gilroy, 1995). However, as Riddick (1996) points out, feedback from teachers is only effective for a student if s/he sees the teacher as a significant other and if the teacher's and the student's perceptions of ability are congruent.

A key element in the reception of feedback from teachers is students' sense of their own intelligence. Stuart (1995) points out that identity involves gender, cultural heritage and family background; that our perception of our intelligence intersects with all these aspects; and that a professional educator's assessment has particular weight. She quotes Mead (1934) as defining the 'significant other', whose ideas about us are highly likely to be internalised, and the 'generalised other': society as a whole. This theory of the self as generated through symbolic interactions was taken up by Goffman (1959), who described the way in which embarrassment is seen in relation to a contrast between shame and esteem: each time we experience embarrassment, we internalise shame and our self-image is confirmed. This process operates in the education system, and can powerfully affect undergraduates (Peelo, 2000a).

Self-representation

Social feedback is part of the overall process of social interaction. If we are to receive feedback, we must first present ourselves to others. What Ivanic (1998:21) calls 'the emotionally fraught, usually subconscious nature of self-representation' Goffman (1959) describes in theatrical terms. Goffman differentiates between a person as 'character' and a person as 'performer'. This can apply to the investigation of dyslexia, with people seen as 'putting on' or reproducing socio-culturally constructed identities. Goffman sees identity as 'a status, a position, a social place' (*op. cit.* 31).

Interviews of any kind, but particularly those which invite the respondent to remember the past, as in a learning life history, involve the representation of the self to the interviewer. Summerfield (1998) is a valuable source on the nature of self-representation. She refers to what she terms the 'inter-subjectivity' involved in the production of memory: 'the relationship between the narrator and his or her audience' (*ibid*, 23). In terms of the research process, an interviewer may be constructing an identity for him or herself in each interview, and so may an informant.

Inter-subjectivity encompasses the 'assumption of consciousness, under-standing and self in others' (Stevens, 1996a:169). It is thus part of the experiential perspective on the self. On the other hand, object relations theorists such as Klein propose that being attached to and confirmed by others is essential to the determination of the self, and this places inter-subjectivity in the psychodynamic realm (Klein, 1993). Psychotherapists Salzberger-Wittenberg *et al* (1983) believe that psychodynamic theory has a great deal to offer the study of learning and teaching situations. They list the expectations students might have of a teacher. They might see her as: the source of knowledge and wisdom; a provider and comforter; an object of admiration and envy; a judge; an authority figure. Conversely, the teacher might have fears of criticism, hostility or losing control. Either way, say Salzberger-Wittenberg and her colleagues, the teacher-student relationship is loaded with opportunities for transference (*ibid*, Chapters 2 and 3), but they do tend to pathologise this agenda.

In her interview study of the experiences of women during the Second World War, Summerfield (1998) attached labels to the types of attitude adopted by her informants ('heroes' and 'stoics'), seeing these as the images of women prevalent at the time. Summerfield's informants are talk-ing about a relatively short period in British history and looking at their roles within it, whereas obtaining dyslexic students' learning life histories involves them in looking back over their whole lives, educationally speak-ing. Nevertheless, similar processes can be seen to be taking place.

Summerfield is using personal testimony for the purposes of historical study. 'Women speaking for themselves through personal testimony', she says (1998:11), 'are using language and so deploying cultural construc-tions'. So such personal testimony cannot represent a truth which is independent of discourse. This is because, explains Summerfield quoting Scott: 'we are dependent on language for understanding who we are and what we are doing' (*ibid*, 11).

Summerfield proposes that the processes which affect people's memories of the past, far from having the negative effect of distorting the truth in historical terms, can create layers of meaning which are worthy of study. Students' words about their experiences of dyslexia can similarly be examined for evidence of the discourses which they represent, since cultural constructions form the discursive context not only within which people express and understand what happens to them, but also within which they actually have those experiences. (Summerfield, 1998:12).

Hence the task of the historian working with personal testimony is akin to that of the researcher into the learning life stories of dyslexic students: 'to untangle the relationships between discourses and experiences' (*ibid*).

Summerfield observes that 'there is not likely to be a single discourse at any one time which directly determines consciousness' (*ibid,* 15), and this is also true of students' use of discourses. She refers to 'the discursive formulations from which understandings are selected and within which accounts are made' in oral history. Her interviews showed women using multiple discourses concerning their wartime lives to 'constitute themselves'. Their testimony is inter-subjective in that it draws on 'the generalised subject available in discourse to construct the particular personal subject' (*ibid,* 15). Both these aspects apply equally to learning life history interviews.

However, Summerfield identifies another way in which the process is inter-subjective: the narrator or interviewee is aware of an audience. That audience has two parts: the immediate audience of the interviewer and the public or imagined audience for the research:

> Inter-subjectivity, understood as the relationship between the narrator and his or her audience, is a necessary and inescapable part of the production of memory. (*ibid,* 23)

The socio-emotional aspects of the dyslexia concept

Salzberger-Wittenberg *et al* write about dyslexia, describing the label as a 'psychiatric' one. One of their studies concerns a child whom they call Maurice who was failing to learn to read. His mother had taken him to a clinic and 'obtained a certificate of dyslexia':

> The diagnosis had been carefully made but later discussion with Maurice showed that he had interpreted the word to mean that he had a nasty, infectious illness and that his brain did not work properly. The sad effect was to make him feel at the mercy of his handicap, reduce his own feeling of control, and, as his teachers reported, seemed quite destructive of his efforts to learn to read. (Salzberger-Wittenberg *et al*, 1983:133)

Ravenette (1979) found that the label dyslexic led families to see children as disabled. Miles, on the other hand, has written at least once per decade (Miles, 1970; Miles, 1988; Miles, 1993) of the value of the label in giving children and their families a way of making sense of what is happening and a route out of self-blame.

A report on a British national inquiry into responses to dyslexia was carried out with a working group of EPs, and included contributions from

Local Education Authorities and statutory and voluntary bodies (Pumfrey and Reason, 1991). It was one of the first studies on dyslexia that had a chapter on social and emotional factors. The chapter concluded that

> labels, limited to within-child variables, can detract attention from policies and organisation that take account of the full social and interpersonal context in which the learning difficulties arise. (Pumfrey and Reason, 1991:73)

The report noted 'the need to take account of the sense the child is making of the situation and the perceptions of family members' (*ibid*). Importantly, Pumfrey and Reason recommended that 'specific learning difficulties be examined in the context of personal experiences and interpersonal relationships, recognising the emotional impact of a prolonged struggle with literacy' (*ibid,* 73).

My study at a special school for dyslexic students (Pollak, 1993) was partly a response to this. I found that by the end of their first year, new students' self-esteem had improved markedly. Using personal construct psychology, the study revealed that they associated reading and writing with positive aspects of their lives. Personal construct psychology also showed that the staff construed the students in widely differing ways, but that they acknowledged that such constructs were 'part of the informal baggage they [brought] into the classroom' and that 'a child's progress depends on how good s/he feels' (Pollak, 1993).

In what was probably the first published response to Pumfrey and Reason's call for further research into socio-emotional aspects, Edwards (1994) examined the 'emotional reactions' of eight 16 to 17 year-old boys who were also attending a special school for dyslexic students. Her case studies reveal uniformly negative relationships with subjects' previous teachers; two thirds of them had been physically attacked, and all had 'suffer[ed] inadequate help or neglect' (Edwards, 1994:161). On the basis of the boys' response to 'special' schooling, she concludes that 'failure and scarring is not an innate and integral feature of the dyslexic' (*ibid,* 162). However, both this and Pollak (1993) focused on students who had been extracted from mainstream schools and given intensive attention, including deliberate efforts to boost their self-esteem.

Riddick's *Living with dyslexia* (1996), sub-titled the social and emotional consequences of specific learning difficulties, also responds to Pumfrey and Reason. She points out that many studies of self-esteem and 'learning difficulties' (such as Butkowsky and Willows, 1980) have focused on reading delay rather than dyslexia and have studied self-esteem only in relation to reading competence.

Riddick (1995a) points out that the relationship between teachers and parents of younger students can be particularly stressful for all three parties when there is disagreement over the nature of a child's difficulties. Part of the problem can be, as Pollock and Waller (1994) observe, that the concept of dyslexia is rather like a religion: people are either believers or they are not.

A notable exception to studies which focus only on reading is Rawson's *Dyslexia over the lifespan – a fifty-five-year longitudinal study* (Rawson, 1995). This study is of 56 boys, both dyslexic and not, who attended a small private school in Pennsylvania. Rawson states:

> The problem of low self-concept was more prevalent and persistent among the boys who were diagnosed and given help after they had experienced failure, for then it was hard for them to believe that they were as capable and likely to succeed as the accumulating evidence of their competence indicated. (*ibid,* 58)

This appears to contradict Miles' belief in the value of the dyslexic label, although the potential problem might be avoided if screening for dyslexia were a normal, non-stigmatising procedure. Rawson adopts a medical view of dyslexia, quoting in full what was then the Orton Dyslexia Society's definition with its reference to a 'neurologically-based disorder,' and stating that the 'diagnosis' must be 'clinical' (*ibid,* 149). So it is not surprising that some of her students did not at first believe they could succeed.

However, it seems that Rawson's school adopted the same philosophy as those referred to above (Pollak, 1993; Edwards, 1994):

> It may be that one of the school's most valuable contributions was to the self-concepts of the dyslexic boys, a persistent faith in their intelligence and capacity to achieve, transmitted to the boys directly and indirectly. (Rawson, 1995:110)

Bat-Hayim (1997) reports on a course at an American college designed to tackle learned helplessness in students with 'learning disabilities' and 'by-pass long-standing emotional and linguistic barriers to learning'. She refers to one student who failed the course, and later thanked the tutors for the fact that 'he was not permitted to use his well remediated dyslexia as a crutch' (*ibid,* 230).

Hales (1994) attempted a quantitative study of 'some personal aspects of the personal functioning of dyslexic people,' using a personality factor questionnaire. He found that infants appeared tense and frustrated, children in the middle school years showed low motivation and high anxiety, whereas at secondary school they wanted to be as unobtrusive as possible. Hales found an inverse relationship between anxiety and IQ, which tends to counter the common belief that intelligent dyslexic children find school life more difficult than their peers.

More than twenty years earlier, a report in the *British Medical Journal* (Saunders and Barker, 1972) had found 'a recognisable neurotic pattern' in a group of dyslexic adults. One had said: 'I want to be a normal person'. This comment may hide a great deal. It suggests a kind of Hawthorne effect in which the experience of being the subject of such research makes people feel abnormal and anxious. Rourke *et al* (1989) listed nine 'neuropsychological characteristics' of children with 'nonverbal learning disability' and used such words as disability, disorder, dysfunction and disease. Their subjects were found to be depressed and suicidal in later years.

Some studies show depression in dyslexic children and adolescents. Maag and Behrens (1989) found that of a sample of 465 high school students, 21 per cent experienced severe depression, although this finding, based on self-report inventories, is complicated by the fact that some of the students had already been identified as 'seriously emotionally disturbed'. A Texas inquiry (Wright-Strawderman and Watson, 1992) found that 35 per cent of the subjects (aged 8 to 11) scored in the depressed range, again using a self-report inventory.

Michaels and Lewandowski (1990) used structured reports by the parents of child subjects. They found that a greater than average proportion of boys with 'learning disabilities' were at risk of developing 'psychological adjustment problems' such as anxiety, depression and obsessive-compulsive behaviour. On the other hand, an Israeli study (Lamm and Epstein, 1992) which used a 'symptom checklist' filled in by teachers, found no difference in terms of 'emotional status' between a dyslexic group of young adults, psychiatric patients or controls. All this supports Little's (1993) strictures as regards generalisability.

Emotional support in higher education

Gilroy (1995), an experienced educational practitioner, makes a practical, realistic contribution. Her chapter in the book *Dyslexia and stress* is called 'Stress factors in the college student'. She writes of the effect of past experiences like these on self-concept:

> ... having been branded as 'thick', ... being ridiculed and misunderstood, ... having struggled hard at school without efforts being recognised. (Gilroy, 1995:66)

In conversation between members of a student support group at her university, Gilroy notes the frequency of expressions such as 'hopeless at', 'could never' and 'typical me'. She observes that:

> There are certain times in a university career that are particularly stressful for the dyslexic student. The very early days at university can place heavy demands on memory, organisation, orientation. There is the stress of the new environment and the anxiety of coping with new names, relationships, activities and a new lifestyle. (*ibid*, 59)

But this is true for all new students, as others have pointed out (Raaheim *et al,* 1991; Earwaker, 1992; Peelo, 1994). A recent report by a British Heads of University Counselling Services Working Group (Rana *et al,* 1999:1) found that there was 'broad agreement from counselling services that the severity of emotional and behavioural disturbance amongst university students is increasing'. Peelo (2000a, 2000b) believes that learning support tutors must address not only cognitive processes but also affective and social ones.

Gilroy (1995:56) argues that dyslexic students have 'a specific language disability' the history of which, when combined with associated working memory difficulties, makes them liable to develop stress symptoms more quickly. She admits that those who regard themselves as dyslexic sometimes fail to see that all students must accept negative criticism in order to develop academically. They may 'blame everything on dyslexia' (*ibid,* 62):

> Dyslexia is ever-present in the students' minds; it makes them egocentric, and they cannot think out from themselves. As a result, they become quite demanding over their 'rights' and may go bluntly into a tutor's room to seek 'justice'. (*ibid,* 62)

Goodwin (1996) suggests that tutors need counselling skills to help students 'move on from' feelings of bitterness and anger, as well as from fearing that they will not succeed. She believes (Goodwin, 1998) that individual counselling for dyslexic students should be of the humanistic or 'person-centred' type, as Rogerian positive regard and empathy are essential for clients who are experiencing anxiety and self-doubt. On the other hand McLoughlin *et al* (1994:47), while acknowledging the importance of Rogers' 'core conditions', propose that what they call 'generalist' as opposed to 'specialist' counsellors might successfully use a cognitive approach. They explain that 'a dyslexic's understanding of the nature of their difficulties is central to overcoming those difficulties' and that 'maladaptive feelings are caused by irrational beliefs' such as that most other students are very good at spelling or rapid reading.

McLoughlin *et al* go on to describe a vicious circle, in which the memory of being called unintelligent by significant others such as relatives or teachers increases negative feelings; this in turn leads to poor self-esteem and lack of confidence, which reduces motivation; this is then interpreted by others – and probably by the student as well – as evidence of low intelligence. They posit four levels of awareness in adult dyslexic people, claiming that supporting them requires consciousness of their starting point:

> People at level 1 are not aware of their weaknesses and have developed no strategies to overcome them.

Those at level 2 are aware of their weaknesses but have not developed strategies to overcome them.

People at level 3 are aware of their weaknesses and have developed compensatory strategies, but have developed them unconsciously.

Finally, people at level 4 are aware of their weaknesses and they have consciously developed strategies to overcome them. (McLoughlin *et al,* 1994:50)

As regards 'starting points', the report of the NWP differentiates between counselling newly enrolled students and such work with newly identified students. The suggestion is that identification as dyslexic is central: newly admitted students may have recently experienced stressful dyslexia assessment, or be fearing that they will have to go through it, whereas those who have just been identified may need emotional support because 'they need to come to terms with new aspects of themselves' (Singleton, 1999:134).

The discovery that one has dyslexia can produce feelings of relief, but it can also generate anxieties. Students exhibit confusion and loss of confidence *because they have only a vague understanding of the nature of the condition at this early stage.* (*ibid,* 134 – author's emphasis)

This part of the Singleton report raises two issues. One is concerned with the use of the word 'identify'. In some quarters it has become the norm to try to avoid medical language in connection with dyslexia in adults (Hunter-Carsch and Herrington, 2001; Hunter-Carsch, 2001; McLoughlin *et al,* 2002); the Singleton report itself states that the term 'diagnosis' 'will be avoided as far as possible because of 'disease' connotations' (*ibid,* 81). The preferred term is 'identification', the root word of which has clear implications for the present study. Yet on the same page as this passage, the NWP report uses the expressions 'students with dyslexia' and 'a student has dyslexia'; in its preferred definition it refers to dyslexia as a 'condition'. The other issue is the assumption that it is necessary to expound a discourse of dyslexia to a student; the report also recommends that this should be done as part of staff development (*ibid,* Chapter 13).

Summary

This chapter has considered models of self-concept and of self-esteem, and the role of these in self-representation. It has linked them with the socio-emotional aspects of dyslexia, and of learning support in HE.

Chapter 4 describes a research project designed to explore these issues via the investigation of students' learning life histories.

Chapter 4
An HE-focused research project

The report on a UK national inquiry (Pumfrey and Reason, 1991:73) recommended that 'specific learning difficulties be examined in the context of personal experiences and interpersonal relationships'. How might this be approached? The research project (Pollak, 1993) referred to in the last chapter tackled self-esteem development quantitatively by using an inventory, and also qualitatively, by using personal construct grids to make individuals' attitudes and beliefs manifest. Two British authors have since published interview studies: Edwards (1994) calls hers 'eight case studies in emotional reactions', which relate to young teenagers, and Riddick's accounts focusing on children and adult students include the social and emotional consequences of 'specific learning difficulties' (Riddick, 1996; Riddick *et al,* 1997).

In the US, Kurnoff (2000) entitled her book *The human side of dyslexia: 142 interviews with real people telling real stories.* The people interviewed (in the US and the UK) ranged in age from young children to college students, and Kurnoff states early on that: 'It's not medical, it's social'. The book is discussed in Chapter 8.

Rodis *et al*'s (2001) *Learning disabilities and life stories* also stresses the social dimension. This set of autobiographical accounts and scholarly essays is designed to provide education professionals and family members with insights into 'improving the lives' of dyslexic people. Unlike Kurnoff, Rodis *et al* do not focus on educational experiences. The same might be said of a third American book, Rawson's *Dyslexia over the lifespan* (1995). Rawson's unique achievement is to have followed the lives of a group of more than 50 people over 55 years; half the book is devoted to their careers as adults.

What has been lacking is work focusing on the experiences of dyslexic students in HE. An exception is Riddick *et al*'s 1997 study of undergraduates, sub-titled *Growing up with a specific learning difficulty.* They report on respondents' perceptions of their school experience in terms of the presence or lack of 'protective factors' such as supportive parents. They examine respondents' perceptions of the label 'dyslexic' and what they call their 'understanding of dyslexia' and report their statements about reading, writing, spelling, speaking and coping strategies. After a report on self-esteem, Riddick *et al* give a brief summary about university experience. They call for further research into five areas, including the evaluation of individual coping strategies and of the efficacy of different types of support (*ibid,* 184-185).

The NWP report (Singleton, 1999) includes the latter point, listing as 'current controversies':

■ whether students with difficulties in literacy rightfully belong in higher education

■ how students with dyslexia may be reliably and consistently identified and supported (Singleton, 1999:17).

The report calls for 'promotion of a better general understanding of dyslexia amongst staff and students in higher education, and amongst the population generally' (*ibid,* 166).

How well are universities dealing with dyslexic students? Riddick *et al* (1997:185) call for work on 'the lifetime course of the emotional and social development of dyslexic individuals'. Their reasons are two-fold: to improve learning support provision, and 'to develop our understanding of cognitive and socio-emotional development generally' (*ibid,* 185). Such learning life history work is also valuable because the label 'dyslexic' is more than a matter of reading and writing, raising as it does issues of identity, in particular 'defect' and 'difference'.

Increasing numbers of students in HE believe they have a condition called dyslexia, the existence of which is enshrined in legislation (Singleton, 1999; HESA, 1997). Inclusivity and diversity in HE are worthy notions, but higher education institutes (HEIs) must be prepared to deal with the variety of students they are admitting, and dyslexic people constitute a majority of those undergraduates who are regarded as having special needs (Singleton, 1999).

In order to promote the 'better general understanding' of dyslexia by the HE sector which the NWP report calls for, a research project was set up to inquire into students' views of dyslexia and the consequences of those views. The two-part umbrella question was: 'How do students who have been identified as dyslexic define dyslexia and describe their own experience of it?' Answering this involved finding out from dyslexic students how they saw dyslexia as having affected both their route to University and their ability to deal with its challenges. So additional questions were: How do the various influences which have been brought to bear on these students impact on their identity and self-concept as participants in Higher Education? And how did the informants' sense of identity affect their ability to manage the pressures of studying for a degree, in terms of their cognitive, affective and social experience?

Chapter 2 made a case for the social constructionist view of identity. This is constructed through discourse, although as Ivanic (1998:27) points out, 'several types of socially available resources for the construction of identity operate simultaneously'. Ivanic sets out four aspects of what she calls 'writer identity': autobiographical self, discoursal self, self as author and possibilities for self-hood (*ibid,* 23). In terms of dyslexia it is useful to look for a modified version of Ivanic's four aspects; these could be called four facets (for a dyslexic person) of identity as a student:

- ■ Autobiographical self: the identity people bring with them to the act of being a student, shaped by their earlier social experiences
- ■ Discoursal self: the discourse of dyslexia with which they identify
- ■ Self as a student: the level of confidence with which individuals see themselves as readers, thinkers, note-takers, writers, contributors to seminars and similar activities
- ■ Possibilities for self-hood: social, cultural and institutional options; issues of power, values and beliefs.

These aspects of identity as a student may emerge from interviews if respondents are asked to reminisce about their educational experiences. Summerfield (1998) identifies a dual role of reminiscence, firstly as a life review, in which one makes sense of one's life, and secondly for the maintenance of self-esteem, by re-telling self-affirming stories to help deal with losses and memories of struggle. This is important, because it means that the interview process can benefit the student as well as the researcher. The key point is that people's understandings of their own experiences form a vital part of knowledge about the phenomena labelled dyslexia.

The epistemological position of this work includes seeing the researcher as actively constructing knowledge about the educational scene, and not as a 'completely neutral collector of information about the social world' (Mason, 1996:36). The researcher requires sources (i.e. informants) with whom he can generate data, as opposed to collecting it.

The research questions above are exploratory, indicating that generating valid data calls for a qualitative approach (Miles and Huberman, 1994). My study is concerned with individuals' own accounts in interview of their attitudes, motivations and behaviour: their perceptions, attitudes, beliefs, views and feelings (Hakim, 1987).

A project which focuses on learning life history draws on Plummer's seminal *Documents of Life* (Plummer, 1983, 2001). Plummer began what has become mainstream life history research, focusing on comprehending how one constructs and makes sense of one's life at a given moment. The present study aims to elucidate the ways in which dyslexic university students make sense of the process of studying.

Using interviewing is an innovative approach. Comparable interview data were used in Riddick *et al* (1997), which was published after I had carried out my interviews. But before that there was no published exploratory work in the UK on the experiences of dyslexic undergraduates. And such work requires an audience, as memory and reflection are greatly facilitated by engagement between the narrator and a responsive listener (Summerfield, 1998,1999).

This project is not focused on the views of academics or of the relatives of students labelled dyslexic. Nor does it seek information about students who are wondering whether the label applies to them. The focus is on university students who accept the label dyslexic – they are the subjects. The research questions involve the process of identification as dyslexic, so informants must have experienced this and be willing to talk voluntarily about their experiences.

Many authors (Klein, 1993; McLoughlin, Fitzgibbon *et al*, 1994; Cairns and Moss, 1995; Krupska and Klein, 1995; Reid and Kirk, 2001) state that assessment of the needs of a dyslexic student should begin with an educational or learning history. Klein (1993) comments that adults can usually describe their difficulties fully. 'A learning history offers evidence of patterns of difficulty that can be scrutinised' Cairns and Moss (1995:48).

'How do students who have been identified as dyslexic define dyslexia and describe their own experience of it?' was the umbrella research question. This implies a 'homogeneous sample ... covering a narrow range or single value of a particular variable' (Robson, 1993:142). In order to find out whether the label dyslexic applies to them, and to gain access to funded learning support, UK higher education students have to approach a department which is generally part of Student Services (DfES, 2004; Gilroy and Miles, 1996). Accordingly, potential informants were contacted via these departments. To achieve a variety of university experience, they were taken from a new university in the Midlands and an old university in the North of England, plus two corresponding institutions in the South.

Cohen and Manion (1989) and Oppenheim (1992) all recommend that a sample size of at least thirty is necessary for this kind of research. It was hoped that a cohort of students of this size would between them exemplify a range of experiences relating to dyslexia. To widen the range of possible experiences on the way to university required a sample who had arrived via a variety of routes. To cover the range of experiences of dyslexia, the sample had to include students whose home backgrounds had been supportive of their educational endeavours and some that had not. I approached seven students I knew at two universities in the South of England who had been admitted via Access courses and other non-traditional routes and who had experienced a variety of levels of academic support. The sample also met the diverse backgrounds criterion, as fifteen had arrived via A Levels, six via Access courses and the rest via various routes including accreditation of experiential learning. (In the UK, an Access course prepares people with little post-16 educational experience for entry into HE.)

A wide age range was also required, to maximise the potential for differing points of view (Robson, 1993) and the age range of those coming forward was 18 to 53. There were 13 males and 20 females, which appeared unrepresentative of the dyslexic population, as until recently the assumed ratio was at least 4:1 male to female (Naidoo, 1972; Doyle, 1996). It has now been suggested (Fink, 1998; Morgan and Klein, 2000) that both sexes are equally involved. However, the research questions were not focused on gender, and self-esteem can evidently be a problem for either sex (Pollak, 2004).

Because the students attended four universities, a range of institutional approaches to dyslexia was likely. I have called the universities:

Burtonforth – an older 'traditional' university in the North

Axbridge – a 'new' university in the Midlands

Spenceton – a younger 'traditional' university in the South

Belleville – a 'new' university in the South.

Learning support departments and welfare officers who worked with dyslexic students at the universities distributed letters inviting students to take part in the research. Consequently, the sample was a self-selected group. It included the kind of people the project required in HE, identified as dyslexic and willing to talk about their experiences.

The letter to prospective informants declared that they would not be subjected to tests or questionnaires, but would be interviewed about their learning histories.

Some students who made appointments failed to attend, so the final sample, including the pilot group, amounted to 33, made up as follows:

Burtonforth 17   Axbridge 8

Spenceton 5   Belleville 3

Interviews lasted about 90 minutes, and were transcribed. Transcripts were sent to the informants, with copies of the tape recordings, so they could clarify what they had meant to say and add further thoughts. The text was analysed with the help of a qualitative research software package called 'NUD.IST,' an acronym for non-numerical unstructured data indexing searching and theorising (Richards and Richards, 1996).This allows the researcher to build up an interlocking network of labels for sections of text (known as 'coding'), and to search the transcripts in sophisticated ways.

The data also included two types of documentary evidence: EPs' reports on informants, and information for students about dyslexia published by various universities. The EPs' reports on the informants, provided voluntarily by 22 of them, varied in length from less than one page to eleven pages. All were written to a formula widely practised by such psychologists: an introduction covering the educational background of the student and reason for referral; results of normative tests; outcomes of any criterion-referenced tests; conclusion in respect of dyslexia and recommendations. The dyslexia information booklets and leaflets bore titles such as *The Dyslexia Handbook, Support for students with specific learning difficulties (including dyslexia)* and *Student's Handbook: disabilities, dyslexia and special needs.*

This material was coded in two ways: literal and interpretive (Mason, 1996). The literal included noting any direct statements such as definitions of dyslexia or opinions about what constitutes evidence of it. The psychologists' reports also commented on the subject's emotional state or personality. My interpretive coding referred to the model of dyslexia being used.

Table 4.1 shows the basic facts about informants in alphabetical order: age, university, route to university and degree subject:

The cohort comprised 13 men and 20 women who ranged in age from 18 to 53 and reached higher education (at four universities) via a variety of routes. There is no pattern in the subjects informants were studying and these were very varied. This table is gradually expanded in subsequent chapters, as further information about each informant is elucidated.

A detailed report on the research method is not necessary here. But it is important to point out that the adoption of an interpretivist approach generated interview data which revealed valuable material about the cognitive, affective and social aspects of life in HE for dyslexic students.

Summary

This chapter has set out the antecedents, rationale and methods adopted for the research project presented in this book. It has also introduced the students involved; Appendix II gives brief 'life maps' for each of them.

Chapters 5 to 8 explore the findings of the project.

Table 4.1 Basic facts about informants

Informant	Age	Route to Univ.	University	Subject
Adrian	25	BTEC	Belleville	Engineering
Alice	37	A Levels	Axbridge	Education
Alison	20	A Levels	Axbridge	Computer science
Aarti	22	A Levels	Burtonforth	Media & drama
Ann	21	A Levels	Burtonforth	Zoology
Arnold	20	US grades	Spenceton	Anthropology
Betty	49	APEL	Axbridge	Health visiting
Bruce	24	A Levels	Burtonforth	Biology
Charles	44	APEL	Belleville	Building surveying
Charlotte	21	A Levels	Spenceton	Social policy
Chuck	34	APEL	Belleville	Engineering
Eliza	22	Canadian grades	Axbridge	Hotel management
Enid	20	A Levels	Burtonforth	Archaeology
Fenella	44	Access	Spenceton	Social anthropology
Gary	20	A Levels	Burtonforth	Computer science
Geraldine	53	A Levels	Axbridge	(Lecturer)
Harry	27	A Levels	Burtonforth	Economics
Jemima	20	A Levels	Burtonforth	Occupational therapy
Jeremy	19	A Levels	Burtonforth	Biochemistry
Lance	24	A Levels	Burtonforth	Politics
Lisa	50	APEL	Burtonforth	Sociology
Mel	32	A Levels	Axbridge	Education and I.T.
Patrick	25	A Levels	Burtonforth	I.T.
Peggy	38	Access	Spenceton	Geography
Phoebe	21	A Levels	Burtonforth	Classics
Rachel	20	A Levels	Burtonforth	Occupational therapy
Robert	31	Access	Burtonforth	Law
Ron	41	Access	Axbridge	Adult nursing
Sally	19	A Levels	Burtonforth	Business studies
Stephen	22	A Levels	Burtonforth	Geology & geography
Susan	45	Access	Spenceton	Psychology
Victoria	50	Access	Axbridge	Social work
Will	18	A Levels	Burtonforth	Geophysics

Chapter 5

Socio-emotional and identity issues in compulsory and higher education

Introduction

How do dyslexic students define dyslexia and describe their own experience of it? The literature on dyslexia is overwhelmingly cognitive (Stanovich, 1982; Seymour, 1986; Dockrell, 1992; Fletcher *et al*, 1994; Nicolson and Fawcett, 1994). By inviting informants to describe their learning histories, the project obtained data rich in affective and social material, as well as cognitive; this provided answers to the question about informants' sense of identity and self-concept. Informants also talked extensively about their learning experiences at school and at university. Brief illustrative extracts from each interview are given in Appendix I.

This chapter begins by proposing a descriptive typology: a model showing the pathway for the individual from the definition of dyslexia to the student's sense of identity, and thence to the socio-emotional effects of the self-concept and their relevance in HE. The typology provides the structure for this and the next two chapters, in which the basic table of informants (Table 4.1) is gradually expanded.

A descriptive typology

In the process of putting their experiences and feelings into words, informants were employing cultural constructions and making use of available cultural representations (Summerfield, 1998) as they tried to make sense of education-related events in their lives. The interview data and documentary evidence show that the informants' beliefs about dyslexia have a profound effect upon their sense of identity, that this process produces emotional outcomes, and that these influence the students' University careers. This model is set out in Figure 5.1 below:

Figure 5.1 : Pathway from the definition of dyslexia via identity and socio-emotional factors to experience of Higher Education

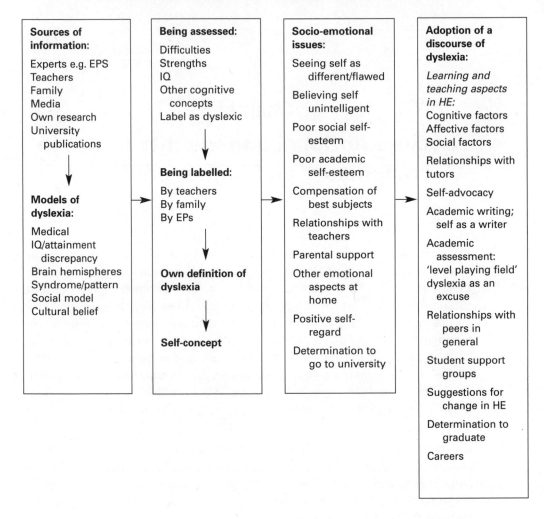

Sources of information:

Experts e.g. EPS
Teachers
Family
Media
Own research
University
   publications

Models of dyslexia:

Medical
IQ/attainment
   discrepancy
Brain hemispheres
Syndrome/pattern
Social model
Cultural belief

Being assessed:

Difficulties
Strengths
IQ
Other cognitive
   concepts
Label as dyslexic

Being labelled:

By teachers
By family
By EPs

Own definition of dyslexia

Self-concept

Socio-emotional issues:

Seeing self as
   different/flawed

Believing self
   unintelligent

Poor social self-
   esteem

Poor academic
   self-esteem

Compensation of
   best subjects

Relationships with
   teachers

Parental support

Other emotional
   aspects at
   home

Positive self-
   regard

Determination to
   go to university

Adoption of a discourse of dyslexia:

Learning and teaching aspects in HE:
Cognitive factors
Affective factors
Social factors

Relationships with
   tutors

Self-advocacy

Academic writing;
   self as a writer

Academic
   assessment:
'level playing field'
dyslexia as an
   excuse

Relationships with
   peers in
   general

Student support
   groups

Suggestions for
   change in HE

Determination to
   graduate

Careers

The pathways vary, as the following four examples illustrate:

1. Belief in her own intelligence (supported by her family) in spite of poor academic performance at school leads a student to focus on her own strengths of oral expression and visualisation, which make her determined to go to university and succeed on admission. Informants with similar stories: Rachel, Robert

2. A received definition of dyslexia as a neurological deficit causes poor self-esteem, which results in social withdrawal, a tentative approach to university admission and lack of confidence once admitted. Informants with such stories: Ann, Fenella.

3. Belief that dyslexia is a recognised pattern of difficulties creates expectations of learning support. When this is not forthcoming, anger and frustration begin at school and provoke a strong-minded effort at university to obtain special arrangements. Informants with similar stories: Lance, Mel.

4. A received definition of dyslexia as principally a discrepancy between intelligence and academic attainment leads to a self-concept which focuses any difficulties on educational activities. The self may be seen as flawed, and experience at school and university may include intense awareness of taking longer than peers to complete study tasks. Informants with similar stories: Alison, Alice.

The average age at assessment of the cohort as a whole was approximately 24. However, comments such as Eliza's: 'they started saying that there was something wrong with me .... how old was I then? um, nine' indicate that the process of labelling happens in areas outside the psychologist's office, and can begin quite early in a student's life.

Miles and Huberman (1994:70) refer to four kinds of pattern arising in qualitative research data: themes, causes/explanations, relationships among people and emerging constructs. The typology shown in Figure 5.1 (page 52) includes examples of all four of these patterns at each stage of the pathway, as set out in Table 5.1.

The theme in the top row of this table is the role of experts, with the concomitant belief by the student that her deficiencies must be identified and supported by such figures as EPs, counsellors and learning support tutors. The second row exemplifies the way dyslexia is often welcomed as an explanation for academic failure (Miles, 1993). In the third row, a pattern of relationships shows how deference to authority figures can be diminished by a perception of poor treatment, such as an EP being uncommunicative or a teacher sarcastic. The fourth row shows a pattern of reframing the dyslexia concept (Gerber *et al,* 1996), in which awareness grows that there are other ways of construing it. We see examples of these patterns in this and the next two chapters.

Table 5.1 : Patterns at each stage of the pathway model

Pattern	Definition of dyslexia	Identity	Socio-emotional effects	Experience of HE
Themes	The definition comes from people who know	You have to go to an EP to be identified as dyslexic	I get depressed about my difficulties, so I go to counselling	I spend more hours on tasks than peers, but it is my problem and I need to consult a learning support tutor
Causes or explanations	Dyslexia is a defect or a difference	My brain is different, and in some ways deficient	I need a lot of support	I did badly in the exams because I am dyslexic
Relationships among people	Experts are right, but EPs don't always treat you well	People call me lazy	Role of teachers can be positive and negative	Role of lecturers can be positive and negative
Emerging constructs	People can be ignorant about dyslexia	I can change my view of dyslexia	Dyslexics can go to university; I am determined to go	I need to be taught and examined differently

Available definitions of dyslexia

Having set out to look for ways in which informants defined dyslexia, one could make assumptions about their likely reference to neurological concepts. The literature, and hence the dyslexia profession, has been full of these throughout its hundred-year history (Miles and Miles, 1999). This project's research questions, however, involve affective and social, as well as cognitive areas. Informants talked about a range of factors which influenced their definition of dyslexia (see Figure 5.2 opposite – letters in brackets refer to overlap with affective and social aspects).

Informants spoke of many more areas which were more cognitive than affective or social. This is not surprising, as the focus of the interviews was their learning histories, and they were studying at university. The three areas cannot be completely separated. For example, when talking about her difficulties, a student may be describing a cognitive process, but she will probably use emotional language and refer to social aspects such as peer or parental pressure, or university teaching and learning policy. And social aspects tend to have an affective dimension and vice versa.

As the interviews had been transcribed, text searches enabled me to focus on all three aspects. Text searches on the cognitive aspects forming part of an informant's definition of dyslexia explored the following:

Figure 5.2 Cognitive factors which influenced informants' definitions of dyslexia

Three-dimensional thinking
Use of visualisation
Art and creativity
Speed of information processing
Sequencing/linear thought
Memory
Receptive and expressive language

Study skills in general (s)
Personal organisation and time management (s)
Learning support (s,a)
Reading
Writing
Spelling
Mathematics

Academic assessment (s,a)
Cognitive style
Best and worst 'subjects' (a)
Their own strengths (a)
Their difficulties (s,a)
IQ/attainment discrepancy (a)

■ Did students see dyslexia as a problem? Which aspects of their learning histories did they associate with problems? A text search of all transcripts for the word 'problem/s' revealed that the term was used almost exclusively by the interviewer, so this thread did not 'pan out' (Miles and Huberman, 1994).

■ A search for the word 'dim' yielded a similar result, although 'bright' was used by many students to denote 'intelligent,' usually in a context of implying that they themselves were not.

■ A search for the word 'thick', on the other hand, showed it was used in 23 interviews; in 15 cases, the student used it about herself, to denote that she lacked intelligence. Four informants commented on their achievement in reading a 'thick book', in one case quite recently, even though 'remedial' texts are usually short.

Detailed exploration of the definition stage of the pathway shown in Figure 5.1 involves a number of cognitive and some social factors. The 'sources of information' in the first column of Figure 5.1 are explored first.

The role of parents

Parents were an important source of information about dyslexia, especially for younger informants. For brief 'life maps' of informants, see Appendix

II. Enid said that both her parents were teachers, and had consulted colleagues, including 'a psychiatrist', about dyslexia. Will's mother worked at a special school, and consulted a colleague there whose son had been identified as dyslexic. Eliza's parents 'started reading up' on dyslexia and told her that 'you have a very high IQ, you're very smart, you just have to be taught in a different way'.

The parents who were relatively well educated tended both to inform themselves about dyslexia and to pressure their child's school to act, whereas those who were not tended to be fatalistic or uninvolved with their children's schooling. A similar contrast was found in a study of dyslexic undergraduates carried out at the same time (Riddick, Farmer *et al,* 1997). In all, ten informants cited their parents as sources of information about dyslexia.

The role of teachers
Nineteen of the students were aged between 18 and 25, so would have been at primary schools in the 1980s. Their teachers were thus likely to have been influenced by the Warnock report (1978) and the subsequent Education Act (HMSO, 1981). But no student reported that a teacher had ever spoken of 'special educational needs' and only one (Lance) remembered having been referred by a teacher for extra help, which would have given an implicit definition of dyslexia as something 'other' which had to be dealt with outside the classroom. Lance was referred by his junior school class teacher to a learning support teacher who described herself as dyslexic and said that she had dyslexic children of her own. She told him: 'You can make it. You're dyslexic, but you can get there'.

Lance's support teacher taught him what he called 'tricks of the trade' for reading and spelling, which sounded like having been treated with solidarity. Eliza, a Canadian, on the other hand, used the expression 'something wrong with me' three times when she talked about the first teacher who commented on her difficulties. Jemima differentiated between a 'special dyslexic teacher' at her primary school and another who 'just didn't understand' and 'just thought I was stupid'. At her secondary school 'they didn't believe in dyslexia at all'. This suggests a notion of dyslexia as a cultural belief (Barton and Hamilton, 1998).

The role of the media and the informants' own research
Some of the respondents used their own research to find out about dyslexia. The youngest was Mel, who at the age of nine was aware of a classmate who was 'badly dyslexic', particularly in respect of handwriting. Mel was often paired with this boy, as she could read his writing fairly easily. She knew he was labelled dyslexic, and when she came across a magazine article on the subject, she thought:

Ah, that's me. What's more, that is definitely what he's suffering from.

This was in 1972, the year the British Dyslexia Association was founded and interest in dyslexia was being promoted (Scott, 1991). Alice was in her teens in the 1970s, and remembered newspaper articles about word-blindness. Geraldine recalled an article in the late 1960s which 'gave a list of things that dyslexic people do'. She had had the same response as Mel: 'Hey, but that's me!'

Lisa was a similar age to Geraldine. She spoke of seeing actress Susan Hampshire on television in 1975 and thinking 'Oh, I wonder, you know, if that's been my problem'. Another student who spoke about Susan Hampshire was Victoria, but when she read about Hampshire's difficulties, 'it still didn't register'. She did not recognise herself, even when she read other newspaper articles about dyslexia. However, a friend saw how she struggled at a Scottish dancing class and suggested that she might be dyslexic. Victoria 'looked it up' and 'could see the patterns'. She explained:

> I read somewhere that um dyslexia is often associated with um the child's mother, who had a very long delivery ... I think my mother said it took me nearly 36 hours to come into the world.

Perinatal anoxia was for some time thought to be a cause of dyslexia (Critchley, 1970; Naidoo, 1972).

Ron also sought information about dyslexia when he realised it applied to him. He read about the male/female ratio among dyslexic people, and looked the word up in a dictionary, about which he remembered only 'spells b and d back to front'.

At the time the data for this study were generated, British informants would have had little opportunity to see published material on dyslexia in Higher Education other than literature put out by their own universities, except for two publications by Gilroy (Miles and Gilroy, 1986; Gilroy, 1991). In its first paragraph, the earlier one refers to 'diagnosed dyslexics', 'their problems' and 'their difficulties' and describes dyslexia as 'an anomaly of development' (Miles and Gilroy, 1986:1). The second edition (1996:1) replaced the latter phrase with 'a distinctive balance of skills' but it had not appeared when most of these interviews were carried out. The work of Davis, a dyslexic man with a mission to spread the word about his personal way of tackling it (Davis, 1995) had been published, but by an obscure publishing house. Davis' work has since received widespread publicity and his 'method' is being taught in several countries (Davis, 2001).

The work of the UK National Working Party on Dyslexia in Higher Education had begun in 1995, but the report (Singleton, 1999) was not published for several years. In terms of models of dyslexia, Gilroy and Miles (1996) and the Working Party report similarly offer mixed messages.

Gilroy and Miles (1996) refer to dyslexia as a 'condition' with a 'physiological basis' and as a syndrome, but also speak of dyslexic people being 'gifted' and 'creative'. They imply re-framing when they write of 'tasks at which dyslexics are likely to be successful' (Gilroy and Miles, 1996:8). The Report of the National Working Party, of which Gilroy was a member, also mixes its language, describing dyslexia as a syndrome and a condition with neurological bases, but including reference to West's list of positive aspects such as visualisation and holistic thought (West, 1997).

The National Working Party was not writing for the students. It was motivated by the awareness of increasing numbers of dyslexic students in HE that also generated conferences for professionals in the mid 1990s (Stephens, 1996; Waterfield, 1996). Whether or not publications were available to my informants, most of them insisted that they read as little as possible. Home internet use was in its infancy then and none of the students mentioned finding information about dyslexia on the world wide web. Their sources were clearly human, except for some mature students who had seen items in the press.

The role of university publications and tutor feedback

Just as a university presents students with a model of academic literacy (Lea and Street, 2000), it also presents them with a model of dyslexia, if it acknowledges the phenomenon. Stephen recalled seeing a poster at Burtonforth inviting students to come forward for dyslexia assessment. The words 'IF YUO CAN READ TIHS you might be dyslexic' had puzzled him for some time, because he could not see what was wrong with them. Such a poster implies that the key to dyslexia is visual perception of letter sequence.

Spenceton presented a medical model of dyslexia to students. A leaflet about the work of the Learning Support Unit announced on the first page (original emphasis):

Assessment for Specific Learning Difficulties (including Dyslexia)

If you are seeking assessment for specific learning difficulties you *must* leave the following items with the receptionist at the time of making the appointment:

1. a letter of referral from your Sub-dean or a tutor who has experience of your work

2. a sample of your written work

3. a completed application form which can be obtained from Counselling and Psychotherapy, your School Office or your Sub-dean

4. any previous assessments you may have had.

In contrast, Belleville's Dyslexia Handbook began:

'Belleville University welcomes students with dyslexia for the special skills and motivation that they bring to their studies'. The handbook page headed 'What is dyslexia?' stated:

> Adults with dyslexia experience a marked and unexpected discrepancy between their general intelligence and the ability to perform tasks involving written language.

It went on to offer pages headed 'Special skills of people with dyslexia' and 'An effective learning programme', as well as 'Help from teaching staff' on four pages marked 'You may want to give a copy of this to your lecturer'. Having thus espoused the IQ/attainment discrepancy model, Belleville seemed to be inviting students to advocate for themselves.

Burtonforth's *Student's Handbook – Disabilities, Dyslexia and Special Needs* sought to differentiate between disabilities and dyslexia. The dyslexia section made a distinction between 'general learning difficulties' which students might experience for a variety of reasons, 'such as gaps in their education or returning to education after a period at work or bringing up children,' and dyslexia. Dyslexia was exemplified by 'a cluster of the following symptoms' and the nine bullet points which followed all began with the word 'difficulties'.

Another university in the same city as Burtonforth was even clearer about its espousal of a medical model of dyslexia. Its booklet for students, *The dyslexia support service* said of dyslexia: 'It's like having measles – the difficulty can be mild through to severe'. This model appeared in more formal language in a Midlands university's contemporaneous *Guide for staff* about dyslexic students: 'It is a chronic neurological disorder that inhibits ... Its most common symptoms are ...'

Staff in UK learning support units continue to grapple with informing course tutors about dyslexia in students. Stephen seemed to be aware of a possible difference between the view of dyslexia held by Student Services and that of his course tutors. He said that he always wrote 'I am a dyslexic student' at the beginning and end of his examination papers, but added 'I don't know if the markers understand'. He was thus making the assumption, common to all the students in the study, that there was a clearly definable unitary phenomenon called dyslexia which lecturers could or should recognise.

Spenceton University made it clear to Charlotte that she fell short of the required standard of academic literacy. When her first essay was returned, Charlotte had 'never seen so much red pen in my life'. She recalled her tutor saying: 'This is not the standard we expect at university. Do something about it'. That may be how she remembered it, but it does show the way in which the 'problem' was placed with the student. The importance of dyslexia awareness among support staff is demonstrated by another part of Charlotte's narrative: it was an administrative officer in the School (of study) Office who suggested that she might be dyslexic.

Tutor feedback of various kinds was mentioned by more than half the students, but they referred to this in terms of academic-related comments. No one reported a tutor as having expressed an opinion as to the nature of dyslexia. (The significance of tutor feedback is discussed in Chapter 7.)

The varied sources of information about dyslexia provided the students with four broad models of it: medical, IQ/attainment discrepancy, syndrome and hemispheric preference. No one had been offered a social model. However, this has been included in Figure 5.1, as some informants later adopted it for themselves. (This will be explored in Chapter 8.) One highly influential source of information about dyslexia was the EP, whose role is explored below.

Identity

The experience of being formally assessed, the expression generally used in the UK for the process of identification as dyslexic, is a crucial event in the life of a dyslexic person, because the EP has the power to say whether or not someone is dyslexic. Table 5.2 expands Table 4.1 to show the year and age at assessment.

This table shows that all but one of the mature informants – those over 25 – were identified as dyslexic not long before they were interviewed, whereas most of those under 25 had been so identified in childhood. The effect of such early experience is now examined.

Assessment for dyslexia at school

Chapter 2 referred to the 'abstract expert systems' used for defining people (Giddens, 1991). At present in the UK, the role of the Educational or Occupational Psychologist in deciding that a person is dyslexic is paramount. Full psychological assessment for dyslexia is a critical moment for a dyslexic person (Miles, 1993; Turner, 1997), and is decisive in furthering a person's progress along the pathway set out in Fig 5.1. The socio-emotional aspects of the assessment experience include:

- the way it is presented to the child/student
- fear of being found to be unintelligent and not dyslexic – this applies mainly to those assessed in adulthood
- relationship with the EP
- experiencing pain and pleasure during the tests
- feedback after assessment
- reaction to the label.

Table 5.2 Year of assessment and age at assessment

Informant	Age	Route to University	University	Year of assessment	Age at assessment
Chuck	34	APEL	Belleville	72	c.12, 33
Mel	32	A Levels	Axbridge	81	32
Gary	20	A Levels	Burtonforth	82	6 or 7
Eliza	22	Canadian grades	Axbridge	82	8 or 9
Stephen	22	A Levels	Burtonforth	83	9,17
Phoebe	21	A Levels	Burtonforth	83, 89, 92	8,14,17
Jemima	20	A Levels	Burtonforth	85	9
Sally	19	A Levels	Burtonforth	86	8/9,17
Arnold	20	US grades	Spenceton	88	12
Bruce	24	A Levels	Burtonforth	88	16
Alison	20	A Levels	Axbridge	91	15 or 16
Geraldine	53	A Levels	Axbridge	91	47
Ann	21	A Levels	Burtonforth	92	c. 18
Rachel	20	A Levels	Burtonforth	92	16
Fenella	44	Access	Spenceton	93	42
Lance	24	A Levels	Burtonforth	93	10, 21/23
Will	18	A Levels	Burtonforth	93	c. 10, 15
Betty	49	APEL	Axbridge	93	46
Charlotte	21	A Levels	Spenceton	94	19
Robert	31	Access	Burtonforth	94	29
Jeremy	19	A Levels	Burtonforth	95	18
Enid	20	A Levels	Burtonforth	95	19
Victoria	50	Access	Axbridge	95	49
Peggy	38	Access	Spenceton	95	37
Aarti	22	A Levels	Burtonforth	95	21
Patrick	25	A Levels	Burtonforth	95	24
Lisa	50	APEL	Burtonforth	95	49
Alice	37	A Levels	Axbridge	95	36
Susan	45	Access	Spenceton	95	43
Harry	27	A Levels	Burtonforth	95	26
Adrian	25	BTEC	Belleville	95	24
Ron	41	Access	Axbridge	95	40
Charles	44	APEL	Belleville	96	43

Those who experienced formal dyslexia assessment at primary school had had much longer than other students to become accustomed to the label, but also to come to terms with their emotional reactions. Those assessed in childhood may be more likely to accept the discourse of the psychologist, usually reported via parents and teachers. And they had nothing to gain by being labelled. The prospect of a Disabled Students' Allowance was not part of the picture.

Medical or disability language may have been used by a parent or teacher well before the assessment session. How did informants respond to this? Eliza remembered how when she was eight, her class teacher had 'said that something was wrong with this child'. She was initially taken to a children's hospital for a physical examination and expectated that she would be given a pill, return to school and 'sit down and pass'. But after assessment by two EPs, the family received what Eliza called the 'tremendous boost' of her identification as dyslexic, with its message that 'you're very smart, you just have to be taught in a different way'.

Stephen was first assessed at a similar age to Eliza. He was presented with the discrepancy model of dyslexia: 'I was told my IQ was quite good, but my reading skills were a bit less'. His comment raises an issue affecting many informants: the fear that assessment will reveal not dyslexia but lack of intellectual ability: 'It was nice to know that you're not just – you have got a problem, so it's not just because you can't do it, which is nice to feel'. This was particularly important to informants who were assessed as adults.

Stephen's reward for attending his first assessment was a set of toy cars. Phoebe enjoyed going on a trip to London at the age of eight and experienced the tests as enjoyable puzzles. Alison, 15, 'took great delight in being able to do the puzzle things' although she remembered finding the digit span test hard. Chuck's experience was different. When he was taken to London in the early 1970s – which meant 'various hospitals' – 'no one did me the courtesy to tell me what I was going to all these places for'.

Ann was jealous of what she saw as her mother's higher estimation of her older sister's ability, so she enjoyed hearing the EP saying that both their IQs were well above average. Alison had also been gratified by being deemed to have 'quite high intelligence': 'that was how I had always felt'.

Assessment reports clearly played a role for some informants in helping them to achieve a coherence system in terms of their identity (Linde, 1993; Miles, 1993). Ann was told that there was 'just a little thing wrong' with her, but was happy that 'it was an explanation' for her experiences. Will said that the report made him feel 'much better:' 'I thought ah hah, I see the light'. The dyslexia concept continues to be a crucial one for many students because it offers an explanation for a range of experiences. Fenella, who was assessed at 42, said:

> Although it was scary ... I felt: at last there's a reason why I've had all these emotions about my ability and why I'm so slow at reading.

Ann was being assessed in preparation for her A Levels. So was Rachel, who had, like Stephen, worried lest she was found to be unintelligent. Rachel accepted the 'expert system' gladly: 'It sounds like a professional saying you are OK, and you are'. Rachel's psychologist seems to have avoided medical language, telling her: 'You're just different, you interpret information differently'.

Stephen was re-assessed halfway though his A Levels. He found the psychologist 'rude' and 'patronising' and the whole experience 'demoralising', although the report states that 'co-operation and persistence were maintained throughout the session' and describes Stephen as a 'highly motivated hard working young man'. EPs' reports can be received with mixed feelings, especially by adults, whether they are parents or dyslexic subjects. Phoebe's parents had later told her that her first report at eight was 'really quite degrading' as it said she would be unlikely to pass any examinations. Many of the informants commented on the quoting of reading ages. Jemima described her third EP as 'really really nice', but was 'shocked' by seeing her reading and spelling ages given as 11 years when she was 18. Charlotte was assessed at 19 and had a similar experience; she telephoned her mother in tears when she received the report.

Jemima had been aware that she would have to show her psychologist's report to other people. Rachel's reaction at 16 to identification involved awareness of the opinion of others:

> When I first got told I was dyslexic I was like dead embarrassed, cos I thought, 'Oh my God, everyone's going to think I'm a right 'uhm uhm', you know.

A social constructionist perspective sees identity as the adoption of the beliefs which are available in a person's social context. The examples in this section demonstrate the ways in which dyslexia can be socially constructed for individual young people.

Assessment for dyslexia in adulthood

In the case of adult students following Access courses, fears of what others might think may apply more to course tutors than to fellow students. Fenella was afraid that she should not be attempting any course when there was 'something wrong' with her; Peggy, who was assessed at 37, did not want to approach a University saying 'please let me in with an Access course and by the way I'm dyslexic'.

Fenella had been doing voluntary work with people with learning difficulties; the special needs tutor at her Tertiary College gave her some tests and said that she had 'specific learning difficulties':

> It was embarrassing because we were in a little side office ... I should think the whole of the study skills department must have heard me break down into sobs and tears ... It just felt terribly traumatic.

The vocabulary distressed her: 'I still didn't know who I was'. Peelo (1994) notes that 'diagnosis' at such a stage is a personal crisis. Having decided upon a major change of life direction by going to university, the student is told she is 'deeply flawed'. Victoria's written report, received at the age of 49, made a profound impression on her:

> My golly, I got everything wrong ... An endless list of things I just can't do. No sequencing, nothing. Visual, auditory perception, is it called? That's all gone. There's just so many things wrong, I'm amazed.

Fenella's report was 'devastating ... it knocked me for six'. Having gone through the fear of being found 'not all there' rather than dyslexic, Fenella was relieved but also anxious about what the label meant. But the hardest thing to deal with in the report was the attainment data, the spelling and reading ages. The report of the NWP deplores the quoting of these in reports for adults (Singleton, 1999). Fenella said:

> I already felt like a fish out of water at university and here I am in a grown-up world, a world that I never thought I'd get to because although I wanted to, it's really all beyond me, and who the hell do I think I am, you know, sort of doing this, and to see those ages, it just threw me back into that frightening world that I was in as a child.

Fenella and Victoria were among the older informants who saw themselves as defective (Peelo, 1994), partly because of how dyslexia was described to them, but also because of when they encountered it. As Riddick *et al* (1997) point out, those who have lived with the dyslexic label for some years have had time to work out detailed ideas about the concept. One such in the present group was Geraldine, who had been wondering for some ten years whether she might be dyslexic before arranging to see an EP at the age of 47.

Informants first identified as dyslexic in adulthood often fall into one of two categories: those who had been wondering about dyslexia for many years, and those for whom a tutor's suggestion that they be assessed came as a surprise. Robert's experience was of the latter kind. His Access Course tutor first proposed that he should consult his doctor, which shows that a medical view of dyslexia was still apparent in 1994, but he was eventually seen at a university which had a Dyslexia Unit in its Psychology Department. Assessed at the age of 29, Robert was sent a report which he could not understand because of its jargon.

A link between those who had been wondering about dyslexia and those who had not lies in the IQ/attainment discrepancy model. The informants and their tutors often arrived at thoughts of dyslexia because of an observed or perceived contrast between their oral ability and their reading or writing. Like others, several informants, Rachel, Susan and Ron, had approached meeting the EP with one major fear: that the outcome would be a verdict not of dyslexia but of low intelligence. Susan's EP had explained dyslexia neurologically, and Susan commented:

> It was nice to know that it wasn't a mental ability – well I suppose it was a sort of mental, but the physical side of mental, you know, capabilities.

Identity is partly shaped by the pronouncements which reach us via abstract expert systems. The students were being inculcated with models of dyslexia which had a direct influence on their self-concepts. The way dyslexia was presented in the subsequent EPs' reports may have been more varied than in the examples above, as the following section shows, but it remained highly influential as part of the associated elements which made up the self for those students.

Documentary evidence: Educational Psychologists' reports on the informants

Twenty-two students provided copies of their assessment reports. These constitute valuable evidence in two areas: the model of dyslexia adopted by the psychologist, and the terms in which the student is described.

We have considered the accepted definitions of dyslexia which are based upon (a) a discrepancy between 'intelligence' and scholastic attainment, (b) a recognisable pattern of difficulties, (c) a neurological deficit and (d) the exclusion of other reasons for difficulties, such as lack of opportunity or primary emotional disturbance. As the reports on the students were written between 1983 and 1995, and most in 1994 and 1995, they did not show evidence of the cognitive style model of dyslexia which since has appeared in the literature (Cairns and Moss, 1995; Krupska and Klein, 1995; Reid, 1996; Herrington, 2001a). None referred to dyslexia as a 'difference' or as a preference for certain cognitive processes.

The reports varied in length from 270 words – by an EP who was a lecturer at Burtonforth University – to approximately 2,250 words. Most of those by independent EPs were three to five pages long. Then, as now, most EPs began with a tabulated summary of Wechsler Intelligence Scale results. Only a few provided a glossary or information sheet on the nature of these tests.

Most authors used the term dyslexia (see Table 5.3 below). Some called it a 'specific learning difficulty'. The Principal EP who reported on informant Bruce referred to 'a specific difficulty affecting his communication skills', but reached this conclusion by citing an intelligence/spelling discrepancy and also the exclusion of 'environmental factors'.

Thirteen of the twenty-two reports mentioned intelligence/attainment discrepancy, using phrases such as 'difficulties in spite of superior intelligence' and 'your pattern of performance is quite out of step with your general intellectual level'. The lecturer in psychology at Burtonforth University used terms such as 'specific impairment', 'significant degree of disability', 'developmental dyslexia' and 'dysgraphia,' which was not explained. The reports on my American informant did not use the generally preferred expression in the US, 'learning disability' (Rourke, 1988; Swanson, 1996; Kavale and Forness, 2000) but did refer to 'learning difficulties'.

The second most common model of dyslexia in the reports, used by eleven psychologists, was the pattern of difficulties or syndrome model, although many combined it with other models, as Table 5.3 shows. One author (EP number 11) covered more than one option by writing about 'the syndrome of specific learning difficulties or dyslexia'. Terminology here included examples such as 'profile associated with difficulties of a dyslexic kind' (number 2) and 'fairly marked pattern of dyslexic difficulties' (number 8).

Psychologists who supported their conclusions with cognitive psychometric data used terminology such as 'phonological difficulties' and 'auditory short-term memory'. One referred to 'difficulties with auditory memory and visual processing, which have probably affected the normal development of literacy skills' (number 1). The words 'normal,' 'average' or 'typical' appear in many reports, but not to describe the subjects.

Exclusionary comments (as in the World Federation of Neurology definition of dyslexia published in 1968 – see Chapter 1) appear in only three reports, one of which quotes the WFN text.

Apart from high 'intelligence' where relevant, very few reports mentioned students' cognitive strengths, apart from pointing out any Wechsler subtest scores which were above the mean, although without explaining their significance. However, students of all ages can tell one a great deal about the way they function, before one uses any tests. Although the American report on my US student, written in 1987 when he was thirteen years old, included information from a 'self-administered student profile', few of the other reports referred to any input from the student about how they processed information. The majority of authors presented themselves as experts. One began by stating 'I examined Phoebe on 15th March ...', and another concluded that the subject was suffering from 'a permanent condition'.

The longer reports tended to have most positive features. One independent Psychologist in the South of England for example included paragraphs in italics at the start of each section, explaining what the test was for and what the results might imply. This author also warned that 'all tests have some margin of error' and 'an individual's mood and motivation may also affect the result'.

The most important part of an EP's report may initially be the formal identification of the subject as dyslexic, if s/he needs this in order to obtain funding for learning support, or special examination arrangements. However, the final recommendations, if thorough, can be of lasting value. Certain recommendations were expressed in language which might have influenced the subject's self-image, such as the following:

- 'Chuck is already finding that word processing is helpful to him, although as yet it is terribly time consuming for him'. This not only acknowledges the subject's input into the assessment process, but also conveys to his tutors an element of his life as a student. It also sums up a problem area without using medical language

- One EP recommended additional time in examinations, first describing the student as having 'a lively interest in his particular subject' and as 'imaginative and creative', but 'handicapped' by dyslexia and 'handicapped' again by slow information processing. The student (Charles) took a medical view of dyslexia

- The recommendation that tutors should 'appreciate that the spelling problems reflect a specific impairment, and do not simply reflect carelessness on your part' seems intended to be helpful. The student concerned adopted a medical view of dyslexia, and defined this as 'a fault in your personality'.

The table on page 68 shows the range of models of dyslexia being used by the EPs seen by the students.

These reports were written by thirteen different EPs and were dated between 1983 and 1995. The reports which used a 'pattern' model are especially revealing. In the two reports which used such a model exclusively, the authors based this on the Wechsler Adult Intelligence Scale (WAIS) (Wechsler, 1981) and one other test (either the Bangor Dyslexia Test, Miles, 1982, or the Wide Range Attainment Test (WRAT), Jastak and Jastak, 1978). Only one of these identified any cognitive strengths. Of the reports which based the identification on a combination of discrepancy and pattern models, two authors relied on the subject's self-reported difficulties to identify the 'pattern', and on the WAIS for the discrepancy. One of these reports, dated 1986, was the oldest in this group. Note that all but two of the psychologists in Table 5.3 included an IQ/attainment discrepancy as a key factor, relying on spelling and reading tests to demonstrate this in addition to the WAIS (or WISC in the case of children).

Table 5.3 : Educational Psychologists' models of dyslexia

Informant	EP	EP's model	EP's terminology
Fenella	1	Discrepancy	Specific learning difficulty or dyslexia
Charles	1	Discrepancy + pattern	Specific learning difficulty or dyslexia
Charlotte	1	Discrepancy + pattern	Handicapped by a specific learning difficulty or dyslexia
Peggy	2	Discrepancy + pattern + neurology	Significant specific learning difficulty of a dyslexic type
Mel	2	Discrepancy + pattern	Specific learning difficulties(dyslexia)
Susan	3	Discrepancy	Specific difficulties
Robert	4	Pattern	Dyslexic disability
Sally	5	Discrepancy + pattern	Specific learning difficulties
Enid	6	Discrepancy + exclusion	Developmental dyslexia
Jeremy	6	Discrepancy + exclusion	Developmental dyslexia and dysgraphia
Lisa	6	Discrepancy + exclusion	Developmental dyslexia
Harry	6	Discrepancy + exclusion	Developmental dyslexia
Aarti	7	Discrepancy + pattern	Dyslexic difficulties
Lance	7	Discrepancy + pattern	Developmental dyslexia
Patrick	7	Discrepancy + pattern	Specific learning difficulties
Alice	8	Discrepancy + pattern	Dyslexic difficulties
Victoria	9	Pattern	Specific learning difficulty(dyslexia)
Phoebe	10	Discrepancy	Developmental dyslexia
Chuck	11	Neurology+ discrepancy	Dyslexic
Stephen	11	Discrepancy + exclusion	Specific learning disability or dyslexia
Bruce	12	Discrepancy + exclusion	Specific difficulty affecting his communication skills
Arnold	13	Neurology+ discrepancy	Learning difficulties

The effect of all the EPs' reports was to identify the subjects as abnormal. The common thread running for the students, both as adults and as children, is that they are made to feel they are 'flawed', and that the academy has immutable standards to which they must struggle to conform.

Table 4.1 is combined in Table 5.4 with sources of 'expert' views on dyslexia in the informants' lives.

Table 5.4: All informants, showing sources of 'expert' views on dyslexia

Informant	Age	Year of Assessment	Age at assessment	Source of expert views
Adrian	25	95	24	EP only
Alice	37	95	36	newspapers, LST
Alison	20	91	15 or 16	EP + Ts + LS tutor
Aarti	22	95	21	EP
Ann	21	92	for A Levels	EP: IQ OK/'done well'
Arnold	20	88	teens	various Ts/EP/counsellors
Betty	49	93	c46	D's EP (then went herself)
Bruce	24	88	16	EP
Charles	44	96	43	LST; rdg on word blindness
Charlotte	21	94	19	LSU staff; LST
Chuck	34	72	school, 33	E.Ps ; own rdg
Eliza	22	82	8 or 9	EPs, SNT, parents
Enid	20	95	19	parents, Univ psychologist
Fenella	44	93	42	SNT at college; LS unit
Gary	20	82	6 or 7	class T; LSTs
Geraldine	53	91	47	own research, self-analysis, EP
Harry	27	95	26	Other student; EP
Jemima	20	85	9?	SNT; EP
Jeremy	19	95	18	GF; Univ psychologist
Lance	24	93	21/23(+10)	LST
Lisa	50	95	49	Hampshire, mags, D's EP
Mel	32	81	32	Reader's Digest, EP
Patrick	25	95	24	EP + other students
Peggy	38	95	37	EP (clipboard image)
Phoebe	21	83, 89	14,17	E.P neg; M neg ;E.P no. 3 OK
Rachel	20	92	16	EP +ive
Robert	31	94	29	Access T; Bangor EP
Ron	41	95	40	Access T; EP; own research
Sally	19	86	8/9,17	EP, M
Stephen	22	83	9,17	D.I. T; M+F read books
Susan	45	95	43	LSU staff; EP
Victoria	50	95	49	DI T + EP
Will	18	93	Junior Sch +15	M's rdg; other dyslexic boy

Key:

DI: Dyslexia Institute	LSU: Learning Support Unit	S: sister
EP: Educational Psychologist	T: teacher	neg: negative
SNT: special needs teacher	GF: girlfriend	B: brother
M: mother	sch: school	D: daughter
LS: learning support	ass't: dyslexia assessment	rdg: reading
F: father	ETH: extra teaching hours	+ive: positive

Table 5.4 shows that the predominant source of expert views on dyslexia was the EP (mentioned by 66 per cent). Next came special needs or learning support teachers/tutors (30 per cent). However, several informants referred to printed sources, which they had either stumbled on or actively sought.

The National Working Party on Dyslexia in Higher Education (Singleton, 1999) reported that 43 per cent of dyslexic students had been so identified after admission. As Table 5.4 shows, this was true of 57 per cent of this cohort. This may be because 33 per cent of the informants had been admitted to University via routes other than A Levels, a higher proportion than the national figure (HESA, 1997).

The experience of being labelled

It is clear that 'diagnosis' and labelling powerfully affect the students' lives. Ann talked about the change in her self-image when she was 'diagnosed' with dyslexia: 'Up until then I had just been bad at spelling and there was nothing really wrong with me'. Thereafter, she viewed herself as having a disability. 'That's the image of a dyslexic person'.

Rachel believed that being dyslexic meant being 'really stupid'. Her initial reaction was 'Oh my God', until her EP explained it as a different brain rather than a defective one. (Rachel did not offer a copy of her report.) With this explanation and her reported high IQ, her confidence increased at college. The model offered to Adrian by the psychologist was based on a graph of sub-test results which was 'like the Himalayas', with some scores very high but others very low. The psychologist explained that a 'normal' person would show a relatively flat graph. Adrian rejected this by declaring 'you can say what you want but that doesn't fit me'.

Robert found the label 'a relief', as 'an excuse for everything that had gone before'. Similarly, Victoria said 'there was a label, there was an explanation, I wasn't just a total div'. Stephen said much the same. Others received the label with mixed feelings. Charlotte said that 'half of me was quite chuffed', and Peggy said it was 'the label you don't want and you do want'. Fenella wondered whether she had been grateful for the opportunity to 'hang' her 'lack of ability on a label'.

Alice was seeing a counsellor who questioned her need to label herself, but Alice had completed a special module for dyslexic students at Axbridge University which encouraged group solidarity. Charles also had questions about labelling. He described the outcome of assessment for dyslexia as 'somebody turning round and putting a label on you, as they've done now at the age of 44'. 'Does the label create the person?' he wondered. Although he did not answer his own question, it was clear from other remarks he made that he saw himself as defective.

Bruce, in common with Jeremy and Harry, saw himself as 'not severely dyslexic'. His reaction to the label had been to think: 'I'll bloody show them'.

Thus the informants' experiences of being assessed and labelled differed widely. Their experiences led to a variety of personal views about the nature of dyslexia. These are briefly discussed here. Later chapters go into greater detail.

Informants' own definitions of dyslexia

Chapter 3 presented a model of the self-concept (Marsh, 1992) which divided the global self-concept into academic and non-academic areas. Some of the students, such as Gary and Charlotte, seemed to link dyslexia exclusively with their academic self-concept, but many did not.

Enid was clear about her definition of dyslexia: it was 'a memory problem', which she explained in terms of every-day activities as well as academic knowledge. This view had reached her via her parents and the university psychologist who assessed her. Chuck was equally clear that it was akin to a physical disability, involving 'bad wiring of parts of the brain'. Like Enid, he had received this from an EP, but had also done his own research. Fenella spoke in similar terms to Chuck. Though she had seen a different EP, she referred to 'a break in the communication system' and 'a short in an electrical system'.

Mel seemed to have carried out a great deal of research. She was the only informant to use the terms 'acquired dyslexia' and 'developmental dyslexia'. Mel was aware of the range of factors often taken to form part of the latter term, but had come to the conclusion that in an ideal situation such labels would be abandoned as a range of learning styles became accepted. Geraldine, who worked at the university where Mel was a student, was delivering learning support herself, and had probably in-quired into dyslexia more deeply than any of the others. She was adamant that it was 'not just phonological awareness', and that dyslexic people's thinking was 'not basically linguistic'. Geraldine had been influenced by the pattern of skills and difficulties model (Miles, 1993) and by research into automaticity (Nicolson, 1990). She concluded that 'the dyslexia is a disability, but your thinking strengths are not'.

Harry used a phrase which the others did not, calling dyslexia 'a bit of a barrier' to academic study. From his EP he had picked up the concept of IQ/attainment discrepancy. He also referred to degrees of severity of dyslexia, counting himself as 'not too bad', but did not see it as a disability except in terms of the job market. Harry expected prejudice from potential em-ployers, and a contrast between the world of work and the relatively pro-tected university environment.

Jemima's definition of dyslexia was focused on academic life: 'a difficulty in learning to read and write and sort of communicating in written terms'. Peggy defined dyslexia along similar lines, but added that the difficulties were caused by memory weaknesses which were 'a physiological thing'. Peggy declared that this notion had come from her EP.

Victoria was adamant that she was not 'clever' in the way in which she wanted to be, and put this down to her dyslexia. Eliza compared herself with her older sister, whom she described as 'intelligent', and said: 'You're not stupid, but you continually prove yourself to be'. The concept of intelligence emerged in most of the students' language about dyslexia. Many reported that they had once believed that dyslexic people were un-intelligent, and Rachel was so convinced of this that she had at first been unwilling to mention it to her friends. However, her current explanation of it was that 'it just means that you learn in a different way'.

The definitions of dyslexia set out in this section match the four examples of pathways through the descriptive typology given in Figure 5.1. The informants regarded dyslexia either as a quasi-medical matter, a matter of IQ/attainment discrepancy or as a function of hemispheric processes in the brain. They were deploying cultural constructions which had been offered to them by the education system, and in the process of telling the interviewer about these, they showed that the constructions were influencing the discourses they were using to create their identities.

Summary

Having proposed a four-stage descriptive typology, this chapter has explored the first two stages: the definition of dyslexia and its role in identity formation as a dyslexic student. We have seen that beliefs regarding the nature of dyslexia can be derived from a range of sources, and that the variety of models of dyslexia explored in Chapter 1 remains wide – certainly wider than it was 100 years ago. We have also seen that the process of formal identification or assessment as dyslexic is an extremely powerful and significant one for students.

The next chapter continues the process of examining the descriptive typology proposed in this chapter by considering stage three.

Chapter 6

Identity issues leading to socio-emotional effects

Introduction

This chapter presents findings of the research study about how the identity issues explored in Chapter 5 affect students' relationships and emotional approach to learning during compulsory education. Informants who were identified as dyslexic during their schooldays spoke of similar issues to those who were identified after admission to HE, such as a pervasive sense of being 'different'. Relationships with family members, peers and teachers were discussed. Sources of positive self-regard were also revealed, and the combined result of these factors made approximately 33 per cent of informants determined to go to University. (See Appendix I for brief extracts from each interview, which exemplify the way informants spoke and include the themes of this chapter.)

Problems and compensations in compulsory education: identity issues lead to socio-emotional effects

The research questions for the study covered informants' routes to Higher Education, starting from their experiences at school. Table 6.1 (pages 74/75) shows aspects of school experience which were prominent in the data, with relevant quotations from interviews.

As Riddick *et al* (1997) point out, accounts of schooldays are inevitably selective and memory is random and not always reliable. In their group of informants, it was the older students who tended to recall humiliation, punishment and being labelled as lazy (*ibid,* 160). The present cohort was different. For example, the youngest informant (Will, aged 18) quoted a teacher as saying 'He's lazy, can't be bothered doing the work'. But the study does support Riddick *et al*'s finding that those who are identified as dyslexic relatively early may avoid being labelled as lazy, so escape losing

Table 6.1: Issues ensuing in compulsory education

Issue	Number of informants
Believed self to be unintelligent	15 (12 women)

Well you know, I'm dyslexic, I'm stupid; of course I can't do it (Phoebe)

I think I felt that [I was stupid] kind of deep inside all the way down the line, even when I was working (Robert)

It's difficult to know when I started to think I wasn't intelligent.... (Fenella)

Unfavourable comparison with other children	10

Oh, you're the practical one, whereas your sister's got the brains (Rachel)

Laura was so wonderful and I was obviously a thick child (Ann)

Poor social self-esteem	12

The other students made fun of me because there was something wrong with me (Eliza)

I think most of them were what you'd call the, um the undesirables, my friends (Patrick)

Poor academic self-esteem	19

(...) but things like English I'd just be really quiet and sit at the back cos I didn't want to be noticed (Rachel)

Even when I couldn't read I would look at the picture and explain what was going on from the picture, even if it was a pile of totally different rubbish (Ann)

Support from parents	12

My parents helped me; like we had reading sessions every night (Jemima)

My Mum pressed the school to keep checking, 'check if he's dyslexic' (Will)

Exams	29

There were so many words, and I was going like 'What are they asking me for?' (Patrick)

If anyone threatens me with an exam, I think my answer will deal with sex and travel (Charles)

Table 6.1: Issues ensuing in compulsory education (continued)

Issue	Number of informants
Compensation of successful school activities	22

I used to do a lot of Judo, and I used to fight for the North West team (Robert)

The Biology was good because we did loads on plants and, you know, we dissected things (Rachel)

I had a natural ability at Science (Gary)

I made an intercom system and a light dimmer (Alice)

Relationships with teachers (bad)	19

I had a screaming match with my English teacher at one point, asking him just to give me some help of some sort (Ann)

I ended up getting migraines, because she used to embarrass me in front of the class (Phoebe)

The English teacher said 'You've got a higher IQ than I have, I can't teach you anything' (Mel)

Relationships with teachers (good)	16

They were constantly positively reinforcing you (Jemima)

She would do diagrams – I love diagrams – and make everything colourful as well (Sally)

their self-esteem because of criticism from their teachers. Jemima, Sally, Gary, Eliza and Stephen all reported feeling more positive about them-selves following assessment for dyslexia early on at school.

Failure at school often engendered feelings of shame (Giddens, 1991). Academic failure can make one doubt one's intelligence, although several informants mentioned their success in art or sport. Sometimes they were conscious of an intelligence/attainment discrepancy well before an EP documented it. Others said that academic failure had been counterbalanced by their social success (Marsh, 1992).

The sex distribution of students who had thought they were unintelligent during their schooldays is telling. As Table 6.1 above indicates, they were mostly female. Is a cultural dimension operating here? Possibly more boys are identified as dyslexic because more is expected of boys, more notice is taken of their difficulties, or their academic failure is more likely to be ascribed to special needs (Fink, 1998). In addition, boys may be more likely to become disruptive when frustrated (Morgan and Klein, 2000). Girls, who tend to remain quiet, are first assumed not to be academic. Fenella was specific about her family's assumption that she was destined to be a home-maker, and Rachel's family described her as 'practical'; Susan did badly at school, but said of her parents: 'I think because I was a girl they weren't particularly worried about that side of things'.

Burka (1983:298), writing about his work in a psychiatric clinic, observes: 'It is very difficult for some learning-disabled children to take responsibility for problems they are having in the classroom'. This leaves the difficulties firmly with the student, as if the school played no role. Phoebe, who was first assessed in 1983, remembered her teacher telling her plainly 'it's your fault' when she failed to spell accurately, even though she was a seven year-old in a class of nine year-olds at a full-time boarding school.

By comparing Tables 5.2 and 6.1 it can be seen that the quotations come from students who were identified as dyslexic both at school and at univer-sity. What differs is their determination to go to university; their socio-emotional experiences during compulsory education had much in com-mon. Children want to be the same as their peers (Edwards, 1994), and they are usually acutely aware of how they differ. The composite state-ments that follow indicate the self-concepts of the cohort during compul-sory education:

- those identified as dyslexic at school: 'They could see there was some-thing wrong with me, and I was sent for formal assessment to see what it was'.

- those identified as dyslexic at University: 'There was something wrong with me, but I got by, and never thought I would get anywhere academically'.

Both these statements make reference to 'something wrong with me'. This encapsulates the way in which these people were pathologised by the education system. Examples of this process are given later in this chapter.

Parental support

Riddick et al (1997) describe the 'protective factors' which make schooldays easier for dyslexic students. One is parental support, and this was evident in the present study. Sixteen informants mentioned having support from their parents, ranging from non-specific encouragement to study of dyslexia and putting pressure on schools to arrange assessment and pro-vide extra teaching hours. Riddick et al note that 'parental education level' may explain why only some parents were actively supportive and this too is borne out by the present study. For example, Ron said his parents never read and had taken no interest in his academic progress, whereas Stephen's parents, a graduate engineer and a physiotherapist, had worked on his reading at home and frequently visited his schools.

As well as pressing for a dyslexia assessment, some parents also paid for a private tutor and encouraged their children to continue studying and enter higher education. As might be expected, most of those who had no such support were mature students.

The further additions in Table 6.2 indicate the informants who said their parents helped them with their dyslexia.

Table 6.2: All informants, including input from parents

Name	Age	Year of ass't	Age at ass't	Expert views from:	Parents' support
Adrian	25	95	24	EP	not stated
Alice	37	95	36	newspapers, LST (Univ.)	ETH, emotional
Alison	20	91	15 or 16	EP + Ts + LS tutor	ETH, general enc
Aarti	22	95	21	EP	not stated
Ann	21	92	for A Levels	EP	M sought ass't
Arnold	20	88	teens	Various Ts; EP; counsellors	pressure on him
Betty	49	93	c46	D's EP (then went herself)	not stated
Bruce	24	88	16	EP	not stated
Charles	44	96	43	LST; rdg on 'word blindness'	M typed his work
Charlotte	21	94	19	LSU staff; LST	ETH
Chuck	34	72	school, 33	E.Ps ; own rdg	took him to EPs
Eliza	22	82	8 or 9	EPs, SNT, parents	'all along'
Enid	20	95	19	Parents; Univ psychologist	M (was a T)
Fenella	44	93	42	SNT at college; LS unit	M read to her
Gary	20	82	6 or 7	class T; LSTs	M = emotional support
Geraldine	53	91	47	own research; self-analysis; EP	not stated
Harry	27	95	26	Other student; EP	non-specific
Jemima	20	85	9?	SNT; EP	ETH; special school
Jeremy	19	95	18	GF; Univ psychologist	M non-specific
Lance	24	93	21/23(+10)	LST	M; M+F= LS Ts
Lisa	50	95	49	S. Hampshire; mags; D's EP	not stated
Mel	32	81	32	Reader's Digest; EP	M read with her
Patrick	25	95	24	EP; other students	private T 6 yrs
Peggy	38	95	37	EP	not stated
Phoebe	21	83, 89	14,17	3 EPs; M	Sent to boarding sch
Rachel	20	92	16	EP	M non-specific
Robert	31	94	29	Access T; EP	financially

Table 6.2: All informants, including input from parents (continued)

Name	Age	Year of ass't	Age at ass't	Expert views from:	Parents' support
Ron	41	95	40	Access T; EP; own research	F = help w. h'work
Sally	19	86	8/9,17	EP, M	M 'all the way'
Stephen	22	83	9,17	D.I. T; M+F read books	M+F a lot
Susan	45	95	43	LSU staff; EP	F = reading
Victoria	50	95	49	DI T + EP	not stated
Will	18	93		Junior sch; 15 M's rdg; dyslexic boy	M req'd ass't; ETH

Key

DI: Dyslexia Institute
EP: Educational Psychologist
SNT: special needs teacher
M: mother
LS: learning support
F: father
B: brother
D: daughter
neg: negative

LSU: Learning Support Unit
T: teacher
GF: girlfriend
sch: school
ass't: dyslexia assessment
ETH: extra teaching hours
rdg: reading
+ive: positive
req'd: requested

Self-esteem is another 'protective factor' at school and is fostered by knowing one's strengths and areas of success. Sixteen students (48 per cent) mentioned being good at Art, and eight rated Maths as their best subject. Nine had done well in Science, four of them mentioning practical work in Biology. Sport was also relevant to self-esteem: nine students (27 per cent) described themselves as having achieved success at a sport, and this enhanced their self-esteem.

Difficulties at school

Predicably, the areas of the school curriculum described by the students as causing most difficulty, and hence emotional problems, were reading, spelling and 'composition' or writing. Reading aloud in class was described as painful by eight of them. As Charlotte said:

I suppose I am like every person that used to dread the time it was your turn to read the book in the class and you'd be there going 'Oh my God, is it going to be me next?' – and every time the teacher would look up to check the next person, everyone's head went down.

Charlotte was 21 when interviewed, whereas Lisa was 50. She describes what happened to her:

'Everybody's got to read, you've got to do it, come on get on with it'. So I did it and when I finished, um, I was in quite a state and she said 'that was terrible'. She said 'we won't ask you to read again'. Um, I think that was... after that I just never, never read aloud, ever, to anyone.

Lance's experience was different. As well as being an inaccurate reader, he had had a stammer. He recalled being aware that the teacher was not selecting him to read aloud and resenting it. Mel and Aarti related how they had expressed resentment about what they saw as unfair treatment at school. Both went on to be somewhat combative at university, demanding support from their course leaders. So were Patrick and Lance, who both became involved in student support groups and lobbying the university authorities about dyslexia.

The students were emotional when they recalled reading while they were at school. Robert recalled making a 'huge effort' to learn to read 'because I was the only one who couldn't'. Several others said how thick the books they read at school were, and some even boasted about a thick or complex book they had recently read. They were acutely aware of the issue of speed of reading. Aaron remembered being set 'a very short story' to read for homework at 14 or 15: 'Some people had read it in a night. It had taken me a week'.

Seventy-eight per cent of the informants spoke about spelling at school, and all but three (Charlotte, Fenella and Victoria) described their own ability as 'appalling' and 'atrocious'. This was associated with self-consciousness (Ron, Phoebe), desperate measures such as writing words out many times (Alice, Rachel) and awareness that there were spelling 'rules' which other students could learn (Alison, Mel). That written language ability affected self-esteem was clear from informants such as Ann, who felt 'particularly useless and thick' because she was 'not any good at anything written down'. Will said: 'Every time I started writing, garbage came out,' and others made self-deprecatory remarks like 'sounds messy' and 'what a prat'.

But not all memories of writing were negative. Some students remembered early successes. Charles, aged 44, recounted writing a long story about animals at primary school. Adrian had a similarly vivid memory:

> I wrote about a spaceman that flew around the galaxies, and I filled the book. Literally filled it completely, pictures, everything. And I got a recommendation to the headmaster.

Ron had studied the life-cycle of the bee with his father, and had been delighted to find an examination question on it. Now 41, he said he could recall his essay 'word for word'. Susan's first writing success had been passing English Language GCSE at the age of 38 and she still became emotional about this.

Relationships with peers and teachers

We saw in Chapter 3 that students expect teachers to fulfil a range of roles, being a 'provider and comforter' as well as a source of knowledge (Salzberger-Wittenberg *et al,* 1983). For some students, a teacher may be the first 'significant other' (Stuart and Thomson, 1995) they have encountered outside the home, and her judgement of them is likely to be internalised.

The students, including the youngest whose experience was most recent, reported similar difficulties in their relationships with teachers because of their spelling and writing, including:

■ being embarrassed by having their incorrect spelling or poor composition read aloud

■ being told that their difficulty in finding words in a dictionary was because they were 'not trying'

■ being shown up for producing little work (e.g. half an A5 page in an hour).

The topic of spelling and composition also evoked comparisons with other children that might have raised the image of 'myself-as-I-would-like-to-be' (Kelly, 1955). Their contrast with other children took various forms, such as:

■ coming bottom in weekly spelling tests

■ covering over their writing with one arm

■ being amazed that other children could remember spelling

■ making their handwriting very small

■ being the slowest at copying from the board.

But some informants recalled successes:

■ several described writing stories at primary school which had been praised

■ many remembered succeeding at oral activities

■ some spoke of the compensation of success outside the classroom in activities such as sport.

When teaching approaches were unsuccessful, some of the students had responded emotionally:

■ they became frustrated by the contrast between their oral and written ability

■ Arnold said he had to 'labour and cry' over spelling homework.

Patrick, Alice and Charles had all seen counsellors when adults, but only Arnold, the American, had seen one when he was a child. His behaviour had been judged sufficiently disturbed for him to be withdrawn to what he called the 'rubber room' for play therapy. Arnold described the events which led to this as being connected with his anger and frustration over his difficulties in class, but also with his relationship with his father, whom he described as capable of 'explosive anger'. Arnold spoke a great deal about his father, in ways that suggested that he had not experienced the 'mirror' of positive regard (Kahn, 1991). In a recent book of autobiographical essays by Americans with learning disabilities (Rodis, 2001), Arnold continues to discuss his father, but seems to have made peace with him.

Socio-emotional and identity issues at home

Table 6.2 above shows the informants whose parents were supportive. Seven of them, Adrian, Betty, Aarti, Harry, Jemima, Lisa and Ron, did not mention their mothers at all. Nine, Ann, Aarti, Chuck, Patrick, Harry, Will, Peggy, Bruce and Ron, made no reference to their fathers. Neither Aarti, Harry nor Ron mentioned either parent. Aarti said only that her parents were born in India.

There were seven students who reported something like: 'My mother noticed that there was something wrong and pressed the school to have me assessed or given extra help'. The language they used about themselves was 'having difficulties' or 'something wrong'. Text searches within the NUD.IST software package reveal tellingly that every informant used the word 'wrong'. With one exception, all used the word 'difficulty' in connection with themselves, as in 'I had difficulty with reading'. Use of the word 'wrong' was more varied – 'I was doing the wrong course;' 'I got it all wrong;' 'they said there was something wrong with me'. Most of the students who talked in this way approached university admission with little confidence, which bears out Rawson's (1995) observation about low self-concept among boys who were diagnosed after they had experienced failure.

Several informants described how their parents encouraged them to practise reading and writing at home. Stephen's mother made him flashcards. Jemima read aloud to her parents in the evenings, even when she went to secondary school. Robert recalled sessions with his father on multiplication tables: 'I mean he did, every single night: persevered hour after hour after hour, night after night after night'. Robert said this was frustrating for both of them, and the same word was used by Arnold, whose parents did his homework with him:

> We would just labour and cry, trying to memorise how to spell words, and they would test me every night and I'd get angry and cry.

Gary described his mother as being 'quite alarmed' when he told her how distressing he was finding his A Level courses, and she encouraged him to abandon them. The determination to persist came from him, and persevere he did, although he 'did cry on her shoulder many a night'.

Table 6.3 : All informants, adding family members

informant	age	yr of ass't	age at ass't	expert views from	family dyslexia	parents' input
Adrian	25	95	24	EP	not stated	not stated
Alice	37	95	36	Newspapers; Univ. LST	F, B	ETH
Alison	20	91	15 or 16	EP; Ts; LST	S; M; uncle	ETH, gen enc
Aarti	22	95	21	EP	not stated	not stated
Ann	21	92	for A Levels	EP	not stated	M req'd asst
Arnold	20	88	Teens	various Ts;EP;counsellors	not stated	pressure
Betty	49	93	c46	D's EP (then went herself)	2 Ds	not stated
Bruce	24	88	16	EP	B? S? Cousin?	not stated
Charles	44	96	43	LST; rdg on 'word blindness'	not stated	M typed his work
Charlotte	21	94	19	LSU staff; LST	not stated	ETH
Chuck	34	72	School, 33	E.Ps; own reading	3 siblings	Took him to EP
Eliza	22	82	8 or 9	EPs, SNT, parents	no	'all along'
Enid	20	95	19	Parents; University psychologist	F; GM	M (= T)
Fenella	44	93	42	SNT at College; LS unit	not stated	M read to her
Gary	20	82	6 or 7	class T; LSTs	not stated	M= emot. support
Geraldine	53	91	47	own research; self-analysis; EP	not stated	no
Harry	27	95	26	Other student; EP	not stated	non-specif
Jemima	20	85	9; GCSE; for A Level	SNT; EP	M (probably)	ETH, spec sch
Jeremy	19	95	18	GF; psychologist	not stated	M non-specif
Lance	24	93	21/23(+10)	LST	not stated	M; M+F=LSTs
Lisa	50	95	49	Hampshire, mags, D's EP	B, D	not stated
Mel	32	81	6th Form + 32	Reader's Digest; EP	nieces	M did reading
Patrick	25	95	24	EP; other students	not stated	private T 6 yrs

Table 6.3 : All informants, adding family members (continued)

informant	age	yr of ass't	age at ass't	expert views from	family dyslexia	parents' input
Peggy	38	95	37	EP	not stated	no
Phoebe	21	83, 89	14,17	3 EPs; M	M	sent to bdg sch
Rachel	20	92	16	EP	F	M non-specif.
Robert	31	94	29	Access T; EP	not stated	financially
Ron	41	95	40	Access T; EP; own research	B	F = help w h'wk
Sally	19	86	8/9,17	EP, M	B	M 'all the way'
Stephen	22	83	9,17	D.I.T; M+F read books	not stated	M+F a lot
Susan	45	95	43	LSU staff; EP	M = illiterate; 2 Ds	F = reading
Victoria	50	95	49	D.I. teacher; EP	not stated	not stated
Will	18	93	Junior Sch +15	M's reading; other dyslexic boy	not stated	M req'd asst; ETH

Key

DI: Dyslexia Institute
EP: Educational Psychologist
SNT: special needs teacher
M: mother
LS: learning support
F: father
B: brother

LSU: Learning Support Unit
T: teacher
GF: girlfriend
sch: school
ass't: dyslexia assessment
ETH: extra teaching hours
rdg: reading

D: daughter
neg: negative
+ive: positive
req'd: requested

If any family member, especially a parent, identifies themselves as dyslexic, a special kind of support can arise. Seven informants stated that one of their parents was dyslexic; Table 6.3 (page 83/84) expands the previous Table to show those who said that family members were dyslexic.

The reaction to such information varied considerably. Enid's father presented dyslexia to her as a memory difficulty with spelling, and tried to pass on his strategies to her when she was 13. Alice and her father never mentioned his dyslexia until she was an adult, when she raised the subject, only to be told that her father had avoided telling her, because 'If I talked to you about it, you might see it as an excuse not to try, and I didn't want to put you off because you were trying so hard.'

On the other hand, Phoebe had 'always been quite familiar' with dyslexia, because her mother was open about her own identification. But her mother believed that she herself had been discriminated against in employment, and did not want Phoebe assessed at first, because of 'that stigma'. Apparently Phoebe's mother's view had changed, and she was 'very sort of self-confident now and loud' about dyslexia.

For Rachel, the knowledge that her father was dyslexic was confused with the intelligence question. Rachel's sister was 'always the exceptional star' and Rachel was 'the practical one'. Their father ran his own business but his wife wrote letters for him, and Rachel 'wondered why my mum was with him because my Mum is really intelligent'. She quoted their father as telling her:

> You're very like me. You know it, you know your stuff; it's just – you find it hard to express yourself.

Robert and Victoria were both punished by their parents for school reports that described them as lazy or not trying, whereas Sally's mother believed her daughter needed support for dyslexia. When she was asked whether her teachers had heard of this, she replied 'I'm sure they had by the time my Mum had finished'. Stephen expressed similar pride in his parents. His school had wanted him to drop an A Level, but: 'Luckily good old Mum and Dad came in again and bollocked everybody and sorted it out'. Barton and Hamilton (1998:105) describe how some parents feel 'shut out of their children's schooling' and become campaigners for dyslexia support. Joining a Dyslexia Association can make dyslexia into what Barton and Hamilton call a 'cultural belief'. This is discussed in Chapter 9.

Pride

There is straightforward pride in success, as in the examples of creative writing success quoted above, or pride in one's own cognitive style – and there is pride in the shape of sensitivity about one's dignity.

There were several examples of the informants' dignity being wounded during their compulsory education:

- Phoebe's teacher read out her spelling mistakes to the class
- Robert's French and Maths teachers told him to stop attending their classes
- Lisa's teacher commented publicly on the poor standard of her reading aloud.

Pride in their own cognitive style was not shown by many of the students when they spoke about their schooldays. But there were some examples:

- Charlotte successfully used mnemonics to remember mathematical facts
- Geraldine described herself as 'a very good patterner'
- Jemima recalled colours used in her GCSE revision notes
- Sally found she could remember the diagrams one teacher used
- because he could picture the real world, Stephen did well in Physical Geography, as opposed to the more theoretical aspects of Human Geography

Frustration and anger

Several students expressed anger when they recalled their frustrations at school: Aaron, Robert, Aarti, Enid, Ron and Alice. Alice believed that she had difficulty expressing her anger over how all her educational experiences had been a struggle, because she had been brought up to believe that one should not show anger. Victoria, on the other hand, was vehement about her anger that dyslexia had prevented her from achieving what she felt she might have.

'Frustration' was the first thing Ron recalled when asked about his principal memory of primary school. He had disliked 'special lessons' for reading, and took deep breaths to calm himself as he spoke of a teacher whom he reported as pretty much saying 'don't bother too much, you won't sort of go that far'.

Chuck, Jemima and Jeremy all described feeling that teachers were frustrated with *them*, but eight others applied the word to their own feelings. Arnold used it most frequently of all of them, about how he used to argue with his father about his homework, and with teachers about his frequent 'demerits' and 'checks off'. Arnold was also frustrated about being kept back a grade, and about often submitting assignments late.

Robert was also voluble about his frustration. Like Ron, he used the word very early in his interview, first in connection with his father's efforts to teach him multiplication tables. Later, Robert recalled the mutual frus-

Table 6.4 : All informants, showing approaches to University application

informant	age	expert views from	family dyslexia	parents' input	approached Univ.
Adrian	25	EP	not stated	Not stated	not stated
Alice	37	Newspapers; LST (University)	F, B	ETH	v . keen
Alison	20	EP; Ts; LST	S; M; uncle	ETH, gen enc	'have a go'
Aarti	22	EP	not stated	No	determined
Ann	21	EP	not stated	M req'd asst	reluctant
Arnold	20	various Ts;EP;counsellors	not stated	pressure	not clear
Betty	49	Ds' EP (then went herself)	2 Ds	Not stated	wanting to improve self
Bruce	24	EP	B? S? Cousin?	Not stated	det. to leave home
Charles	44	LST; rdg on word blindness	not stated	M typed his work	Not clear
Charlotte	21	LSU staff; LST	not stated	ETH	keen; ignorant of dyslxia.
Chuck	34	E.Ps (probably); own reading	3 siblings	Took him to EP	ignorant of demands
Eliza	22	EPs, SNT, parents	no	all along	didn't expect to go
Enid	20	Parents; University psychologist	F; GM	M (= T)	'natural thing to do'
Fenella	44	SNT at College; LS unit	not stated	M read to her	kepg up w frnds;nervous
Gary	20	class T; LSTs	not stated	M= emot. support	always determined
Geraldine	53	own research ; self-analysis; EP	not stated	no	not stated
Harry	27	Other student; EP	not stated	non-specif	career interest
Jemima	20	SNT; EP	M (probably)	ETH, spec sch	confident
Jeremy	19	GF; psychologist	not stated	M non-specif	Ambitious for career
Lance	24	LST	not stated	M; M+F=LS	determined
Lisa	50	Hampshire, mags, D's EP	B, D	Not stated	'learning bug'
Mel	32	Reader's Digest; EP	nieces	M did reading	confident
Patrick	25	EP; other students	not stated	private T 6 yrs	not confident, so HND

Table 6.4 : All informants, showing approaches to University application (continued)

informant	age	expert views from	family dyslexia	parents' input	approached Univ.
Peggy	38	EP	not stated	no	very anxious
Phoebe	21	3 EPs; M	M	left at bdg sch	confident
Rachel	20	EP	F	M non-specif.	'Out' at interview
Robert	31	Access T; EP	not stated	financially	determined
Ron	41	Access T; EP; own research	B	F = help w h'wk	Desire to be a nurse
Sally	19	EP, M	B	M 'all the way'	always going to go
Stephen	22	D.I.T; M+F read books	not stated	M+F a lot	engineering like F
Susan	45	LSU staff; EP	M = illiterate; 2 Ds	F = reading	very tentative, but keen
Victoria	50	D.I. teacher; EP	not stated	no	Keen, but anxious
Will	18	M's reading; other dyslxic boy	not stated	M req'd asst; ETH	not stated

Key

DI: Dyslexia Institute
EP: Educational Psychologist
SNT: special needs teacher
M: mother
LS: learning support
F: father
B: brother
det: determined

LSU: Learning Support Unit
T: teacher
GF: girlfriend
sch: school
ass't: dyslexia assessment
ETH: extra teaching hours
rdg: reading

D: daughter
neg: negative
+ive: positive
req'd: requested
kepg: keeping
w: with
frnds: friends

tration of himself and his maths teacher, because Robert wanted infor-mation repeated so many times. His feelings had been aggravated by the way his reports said he was 'exceptionally lazy', when he believed that he had been making a real effort.

At the time when informants of the age of Ron and Robert (41 and 31) were at school, the provision of counselling for UK school students was less available than now (Downey, 1996). This may partly explain why the only informant to refer to receiving counselling during his schooldays was American, although some may not have wanted to discuss this. Some of the students did however seek counselling at University, as discussed in Chapter 7.

Determination to go to University

Table 6.4 (pages 86/87) adds notes on the informants' approaches to University to the existing list.

Phoebe, Patrick, Charlotte and Jemima all remembered being told by teachers that they would never achieve anything academically. Charlotte's response to this was typical. A teacher had told her she would not achieve good A Level grades and 'when I did get the grades for university, I actually called back to say to her 'I've got them and I'm going. See ya''. Patrick's teacher had told his parents that he was not intelligent. 'In some ways I've got [laughs] him to thank for – in one respect that spurred me on to come here, to get where I have done'. Alice had been advised by an employer that an HNC would be too hard for her: 'She just said to me, 'I don't think you'd be able to cope with it, don't do it'. So I did it, of course'.

Other informants, such as Bruce and Robert, also recalled reacting against people's limited expectations of them. Bruce thought 'sod them; the way I'm going to beat you bastards is by doing better'. Robert was advised not to study Law, because it required so much reading. His reaction was 'sod it, yeah, I'll do it!' Robert (aged 31) was one of six informants who had fol-lowed Access courses, which takes determination for any mature student. He described spending a whole weekend writing and re-writing a 1500-word social psychology essay, staying up until 1 a.m. on the Monday and finding the process 'horrendous'. Before his Access course, Ron (aged 41) had attended evening classes and a City & Guilds 730 course, suffering headaches throughout because his Meares-Irlen syndrome had not been diagnosed. But he was determined to become a nurse.

Another Access student, Fenella (aged 44), had been motivated by her feeling that her friends had degrees and she had 'missed out' on educa-tion. Unlike most of the other informants, however, Fenella had not heard of dyslexia:

I'd been keeping to myself for a very long time, thinking that I was ab-normal, that there was something drastically not right, but not knowing what it was.

Susan (aged 45) had not heard of dyslexia either. At her junior school she had fantasised about being a writer, but her academic self-esteem dis-integrated at secondary modern school where, she believed, girls were mainly prepared for marriage, a state she entered at 19. Susan's path to university began with a book-keeping class after her children were born. A succession of classes followed, in which she increasingly enjoyed writing and was encouraged by others to progress further. Her eyes filled with tears as she spoke about passing GCSE English Language at the age of 38, but she expected to be turned down for her Access course even after passing several more GCSEs.

Of the younger students – nineteen were 25 or under (see Table 6.4) – Gary's relationships with teachers seem more positive than those des-cribed above, but he burned with desire to go to University from an early age. So much so that he continued to attend A Level classes even though he had to force himself to enter the school building. Human motivation is never simple. Gary is gay, and felt that at university he could 'come out'. He had been identified as dyslexic so early in his life that he took it for granted.

The admissions process raised several emotional and identity issues. The determination of informants like these to apply for university was inspired by being advised that they should not try or would fail. Others were con-scious of prejudice of a different kind. Some of those on Access courses, such as Peggy, decided not to mention dyslexia at interview in case it damaged their chances of admission. One young woman with A Levels (Sally) was advised by her EP not to say she was dyslexic.

Admissions interviews raised two issues. Anxiety made Charlotte and Fenella confused and they misunderstood questions or muddled their answers. Jemima and Rachel were reluctant to mention dyslexia in a group interview.

A few informants had a totally different experience. The Canadian student, Eliza, had been told by her teachers not to expect high enough grades for HE admission, but had become keen to go when she discovered that her grades were good. She had been advised that a British university would be good because 'Britain is into dyslexia'. Two informants who were studying occupational therapy (Jemima, Rachel) were uncertain as to whether they could manage the course, but had said so at interview and been reassured that the university (Burtonforth) accommodated dyslexic students: 'We can find new ways of you doing things, if you come here'. Some of the experiences and responses reported here were of a kind that made the students feel good about themselves.

Positive self-regard

Riddick *et al*'s (1997) research participants see themselves as different, in that they think in different ways from many other people. Although some of the present informants characterised non-dyslexic people as 'normal', more of them defined themselves as in some way 'different', often with a positive gloss on the term. Geraldine acknowledged that she had had to come to terms with her 'difference':

> I've had hassle, mid-twenties onwards, because I think so differently and I've gradually appreciated that I do think differently and that I need in fact to respect that if I'm going to actually understand something.

She said she was 'a good patterner' who could 'understand by operations' as opposed to abstract thought.

Others differentiated between their inability to remember and manipulate facts, particularly codes such as dates and document references, and their success with global concepts and logistical planning. In some cases (Eliza, Adrian, Stephen), such trains of thought supported Riddick *et al*'s finding (1997:165) that their respondents were 'able to value at least some of their own abilities at school' when they looked back on it.

As discussed in Chapter 2, contrast with others shapes identity more strongly than 'sameness' (Hall and du Gay, 1996; Craib, 1998). The nine students who saw dyslexia as a medical matter (see Chapter 8) and the twelve who saw it mainly as an academic matter certainly focused on difference, whereas the eight who saw it as a particular cognitive style concentrated on group solidarity based on 'sameness'. Although most students who have been labelled dyslexic have been treated as 'different', some have embraced this and others have resented it. The student who says 'I have a disability, and I am entitled to special arrangements if the playing field is to be level' is very different from the one who seems to be saying 'I have a defect and may scrape through my course if I am lucky'.

Summary

This chapter has focused on the third stage of the pathway model set out in Chapter 5. While many students arrive at University with doubts and fears about their ability to manage its demands (Raaheim *et al,* 1991; Peelo, 1994), what this cohort of students share is that they are different. They may have various ways of construing this difference, seeing it as a defect or a distinctive feature. Over half were not formally identified as dyslexic before admission, but they all feel 'other' in their education.

The next chapter examines the fourth stage of the model set out in Chapter 5: the experience of HE.

Chapter 7
Experience of Higher Education

Introduction
Chapters 5 and 6 present a pathway model from the definition of dyslexia to experience of HE and explore it through the third stage, 'socio-emotional effects'. This chapter covers the informants' experiences at university.

The self-concept of the students who had not been identified as dyslexic before admission was powerfully affected by the experience of formal assessment for dyslexia. Other broad socio-emotional themes can also be isolated, and this chapter considers the cognitive, affective and social aspects of learning and teaching in HE which were revealed by the interviews. Brief extracts from the transcripts which include these themes can be found in Appendix I.

Socio-emotional aspects of university life
Many informants spoke of their frustration during their schooldays because they felt there was a discrepancy between their intellectual ability and their academic attainments. This feeling persisted at university for Enid, Victoria and Stephen. Their colleagues did not realise what long hours of work they had to put in in order to comprehend text or write essays. Even those who were determined not to feel stigmatised, such as Patrick, complained about how this made them feel different.

The students were interviewed at their universities about a topic labelled 'learning life history'. Much of what they said referred to cognitive aspects or, in affective terms, academic self-esteem. Social self-esteem also featured in most interviews, and was stressed strongly by Charlotte, Mel, Bruce, Stephen and Rachel. They linked their perception of their difficulties with their dyslexia, and this underlined their self-concept as 'different'.

One difficulty concerned memory. Alison said:

> When they say 'short-term memory is a problem', boy do I know it! ... I forget things like the moment they're said to me.

Mel and Ann saw this problem in terms of the need for their boyfriends to be patient and understanding, but when asked about 'coming out' to prospective boyfriends, Phoebe declared that it did not matter because she saw dyslexia only in academic terms. (See page 100 for an extended quotation from Ann about working memory.)

Rachel was also concerned about social effects of her poor memory:

> So people just look at you and, you know, if they don't know you very well 1. they take you as being stupid anyway, because you don't seem to be able to have a normal conversation and 2. you can never remember to do anything, you can't remember what happened on Saturday night.

Canadian Eliza used the word 'stupid' with some vehemence. She was studying hotel management. When on work experience in a restaurant, she had had great difficulty remembering what customers had ordered, and giving change at the bar. She described this as:

> little things that you can't do that people can't understand why you can't do them and put it down to stupidity, and you've gotta prove that it isn't.

She defined her problems in the restaurant as 'like a stupid person, stupid stupid stupid'. She had recently confused the digits in a telephone number, and blamed dyslexia for it, 'so dyslexia has got back into my life'. This is an example of an ontological security issue (Giddens, 1991), where one needs acceptance by others as competent, and it is often closely linked with feelings of shame.

Will said that he lacked confidence in his spoken language ability, and sought to avoid shame by mixing with the international students because 'they're learning the language'. Bruce ostensibly felt quite different; he described himself as 'a cheeky chappy kind of prat' who charmed girls with his humour. But like Alison, he was worried about his memory. He sent me this email (unedited) after his interview:

> The slight dyslexia I seem to have may well have harmed my chances with girls a teenager as I pretty useless at memorising telephone nos. and so I had to find someone pretty keen if they were going to go a get a paper and pencil for me!

Stephen's reaction was to withdraw socially. He described himself as 'quite a big loner', adding: 'maybe partly due to the dyslexia, you feel a bit different, so you keep to yourself'. Whereas Gary was quite open with friends about his dyslexia, laughing confidently when telling how a flat-mate had left him a telephone message spelled deliberately bizarrely.

Chuck exemplified the understanding of dyslexia as medical. He saw a parallel between the 'does he take sugar?' approach to people with disabilities and the way he had been treated as dyslexic:

You tend to suffer from the problem that all disabled people have, this want to be treated as normal, like a normal person. ... You get accepted as normal and then they find that you have dyslexia and then their mouth drops and their attitude changes completely, and you get, you get the endearing patronisation.

These examples show that students who had differing views of dyslexia coped socially in different ways.

In terms of seeking help for serious emotional difficulties, only Patrick, Alice and Charles told me that they had seen counsellors at University. Each had a different view of dyslexia. Patrick had suffered what he described as 'bad lows' during his first degree, before he was identified as dyslexic in his third year and had this taken into account in academic assessment. Although he was involved in student support groups while working for his MSc, he had 'never been to counselling so many times'. Alice's self-esteem focused on achieving qualifications, and she had driven herself so hard that she had what she described as 'a total breakdown' and spent a month in hospital. Counselling sessions had led her to believe that 'a lot of the root of the problem is me and the way I focus on life'. Alice, who saw dyslexia as a purely academic matter, was convinced that she must obtain qualifications at the highest level she could, in order to prove that she was intelligent. The third student to have attended counselling, Charles, took a medical view of dyslexia and had suffered from severe examination phobia.

Patrick described how he had almost become 'really really depressed' during his placement year. Work experience seems to have caused emotional problems for several students, often connected with written reports. Patrick spoke angrily and at length in his interview about what he had believed to be a thorough report on his placement project, which had been marked down because of grammar and spelling. Jemima, who had not mentioned being dyslexic on her first occupational therapy placement, described the supervisor as 'frustrated' by her spelling, until she was 'embarrassed' by learning that Jemima was dyslexic. On her second placement, Jemima had mentioned her dyslexia at once, but had remained quiet in the staff common room, because 'I tend to rabbit a bit and then get my words all mixed up'.

References from his tutor caused a problem for Jeremy on his industrial placement. As he was studying applied biochemistry, Jeremy needed to work in the chemical industry, and his tutor said he was 'obliged' to refer to his dyslexia in references: 'He didn't ask my permission; he said 'I'm telling everyone that you're dyslexic." Jeremy believed that some companies would not understand the word dyslexic and would assume that he could neither read nor write. He said 'I'm not going to put myself down if

I don't have to'. He had taken to explaining dyslexia in his applications and minimising its effects, but it took many attempts before he found a placement.

Some of the students worried about whether their future employment prospects would be affected by their difficulties with memory and literacy. As Phoebe put it:

> In certain areas of work it might be a problem. Like say if somebody comes in, and like tells me their name, and what they want or something, I'm likely to forget that.

She nevertheless did not intend to mention dyslexia in what she called a professional situation, unless it became 'embarrassing' not to do so. Susan, who was much older, felt the same:

> I do worry if I got to the field of work and had to, you know, write fairly rapidly things...Then I think it would all disintegrate, that's what worries me.

Victoria was angry about her dyslexia:

> I just regard it as a damned nuisance that's impinged on my life. I'm afraid that's how I look at it. I feel angry about it, I have to tell you, I do feel angry about it. It's stopped me doing things I could be really good at. In fact it's really blocked my life.

She would have liked to be a broadcast journalist or a barrister, but felt handicapped by her inability to remember conversations or order her ideas orally and on paper. Victoria and Alice both used the word 'clever' to describe the sort of ability they felt they lacked.

The students' experiences of being assessed for dyslexia varied considerably, but all of them were identified both as 'different' and as having a problem. The expert figure who made this assessment had the power to influence their lives lastingly, affecting not only their view of themselves and the nature of dyslexia but also their educational experience. This could be positive – for Liam, Alison, Eliza and Stephen the assessment process at school, while identifying them as having a problem, improved their self-esteem because it meant their needs had been recognised (Miles, 1983) and they would no longer be accused of laziness.

Students often revealed their poor self-esteem during the interview. Some laughed as they spoke about unpleasant experiences, or made self-deprecatory comments like 'sounds messy', 'rather stupid' and even 'what a prat'. But some were confident enough to express their anger about the way they had been treated at school and university.

The socio-emotional effects of identity as dyslexic can be divided into two broad categories: those which stem from an internal locus of evaluation (Mearns, 1994) and those stemming from an external locus. The students for whom the locus was external tended to perceive themselves as defective and as second-class citizens in the world of education. Those whose locus of evaluation was internal focused more on the need as they saw it for educational institutions to change their ways so as to accommodate dyslexic people. In both groups there were students who saw themselves as unjustly treated or misunderstood. At university, this tended to be focused on academic assessment.

Learning and teaching issues at university

Sanderson and Pillai (2001) observe that learning support in HE is a lottery. Arrangements for and response to dyslexic students varied widely between the universities attended by the informants in this study. But the students themselves approached HE with various definitions of dyslexia or acquired them after admission. Their self-concepts varied, but so did their personality traits – their experiences at university cannot be attributed entirely to their having been identified as dyslexic. The findings about the informants' academic life in HE can usefully be grouped under cognitive, affective and social (Peelo, 2000a; Peelo, 2000b).

The cognitive aspects of university

Each student's approach to university life depended in part on their previous experience of coping with academic study. Those who had been identified as dyslexic during compulsory education and had received learning support (Gary, Jemima, Phoebe, Sally) were more likely to approach their university courses with confidence. In some cases (such as Gary), this meant being determined to avoid any repetition of the worksheet approach of much school-based 'remedial' work. Their awareness of the ways they could study successfully was useful to them and showed their metacognition (Hunter-Carsch, 2001).

The findings relating to the cognitive aspects of study are described in two parts: first the informants' own strategies, and secondly their comments on their universities' teaching and learning approaches.

The students' learning strategies

Informants reported more successful than unsuccessful strategies. Ann and Robert both felt that tape recording lectures did not work for them, because they never got round to playing back their piles of cassettes, but Aarti was adamant that a tape recording was essential because she could not listen and write notes at the same time. Arnold had enjoyed studying literature by listening to books on tape, so listened to his recordings of lectures without writing notes. Chuck made sketchy notes in lectures, but took care to include the counter numbers from the tape recorder so he could return later and expand the notes.

The computer (PC) also received mixed reports. Robert was the only student to favour using voice-activated word-processing, because he preferred to communicate orally. Betty and Victoria were both nervous of cutting and pasting, lest the text disappear. They and others were aware that having typed a piece of work, its neatness on the screen made it look perfect and therefore hard to edit. But both Alice and Phoebe, who had previously learned to type, found word processing on a PC easier.

There was clearly still a role for pen, pencil and paper. Geraldine used a propelling rubber as well as a propelling pencil, and wrote on alternate lines so that she could easily add revisions. Will used pens of many colours for revision. Lance made essay-plan diagrams by hand and then typed his work from them. Enid wrote all her essays out four times before typing them. Harry found that copying notes out neatly helped his memory, and Jeremy wrote material out many times as a revision technique.

Three further aspects of study emerged: self-knowledge, human support and visual approaches. Charles knew precisely which times of day were best for him to study: 8 a.m. to midday and 7 p.m. to 10 p.m. – followed by the pub. Enid did not study in the evening at all, because she knew she was more likely to reverse letters when she was tired. Victoria had learned that she tended to collect too many sources for an essay. Geraldine chose to study in the library, because in her room she would be tempted to play music and make cups of coffee.

They also showed self-knowledge about what visual approaches worked for them. Rachel liked to picture a book 'like a film' as she was reading it, and relate theory to real people whom she could imagine. Alice, Rachel and Geraldine all used concept maps for noting or essay planning and Rachel used a large wall planner to help her time management. Such techniques are related to the holistic thought these students exhibited: Geraldine placed a copy of any diagram included in a book alongside the text as she read, Will revised by memorising diagrams, and Rachel learned anatomy by dismantling three-dimensional models with a friend and discussing them.

The students also turned to people for support. Harry was happy to ask his house-mates to check his English; Ann borrowed lecture notes from friends; Stephen and Robert asked the librarian to find them books, because the catalogue baffled them. Geraldine married one of her tutors!

Although the DSA includes an element for 'non-medical help' which is deemed to cover regular individual learning support for dyslexic students, only six students, Charlotte, Chuck, Aaron, Peggy, Susan and Charles, were receiving such support. All were at Belleville or Spenceton. Of the remaining two of the students enrolled at Belleville or Spenceton, Adrian had not requested individual support, and Fenella had been referred to a counsellor who offered 'study skills' but had not found this helpful. There is further discussion under 'Social aspects'.

The learning and teaching approaches in the universities

The students longed at times for recognition or acknowledgement of dyslexia by the academy. Lance put it like this:

> I know I've got a good grasp of the subject, and I know people who've got less grasp are getting higher percentages for their essays and marks. I know exams don't do me justice. I know basically I'm better at speaking, and they don't assess that way.

Thirty nine per cent of the students – Ann, Betty, Harry, Jeremy, Aaron, Rachel, Charles, Robert, Lisa, Victoria, Stephen, Mel and Lance – complained about their universities' styles of learning and teaching, yet all except Mel, Lance, Aarti and Patrick seemed to accept the academy's model of academic procedure as a given (Street and Street, 1991) to which they had to aspire.

Like many students, the informants disliked examinations. However, they had specific problems with them, which they described:

■ they ran out of time, because they had to (a) read the questions repeatedly, (b) plan answers slowly, often with a 'concept map' and (c) write slowly, because of their difficulty in focusing on content and spelling at the same time

■ they suffered from pain in their writing hand, either because they seldom used a pen, preferring a computer or from 'dysgraphia' – a term used by some EPs to denote severe handwriting difficulty

■ they believed that non-dyslexic students receive an unfair advantage because examination technique comes easily to them

■ they knew that their coursework marks were higher than their examination marks

■ their spelling and/or grammar ability declined under pressure

■ they suffered from exam phobia or severe panic.

However, some appreciated being in a separate room – the arrangement for those who are having extra time – and some found the extra time valuable, except Enid, who said re-reading caused her to long to re-write whole answers. Harry said that the extra time gave him the confidence to read the question paper calmly instead of panicking; for Bruce, this confidence meant drawing concept maps and checking his grammar.

The question of extra time for dyslexic students in examinations raised a number of issues. Jeremy thought the examiner would know that he had received extra time, and would not therefore penalise him for spelling and grammar, whereas blind marking means that scripts are not identified. Robert's EP's report had recommended both extra time and non-penalisation for language. When he was only granted extra time, Robert had complained, to be told that the EP's report had no status other than as a recommendation. Jeremy's comments about examinations were somewhat contradictory. He did not want to be penalised for written language, but at the same time felt that dyslexia should not be an excuse, and that having a viva instead of a written paper was 'a cop-out'. Such tensions are made clear in the report of the NWP (Singleton, 1999) and have never been entirely resolved in the UK.

Special examination arrangements raise two further issues: severity of dyslexia and IQ/attainment discrepancy. The DI (Turner, 1997) holds that dyslexia has four levels of severity, and that examination arrangements such as extra time should match these levels. Will's comment that his University asked for his EP's report because 'they wanted to know how dyslexic I was' fits this model. However, the variety of percentages of extra time reported by informants presages the inconsistencies identified by Sanderson and Pillai (2001).

Geraldine stated the argument for extra time which was to be given in the NWP report (Singleton, 1999), namely that 'there is no justification for exam arrangements and extra time, if dyslexic people haven't got gifts that are being masked by the dyslexia'. This assumes an IQ/attainment discrepancy model.

The metacognitive awareness showed by some of the students, such as Stephen, extended to the lecturing style of their tutors. They preferred a diagrammatic, graphic-rich style, particularly when it formed part of a course whose structure was made explicit. Rachel, Jemima and Ann all expressed a preference for three-dimensional, practical work as opposed to two-dimensional drawings and long lectures.

The speed of information presentation was a problem for Chuck, Rachel and Victoria. They were troubled by having to copy from boards and screens very quickly and the hasty removal of overhead transparencies. Victoria and Rachel both used the expression 'too rushed' to describe their courses.

However, no clear preference was expressed for oral assessment. Phoebe and Aarti were clear about their preference for written examinations rather than vivas which are sometimes offered to dyslexic students, believing that their speed of information processing was put under greater strain when responding orally than by the task of writing an essay, however rapidly. Lance, who enjoyed making political speeches without notes, took the opposite view. Jeremy thought oral assessment would be too easy. Opinions were also mixed about discussions, which some enjoyed whereas others felt threatened. Sally liked group discussion because she could contribute without the focus being on her for too long, but Betty found the background noise in 'buzz groups' distracting and felt that she could not sort out her ideas quickly enough.

Not all informants had purely negative things to say about the learning and teaching approach of their courses. Rachel said that students received a helpful response from lecturers when they asked for copies of notes because they could not write everything down. Charlotte noted that all students, not only those who were dyslexic, were given handouts of OHTs. Jemima was pleased her department included a tutor who updated students about the ways PCs could help them, another who showed them concept mapping and a third who offered them informal counselling support. Gary appreciated the way his university automatically sent him details of his extra time for examinations without his having to request it every year. Chuck and his year group had been asked for detailed feedback on the teaching style of the course. Chuck felt that tutors enjoyed it when he asked for clarification or repetition, as it implied engagement on his part. But, like Phoebe and Lance, he believed that his tutors were ignorant of the nature of dyslexia, and did not know which students were dyslexic.

The cognitive aspects of the informants' experiences of learning and teaching were characterised by the way they saw themselves as having different brains. For the majority (21), this difference amounted to a defect, but the remaining twelve saw it broadly as having a different kind of brain which was as good as anyone else's. But many of these informants tended to waver between confidence in this point of view and comments which put them in the 'defect' group. For example, Eliza said at one point that however intelligent she was, she was 'never going to be as good as the other students', but she also said that dyslexic people do things in different ways, and 'you'll get there in the end'.

The affective aspects of university

Robert laughed about the way fellow students called the separate examination room used by those being given extra time the 'incontinence room'. Such humour may be what in Transactional Analysis (Stewart and Joines, 1987) would be called 'discounting': trying to minimise the emotional effect of what is in fact a painful memory. Similarly, Enid laughed frequently throughout her interview, usually when talking about something which had not gone well. Other students made these emotional comments about the teaching and learning they were experiencing:

> When you are constantly failing ... you always take a knock, and cumulatively it can be quite disastrous (Chuck)

> I get near to tears sometimes when I can't remember things (Peggy)

I'm proud of myself, I think, and I do think I should be here now (Rachel)

It dragged me to tears at times; a grown man, you know, going down, but it did – it dragged me very, very low (Charles).

Ann was a responsive informant, but her interventions were seldom longer than about 125 words. But she spoke at greater length about her working memory, describing herself as feeling 'particularly useless and thick':

I forget everything the entire time. Erm, like yesterday I was supposed to meet someone and forgot, totally and utterly and it was so vital to me and it's just very annoying that you forget even the most absolutely crucial things and then, of course, you forget everything that's mundane and you just feel very thick and you can't speak properly, I mean, I haven't had to use any complicated, technical words so, but even little words I forget most of the time. You're sitting there and you're trying to think of the word that you want to say, um, I mean, descriptive I suppose, you know, when you are just talking about yourself it's quite easy, when you're talking about something you've remembered or you saw on TV, you're just hopeless at it, absolutely hopeless. So people just look at you and, you know, if they don't know you very well, (one) they take you as being stupid anyway, because you don't seem to be able to have a normal conversation and (two) you can never remember to do anything, you can't remember what happened on Saturday night, you don't remember anybody's names which straight away makes people feel like you don't want to know them at all, you know, if you can't remember their name you obviously, you know, don't think much of them whatsoever. So, I think the greatest thing outside and within the thing is forgetting absolutely everything, all the time.

Several informants spoke about being embarrassed in contexts other than those already described. For example, Robert had written £28 on a cheque instead of £82, and had been suspected of deliberate fraud, and Charlotte was embarrassed when friends corrected her pronunciation of 'Greenwich'.

Mel described having to leave the room because she could not keep up with a seminar, which illustrates a fundamentally cognitive issue. Trying to follow the ideas being presented while also making notes precipitated powerful affective outcomes of panic and emotional distress. In the affective context of lectures or seminars, it takes a degree of self-confidence to sit at the front of a lecture theatre or seminar room and set up a tape recorder or minidisk machine, or to ask for copies of overhead transparencies.

The experience of assessment was highly significant in affective terms for every informant identified as dyslexic after admission to HE. Peggy became quite tearful as she reflected on the different life she might have had had she been assessed much earlier as dyslexic. We saw how Fenella reacted to the term 'specific learning difficulties': when the EP confirmed that she was dyslexic, she found this 'really shocking'. She recalled having three simultaneous emotional responses: relief that she had not been pro-nounced unintelligent, gladness that her difficulties had been recognised and dismay that she had low reading and spelling ages.

Thus the informants' statements about the affective experiences of univer-sity life relate to the cognitive aspects. They share the feelings: 'I have a different brain, and I feel stupid/am upset by my failures/am frustrated'.

The social aspects of university

There are two broad aspects to the social issues in HE: the inter-personal side involving peers or tutors and the institutional side, between infor-mants and their tutors, as representatives of the academy (Becher, 1989; Peelo, 1994). Four facets of identity as a student for a dyslexic person, based on Ivanic (1998), are listed in Chapter 2:

- Autobiographical self: the identity people bring with them to the act of being a student, shaped by their earlier social experiences

- Self as a student: the level of confidence with which individuals see themselves as readers, thinkers, note-takers, writers, contributors to seminars and similar activities

- Possibilities for self-hood: social, cultural and institutional options; issues of power, values and beliefs

- Discoursal self: the discourse of dyslexia with which they identify.

The findings concerning the social aspects of university life for informants are now discussed in light of the first three of these facets; the fourth is considered in Chapter 8.

Charlotte was identified as dyslexic after admission, and her autobiograp-hical self included awareness that dyslexic people could be the subject of humour. She said: 'I made sure they all told me the dyslexia jokes before anyone told me they didn't know I was dyslexic, so I could answer them – and nearly always got it wrong, I hasten to add'. Stephen took the opposite approach: 'I think I'm really quite a big loner. I don't know if it's partly the dyslexia; I just avoid embarrassments if possible'. Lance's approach was different again; he threw himself into student union politics. His comment that this involved 'giving hell to lecturers' prompted the impression that he might have been displacing his anger about his dyslexia.

Gary had been identified as dyslexic earlier in his life than any of the others. His expectations of university life had been as much social as academic, and he seemed so happy – 'I've probably got more friends here than I've ever had in my life, now' – that being teased about his poor spel-ling by friends sounded positively enjoyable. Enid had discovered that some of her peers found spelling harder than she did, and asked her for help.

Mel was aware that friends failed to understand what she said at times, because of her tendency to 'launch into the middle of it' instead of starting her story from the beginning. She described her boyfriend as having 'put up with her' for ten years. She related how conversation could sometimes be difficult, when for example he said something and 'I can sort of feel the noise went past my ears, but nothing latched anywhere'.

In terms of 'self as a student', perhaps the first social aspect of HE life encountered from the institutional point of view was the admission process. Sally was advised by her EP not to indicate dyslexia in her application form for admission to HE, but to mention it after admission. She was the only informant to receive such advice, in which dyslexia was presented as liable to 'hinder your chances of getting in'.

Lance wanted to use HE as a 'new start', and was also keen to avoid using dyslexia as any form of excuse, such as for poor A Level grades, so he decided not to mention it on his application form. In contrast, Aaron had low SAT scores and applied to various universities in the USA as a 'learning disabled' student. All rejected him except one, and this was the university that offered what he described as 'the best support' for dyslexic students. Unlike Lance, Gary was quite happy to explain that his A Level grades were low because of dyslexia, and he believed that this was why the points criterion had been relaxed in his case.

The students encountered some unhelpful teaching styles. Lecturers spoke too rapidly in lectures, used hand-written OHTs or OHTs with tiny print, refused to explain points and instead referred students to sections of books. Some courses were just 'hours of lectures one after the other'. Rachel said that she fell asleep while a series of OHTs in small print was being shown. Victoria was inclined to 'give up', but knew it was she who would be 'the loser', as she would then have to write her assignment entirely 'out of books'.

But positive experiences of teaching and learning were also reported. Charlotte and Ann each mentioned lecturers who, though they spoke rapidly, gave them complete copies of their lecture notes. Enid and Aarti were offered extensions on assignment deadlines, and were not penalised for inaccurate English after their EPs' reports were received. Rachel's course tutors introduced all students to concept mapping (Buzan and Buzan, 1995), and held sessions for dyslexic students on the use of computers. This course, in Occupational Therapy, also used role playing and the linking of theory to real people as teaching techniques.

Jeremy noticed that those he thought of as 'younger lecturers' asked him for information about dyslexia. One of Lisa's tutors had asked her for feedback on his teaching style. Both Ann and Charlotte had been helped by dyslexia-aware administrative officers; in Charlotte's case, the officer was the first person to suggest that she be assessed.

Charlotte felt one reason she had 'excellent rapport' with lecturers was to do with her 'outgoing' and 'friendly' personality. Fenella, who was at the same University, had hesitated to telephone her tutor for help, although invited to do so 'at any time', because she believed her to be overwhelmed with work. Interpersonal factors of this kind may have arisen more at a small, campus university such as Spenceton than in the relatively impersonal environment of a heavily subscribed course at Burtonforth, which Jeremy, Lance and Patrick attended. Lance felt he was 'penalised for not writing linear stuff'. Patrick was highly sensitive about the relationship between the amount of effort he put in and the marks he was given. He was also aware of the requirement to adopt the prescribed model of academic writing: 'I learned the lessons, so I thought 'let's get this jargon out''.

Personality factors can be independent of dyslexia. Sally liked group discussion because she saw it as 'relaxed' and not focused on herself. Betty said that she would 'freeze up' in such situations and preferred to study alone but that part of the problem for her was that there were 'so many other people talking'. There is a view that being disturbed by background noise, particularly speech, is part of dyslexia (Klein, C, 1993; Miles, 1993).

Speed of information processing is similarly said to be an issue for dyslexic people (Nicolson and Fawcett, 1990). Ann had struggled with an anatomy class, during which a bell was rung at intervals to signal students to move between exhibits. Phoebe preferred essays to oral examination, because they allowed her more time to think.

The students were affected in two ways by being 'different' from others in their learning: 'am I so different?' and 'am I being treated differently?' Chuck was self-conscious enough to notice that he was not the slowest to finish copying and note-taking, as he had been at school. But Victoria, Alison, Alice and Stephen were among those who remarked on the relative ease with which they perceived their peers reading, writing and revising for examinations.

The institutional power that is loaded in the admissions interview affects perceptions of 'self as a student' and the overlapping 'possibilities for selfhood'. Rachel had been wary of mentioning dyslexia in a group interview, but when she knew she was to have an individual interview, she took her EP's report and asked whether she 'would be able to cope'. She, like Lance, had a political motive for applying:

> The thing is, the more people that go that are dyslexic the more people are going to recognise it and they're not going to think you're stupid.

Lance was aware of the potential conflict between his aspirations and the culture of the institution. He thought that his political activities did not appeal to some lecturers: 'Since I've kicked up a fuss, I'm not a favourite person'. Although he was the only one to report such activism, Jeremy, Phoebe and Bruce all shared his rejection of using dyslexia as an excuse for anything. Jeremy was most vehement: 'I don't want special exceptions; if I've got it wrong, I've got it wrong'. He had been reluctant to accept extra time for examinations, in a separate room. Jeremy was also sensitive about what exactly the 'level playing field' was in academic assessment. If, for example, extra time has been allowed, should leniency regarding spelling and grammar be offered as well (Singleton, 1999)?

Lance and Jeremy were not the only students to acknowledge the institutional power of the university. Arnold remarked on the contrast between the 'nice safe world' of high school and the pressure in university life to 'advocate for yourself'. Several of the informants presented themselves as active self-advocates. Victoria reminded her subject's Field Chair to take account of dyslexic students during his lectures, and wrote to other lecturers about this too. Charlotte went to see her Dean to explain her EP's report. Ann also went to see the Dean, only to be told that the Faculty did not have 'a system for dyslexics'.

'Possibilities for self-hood' may overlap with 'autobiographical self', since part of the motivation for such self-advocacy might have been the determination to avoid the negative experiences of school days. Charles, Peggy, Charlotte and Harry all remarked on how the sight of their work covered in red ink reminded them of the past. Charles was aware that text corrections made him 'turn in on [him]self' just as they had 25 years earlier.

There was a tension in the cohort between the desire for all students to be treated in the same way, for example, in respect of copies of OHTs, and the hope that all course tutors would make allowances for their dyslexia. Similarly, they wanted their work to be marked on the same basis as their peers' – that is that all work is anonymous, including papers written with extra time – but they did not feel they should be penalised for spelling and grammar. Betty had noticed that tutors would put ticks next to points they liked in her essays and wondered why structure was called for, if marking seemed to be about looking for certain points to be included.

Institutional aspects of learning and teaching for dyslexic students which impinge upon their possibilities for self-hood include learning support. This can be delivered in groups or individually. Eighty four per cent of the informants talked about learning support in general, and 54 per cent mentioned support groups for dyslexic students. At Burtonforth University, students who declared dyslexia on admission were automatically entered for extra time in examinations and offered extended time on library loans.

Axbridge students were issued with small coloured cards to attach to their written work, announcing that they were dyslexic and it offered a credit-bearing module exclusively for students who had been formally identified. At Spenceton, dyslexic students were supported by members of staff in the Counselling and Psychotherapy unit, and by a HEFCE-funded joint learning support unit which also served Belleville University.

How did these arrangements affect the students' sense of self? The administrator and the support tutor of the joint learning support unit at Belleville were both dyslexic, and used routinely to tell the students so. Charlotte had found this to be both a personal support in terms of empathy and a role model in terms of dyslexic people finding worthwhile profes-sional employment. Chuck described such empathy in line with solidarity between black people, as he believed that people of African-Caribbean origin faced prejudice and ignorance in the same way dyslexics did.

Such personal empathy was in contrast to the learning support arrange-ment at Spenceton, where Fenella and Charlotte were studying. They had been offered sessions billed as 'study skills' from a counsellor, and had been taken aback to find that he wanted them to focus on their emotions.

At Burtonforth, Robert knew the support librarian by name and found her 'very helpful' when he asked her to help him find materials. But Axbridge did not seem to have such a person. Victoria had been paying £20 per hour to a private learning support tutor when she could afford it, and cited help with the library as one of her reasons for booking a session. Also at Ax-bridge, Betty had attended some group support sessions but expressed a preference for individual support. Eliza spoke enthusiastically about the group sessions and how learning about concept maps, use of colour for learning and awareness of the roles of the cerebral hemispheres had helped her, but added that she 'did use dyslexia for its concessions'. Attending the module had led Eliza to understand that 'when I leave academic learning, I'm not gonna leave dyslexia' – in other words, she accepted a model of dyslexia as a lifelong mindset rather than merely an educational matter.

Victoria and Alice both took pride in 'never [having] had anything' in terms of learning support before. But both had attended the module at Axbridge for dyslexic students. At the other universities, Ann, Stephen, Jeremy and Gary were reluctant to attend student-led support groups, saying that they perceived such meetings as 'whingeing' and 'moping', and offering just empty conversations along the lines of, as Stephen put it 'oh, what subject are you doing?'.

Mel, Fenella and Lance had each set up support groups themselves. Lance complained of members who came in order to obtain information about arrangements such as the DSA and never returned, and Fenella soon learned that if she did not remind people about meetings, they did not appear. Fenella's Dean had helped her by personally contacting all the Faculty students listed as dyslexic and informing them about the group, as well as organising a room for them to meet in. Initial meetings had involved a great deal of 'gushing about their feelings, all this sort of pent-up stuff', which Fenella felt was particularly important for mature students such as herself who had only recently been identified. Eliza was also aware of this, but from the opposite perspective: having regarded herself as dyslexic for many years and come to terms with it, she wanted to tell the others 'Cope with it, guys!'

While Jeremy was adamant that he regarded dyslexia as 'not a club, not a social thing', and Gary preferred to make friends for other reasons than dyslexia, Harry had been to a group meeting that left him feeling that 'mine's not too bad' and that other students were more 'severely' dyslexic than he.

To sum up the social aspects of learning and teaching: all the informants seemed to have emotional baggage from their experiences at school. Many were sensitive to being picked out as different, and yet in some ways they wanted this to happen, especially regarding academic assessment.

This chapter has considered the cognitive, affective and social aspects of learning and teaching in HE for this group of dyslexic students. The three aspects are united in six ways:

- Personal history – dyslexic students may have been identified relatively early in life or since admission to university. They may have had positive relationships with teachers, or memories of sarcasm and liberal use of the red pen
- Academic study is a struggle
- Self-awareness, both cognitive and affective, is needed
- Determination is needed to deal with both the struggle to study and the intra- and inter-personal issues
- The power of the academy
- The differing models of dyslexia adopted by students (of which more below).

Informants' suggestions to their universities

Lance, Sally, Chuck and Aarti called for greater staff awareness of the nature of dyslexia, Aarti also including support staff such as computer technicians, who tended to expect all students to read the software manuals effortlessly. Charlotte, Enid and Phoebe wanted there to be communication among the lecturers so they were not obliged to speak to each one in turn about being dyslexic.

Lisa, Lance and Chuck had views on teaching styles, suggesting that there should be greater emphasis on the structure of lectures at the start, preferably with diagrams and flow charts. Others such as Stephen praised lecturers who worked in this way. Fenella wanted greater acceptance of the way 'everything takes longer' for dyslexic students. This was endorsed by Rachel and Victoria, who required lectures to be delivered more slowly.

Technology could also be helpful. Aarti suggested material such as study skills information be available on tape, and Chuck wanted to see course material on interactive CD, because he needed frequent repetition and practice.

On academic assessment, only Peggy, Sally and Lance called for assessed presentation or other forms of oral assessment. Lance was convinced that examinations did not 'do him justice,' that in all assessed work, marking should focus on content rather than on what he called English, and that 'non-linear' writing should be accepted. Peggy thought that using a variety of assessment methods would be equitable for all.

Aarti was the only informant to request individual dyslexia support, though there was none available at Burtonforth at the time. Patrick, also at Burtonforth, was alone in proposing that all students should be screened for dyslexia on admission and that this should be followed by 'allowances' for those identified. Lance added to this the idea that every university should publish details regarding the support available to dyslexic students. The national picture in the UK then was very different from now.

Finally, although the informants at Axbridge University had all attended a special module for dyslexic students delivered by a tutor who identified herself as dyslexic, only Victoria mentioned the need for dyslexic students to have role models in the form of mainstream lecturers who were known to be dyslexic themselves.

Summary

This chapter has considered the informants' experience of HE. They regarded themselves as different from other students and as having specific problems, although they interpreted these in different ways. Most had comments to make about their Universities' learning and teaching approaches, and while the majority seemed to regard these as immutable, some had clear ideas about ways in which they could be changed. These diverse responses seemed to depend on the model of dyslexia the student had adopted.

Chapter 8
Discourses of dyslexia

Introduction

The informants in the study presented here were constructing their identity as students – as readers, thinkers and time managers as well as writers – and their representations of reality involved the powerful influence of the concept of dyslexia, which is both culturally recognised and ideologically shaped. This chapter identifies the major themes running through the data: the informants' discourses of dyslexia. Following Ivanic (1998), a definition of the term 'discourse' is proposed which is wider than language. For the purposes of the study reported here, a discourse of dyslexia is defined as the values, beliefs and power relations associated with the concept. This chapter sets out the discourses of dyslexia evident in the data and then examines their sources, their effects on the informants' routes to HE and the role of such discourses in the students' experiences of university.

From models of dyslexia to discourses of dyslexia

Summerfield (1998) looked at self-representation by women in the second world war (see Chapter 3). A parallel can be drawn between women's sense of themselves in the light of the cultural representations or popular discourse available during the war and present-day students' sense of themselves as dyslexic in the light of the models of dyslexia offered to them. The descriptive typology set out in Chapter 5 proposes a pathway from extant definitions of dyslexia to being assessed as dyslexic and thence to identity. Common images of dyslexia are evident in the language used by informants. The models of dyslexia they adopt have mostly been in existence for decades, some for a century. This chapter shows that just as Summerfield's informants were identifying with popular discourses to adopt different values, beliefs and attitudes to power relations in terms of their self-concepts as women, my informants were doing the same in terms of their self-concepts as dyslexic students. The models of dyslexia they had been offered had become discourses.

Historically, the main models of dyslexia have been:

■ the medical model – dyslexia as a biological defect

■ the IQ/attainment discrepancy model – dyslexia defined by scholastic achievement

■ the brain specialisation model – dyslexia as a group of strengths and weaknesses

■ the syndrome model – dyslexia as a pattern of difficulties, usually found together.

Summerfield (1998) called her informants 'heroics' and 'stoics' according to the self-images they adopted. The students who adopted a mainly medical discourse of dyslexia can be called 'patients'. These students used language such as 'symptoms' and 'diagnosis,' and regarded themselves as defective. The students who adopted the IQ/attainment discrepancy discourse could be called 'students,' and they saw dyslexia as purely concerned with academic study. Any who saw dyslexia as a matter of brain specialisation can be called 'hemispherists', as the literature on this tends to focus on the roles of the two cerebral hemispheres, and any who regarded dyslexia as a pattern of difficulties can be called 'syndromists'.

As in the case of the cognitive, affective and social factors, there is inevitably overlap between these groupings. Many informants spoke of their definition of dyslexia, either directly or indirectly. It was however noticeable that those who adopted a medical view tended to be very clear, almost dogmatic, about this. These students' remarks about the definition of dyslexia were dominated by the disability model, although this is partly explained by the fact that almost all the informants were to some extent influenced by that model. Similarly, most spoke about their study strategies, although interview data was marked by the way some exhibited successful metacognition, rather than simply bemoaning their difficulties, and this often involved awareness about their own diverse cognitive functions.

Although naming these four discourses seems like attributing labels, this is not intended. The word 'dyslexic' is already a major label and this study does not wish to label informants further but to categorise it in a way that will aid understanding. The categories have emerged from the interviews. Those who coined the word dyslexic meant well, but the term covers a broad spectrum of people. The informants have placed themselves in these categories on the basis of what they said in the interviews. As Riddick *et al* (1997:164-165) point out:

> ... individual understanding of the meaning of the label can be seen to encompass a varying range of difficulties. Some see it as purely a difficulty with literacy skills, others see it as far more pervasive, affecting the organisation of many aspects of their lives.

As well as interviews with informants, an important source of discourses of dyslexia is the EPs' reports. Table 5.3, showing the models of dyslexia evident in those reports, is expanded below.

Discourses of dyslexia adopted by informants

Some informants used the language of cognitive psychology and EPs: 'short term memory', 'developmental dysgraphia'. Others used phrases with medical resonance: 'I've got something', 'diagnosed', 'symptoms'. These informants, a total of nine, tended to adopt a skill deficit model of academic writing, seeing difficulties with it as problems within themselves, and poor spelling as a personal defect. Those with the poorest self-image showed a lack of both academic and social self-esteem, and expected to fail in admission to institutions and then in examinations. Those who had a better self-image adopted a disability view of dyslexia (as found in current legislation: HMSO, 2001), seeing it as something to declare when applying to university and for which support arrangements should be in place. This discourse of dyslexia also tends to see short-term memory difficulties as something to apologise for. Such students may continue to believe themselves lacking in intelligence. Calling this discourse of dyslexia the 'patient' reflects its medical nature. It is influenced by contemporary sources which in turn derive their discourse from the early literature on dyslexia. The contemporary sources include the NWP report (Singleton, 1999) and the DI (Dyslexia Institute, 2002), which states that 'dyslexia is now firmly established as a congenital and developmental condition'.

Many aspects of academic study have a social dimension as well as a cognitive one. Students have relationships with teachers and lecturers, and deal with institutional policy on assessment. Academic study for those labelled dyslexic generally also involves affective aspects such as frustration and self-esteem, and the feeling that there is a discrepancy between their intelligence and their academic performance. Frustration may also result from their perception that non-dyslexic peers can read textbooks and write essays much faster than they can. Twelve of the informants regarded dyslexia as confined to academic matters, and as having no relevance outside of their university courses in spheres such as personal organisation or creativity. This discourse of dyslexia is called the 'student'. As with 'patient' discourse, it is influenced by contemporary sources which in turn derive their discourse from the early literature on dyslexia. The contemporary sources include the BDA (2002) and the many EPs' reports which base their identification of dyslexia on IQ/attainment discrepancy.

If 'patients' interpret the cognitive aspects of dyslexia in terms of dysfunctions and 'students' interpret them in terms restricted to reading, spelling and other academic activities, a third group interprets cognitive aspects in a manner more akin to the social model of disability. Such people are often aware of the division of the brain into two hemispheres, and may have strong opinions as to their own cognitive style in terms of functions associated with the left and right sides. Drawing on this analysis, they may see dyslexia as a 'difference' rather than a 'disability', and may identify themselves with successful dyslexic people working as architects or designers. In respect of university study, these students often choose courses which offer alternative forms of assessment such as portfolios or assessed presentations, and seek out lecturers who use diagrams and three-dimensional models. This discourse of dyslexia can be called the 'hemispherist', and eight of the informants adopted it. It is influenced by contemporary sources which in turn derive their discourse from recent literature, as its re-framing aspects are a relatively new approach (Gerber *et al,* 1996). Possibly the earliest reference to it appears in the mid 1970s ('It is not a defect, but an individual difference in cognitive style') quoted in Cairns and Moss, 1995. Today, the Arts Dyslexia Trust (2005) espouses it strongly on its website, stressing visual-spatial skills and divergent thinking.

Not one of the cohort espoused the 'syndromist' discourse referred to earlier. However, a fifth discourse of dyslexia emerged from the data. Four of the informants spoke of establishing or joining support groups, making their own enquiries about dyslexia, and questioning their universities' approaches to learning and teaching. These students were strongly influenced by the affective dimension, but also by aspects of the social. This discourse is characterised by anger, but also by determination to graduate well and to succeed in life by persuading people in authority to accommodate them. This group adopts dyslexia as a political struggle and devotes energy to lobbying education authorities and institutions about provision for dyslexic people. In the light of literature on dyslexia as a cultural belief (Barton and Hamilton, 1998) and as a campaign (Scott, 1991), this discourse of dyslexia can be called the 'campaigner'. The website of the Arts Dyslexia Trust (2005) provides a contemporary source. It states that: ' ... the world is changing fast, [and] the talents of a dyslexic cast of mind may become increasingly necessary and important as we move into a more visually based information-sharing mode'. This view is also propounded by West (1997) and by some dyslexic individuals (Davis, 2001; Sagmiller, 2002). Ivanic (1998:12) asserts that the social constructionist view of identity involves 'affiliation to particular beliefs and possibilities which are available ... in [the] social context' and Thomas (1996:323) observes that if we take such a view of the self, 'we will create and re-create ourselves' (see Chapter 2). The 'campaigner' discourse of dyslexia is an example of such a process.

These discourses of dyslexia are not rigid. More than one discourse can co-exist in the same person's interview data, and can even appear contradictory. Most of the students used medical language about dyslexia at some point, for example. Learning support, to take another example, was an issue for almost all of them. When subscribers to all four discourses spoke of their definition of dyslexia, they included academic aspects such as reading and essay writing. What defines the 'student' group is their statements about dyslexia as a purely academic matter. Similarly, only the 'campaigners' spoke about setting up groups and confronting university authorities.

A text search for the word 'fight' found that three of the four informants identified as 'campaigners' had used the word in a campaigning sense, whereas six others who used it did so in relation to incidents such as playground disputes at school. The word 'struggle' was used by five of the nine 'patients', four of the twelve 'students', three of the eight 'hemispherists' but only one of the 'campaigners' – in all cases about academic difficulties.

Text searches also provide evidence that the 'student' discourse of dyslexia is more aware than the others of a discrepancy between intelligence and academic achievement. The words 'intelligent' and 'bright' were used more frequently by 'students' than the others, generally in the context of such a discrepancy – as in 'they knew I was bright but I couldn't sort of work'. Similarly, the word 'disability' was most used by the 'patients'.

Even so, the four discourses are permeable. Of the informants in the study presented here, the largest group (see Table 8.7) was the 'students', closely

Figure 8.1 : Relationship between discourses of dyslexia

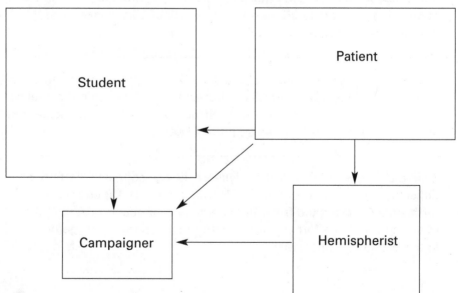

followed by the 'patients'. No group entirely avoided medical language. Figure 8.1 illustrates the relationship between the discourses, the box sizes representing the relative strength of each discourse within the cohort, and the arrows the influences of the discourses upon each other.

A descriptive typology in Fig. 5.1 indicated a pathway from definitions of dyslexia to identity and the socio-emotional effects of identification as dyslexic. Example One below is typical of a 'hemispherist', and Example Two represents a 'patient'. Example Three is a 'campaigner' and Example Four is a 'student'. This chapter explores the discourses implicit within each example.

> Example One: Belief in her own intelligence (supported by her family) despite poor academic performance at school leads the student to focus on her own strengths such as holistic thinking and visualisation. This strengthens her determination to go to university and her success on admission. In this category: Stephen, Rachel.

This discourse focuses on dyslexia as a difference rather than a defect. In the Sixth Form, these people become increasingly aware of their own cognitive style and also of the way they prefer to be taught – for instance with diagrams and concrete examples.

> Example Two: A received definition of dyslexia as a neurological deficit lowers self-esteem. This causes social withdrawal, a tentative approach to university admission and a lack of confidence once admitted. In this category: Ann, Fenella.

Some informants who adopted this discourse had not been identified as dyslexic before university admission. But all had come to see themselves as essentially defective because of their academic failure. Dyslexia had been presented to all of them as an intrinsic defect.

> Example Three: Believing that dyslexia is a recognised pattern of difficulties creates expectations of learning support. When this is not forthcoming, anger and frustration begin at school and take the form of strong-minded effort at university to obtain special arrangements. In this category: Lance, Mel.

This discourse may have some similarity with the others, in that its core belief is 'I am different (or disabled) but I am intelligent'. It goes on to: 'I am entitled to academic success', and often to 'we dyslexics must band together to fight for our rights'.

Example Four: A received definition of dyslexia as principally a discrepancy between intelligence and academic attainment focuses any difficulties on educational activities. The self may be seen as flawed, which affects self-concept, and experience at school and university may be dogged by intense awareness of taking longer than peers to complete study tasks. In this category: Alison, Alice.

The key to this discourse is the person's core belief in her own intelligence, in spite of a perceived defect in terms of academic activities. Self-esteem can be maintained by placing the deficit firmly in the academic domain, and applying the intelligence to study strategies which aim to circumvent it.

Sources of these discourses in the EPs' reports

Since dyslexia ceased to be defined by public authorities as an entirely medical matter, its formal identification has been handed over to EPs. The work of teachers is labelled as merely 'screening'. Psychologists thus have considerable power and influence; it is not surprising that they loom so large in the lives of the cohort. Table 5.3 showed the models of dyslexia evident in the EPs' reports. In Table 8.1 on page 116 it is expanded to show the discourse of dyslexia adopted by each informant.

How dyslexia assessment is experienced evokes 'patient' language and also 'hemispherist' discourse when the EP describes cognitive strengths. This was the case for both Stephen and Robert. When EPs' reports refer only to academic issues and not to personal organisation, general memory difficulties or other non-academic matters, they can also generate a 'student' discourse of dyslexia.

Table 8.1 shows that almost all the EPs include IQ/attainment discrepancy in their models of dyslexia, thus generating the 'student' discourse. The psychologists' reports on these informants reveal statements which may well have encouraged the recipients to adopt such a discourse, focused as they are on the academic aspects of dyslexia:

> On Susan: 'These specific difficulties are creating distinct problems for Susan in coping with the demands of her course in terms of written work'.

> On Charlotte: '.....handicapped by specific learning difficulties or dyslexia, which I consider to be a permanent condition affecting her ability to per-

Table 8.1 : EPs' models and informants' discourses of dyslexia

Informant	EP model	Language used by EP	Informant's discourse
Peggy	Discrepancy+pattern + neurology	Significant specific learning difficulty of a dyslexic type	Patient
Enid	Discrepancy + exclusion	Developmental dyslexia	Patient
Fenella	Discrepancy	Specific learning difficulty or dyslexia	Patient
Jeremy	Discrepancy + exclusion	Developmental dyslexia and dysgraphia	
Victoria	Pattern	Specific learning difficulty (dyslexia)	Patient
Chuck	Neurology+ discrepancy	Dyslexic	Patient
Arnold	Neurology+ discrepancy	Learning difficulties	Patient
Charles	Discrepancy + pattern	Specific learning difficulty or dyslexia	Patient
Phoebe	Discrepancy	Developmental dyslexia	Student
Lisa	Discrepancy + exclusion	Developmental dyslexia	Student
Harry	Discrepancy + exclusion	Developmental dyslexia	Student
Sally	Discrepancy + pattern	Specific learning difficulties	Student
Bruce	Discrepancy + exclusion	Specific difficulty affecting his communication skills	Student
Alice	Discrepancy + pattern	Dyslexic difficulties	Student
Charlotte	Discrepancy + pattern	Handicapped by a specific learning difficulty or dyslexia	Student
Susan	Discrepancy	Specific difficulties	Student
Stephen	Discrepancy + exclusion	Specific learning disability or dyslexia	Hemispherist
Robert	Pattern	Dyslexic disability	Hemispherist
Aarti	Discrepancy + pattern	Dyslexic difficulties	Campaigner
Mel	Discrepancy + pattern	Specific learning difficulties (dyslexia)	Campaigner
Lance	Discrepancy + pattern	Developmental dyslexia	Campaigner
Patrick	Discrepancy + pattern	Specific learning difficulties	Campaigner

form in examinations, where she will be handicapped by her slowness in reading the questions and processing information'.

On Bruce: 'He is almost five years retarded in spelling relative to his age and even more so taking his superior intelligence into account'.

On Lisa: 'The problems that you have with reading are severe and reflect a significant degree of disability. They are likely to lead to problems with written work, particularly under exam conditions'.

On Sally: '....specific learning difficulties ... would be expected to have an effect upon her performance in school and particularly when she is working under timed conditions'.

On Harry: identical language to Lisa. Word processing has obviously been a boon to psychologists.

On Alice: 'What impressed me most was how well adjusted you seem to be to your learning difficulties .... for example, you need to give considerable additional time to extracting meaning from texts'.

On Phoebe: 'Re-assessment of Phoebe's attainments in reading, writing and spelling showed that her learning difficulty is continuing to undermine her performance'.

EP reports apparently played small roles in the students' adoption of 'campaigner' discourse. The reference to 'a very high level of verbal ability' in Mel's EP report may have boosted her self-esteem and it certainly fuelled her anger at her teachers. But the EP said nothing about any methods of learning and teaching which might be most appropriate, other than extra time in examinations. The other three 'campaigners' all had reports from a lecturer at their university who was also a qualified EP. These were among the briefest reports, but all contained statements which seemed to have fed into their sense of injustice. Patrick's referred to 'the residual problems still apparent after much remedial and conscientious corrective work', and how his 'meticulous checking' of his work could not be done under the time pressure of examinations. Patrick spoke at length about how often he had complained bitterly about his grades.

Table 8.2 on page 118 summarises the four discourses of dyslexia and includes quotations from interviews which typify each one.

Crossing the four discourses with interview themes referring to cognitive, affective and social areas produces table 8.3 (page 119).

This table demonstrates the robustness of the four discourses of dyslexia, as interview data from the cognitive, affective and social dimensions can be matched with all four discourses. Interview themes shown in the table were not exclusive to the discourses with which they are associated there; for example, many informants spoke about the definition of dyslexia, and not only the 'campaigners' were determined to go to university. However,

117

Table 8.2 : Four discourses of dyslexia

patient	student	hemispherist	campaigner
Dyslexia as a medical or neuro-logical condition.	Dyslexia as confined to academic matters.	Dyslexia as a difference of learning style.	Dyslexia as a cultural belief, e.g. the need for support groups and mutual solidarity.
Dyslexia as akin to a disease: something which can be 'diagnosed' and has 'symptoms'.	Reading, writing and learning difficulties.	A pattern of strengths and weaknesses as valid as anyone else's.	Dyslexia as a political struggle: the need to lobby education authorities and institutions.
A biological fault or defect.	An issue connected purely with studying, and no other areas of life.	Often a stated preference for right-hemisphere brain functions.	
Something you 'suffer from'.	Often refers to a discrepancy between intelligence and academic performance.	Dyslexia as something shared with successful visualisers such as architects.	
	Often proud of successful paid work which does not involve reading and writing.		
Typical statements	**Typical statements**	**Typical statements**	**Typical statements**
'At least I know I've got something'.	'I've only ever thought of it in academic terms, not in social terms'.	'It's something you're born with'.	'The more people go [to university] that are dyslexic, the more people are going to recognise it and they're not going to think you're stupid'.
'I've got dyslexia'.	'That is my social life – my dyslexia affects only my academic life'.	'You're just different – you interpret information differently'.	'I set up a Dyslexic Society'.
'It's like mis-wiring of parts of the brain'.	'I don't see it as being a problem in the area of work I'm going into'.	'It's nothing to be ashamed of'.	'I learnt from the support of having a group of dyslexic people around me'.
'I've got a smaller clip-board than other people'.	'If I got to the field of work and had to write things fairly rapidly, I think it would all disintegrate, that's what worries me'.	'Lots of designers are dyslexic'.	'I'm hoping to persuade the University to stump up some money'.
'Being dyslexic is just a fault. It's a fault in your personality'.	'I knew it was a reason for having bad English skills, yet still remaining quite bright at the same time'.	'Seeing the model was really good, because it was 3D'.	'We're trying to force the issue, trying to get concessions done'.
		'I'm a right-brained person'.	

Table 8.3 : Cognitive, affective and social aspects of the four discourses

	patient	student	hemispherist	campaigner
Cognitive	Definition of dyslexia Own main difficulties Intelligence issue	Reading, spelling, writing, maths Best subjects Worst subjects Intelligence Oral ability Exams	Cognitive style Creativity 3D thought Memory strategies Own strengths	Teaching and assessment style Early identification
Affective	Academic self-esteem General self-esteem Self as disabled or defective	Stress Strain of IQ/attainment discrepancy	Self-acceptance	Determination to go to university Vocabulary such as 'fight'
Social	Relations with teachers and parents EPs' reports	Laziness issue Outlook on the future	Identifies with famous dyslexics Open about dyslexia	Suggestions for universities Support groups Admissions issues

'patients' used more medical language and showed markedly poorer self-esteem than the rest, and 'hemispherists' were the only informants who talked about patterns of thought associated with the right cerebral hemisphere. 'Campaigners' were the only ones to mention political activism in respect of dyslexia, and it was mainly 'students' who emphasised their awareness of an ability/performance discrepancy.

Linking concepts of identity with discourses of dyslexia

Chapter 2 explored the ways identity is conceived. The four discourses of dyslexia distinguished among the informants may be mapped onto the ways identity is conceived:

Table 8.4: Concepts of identity and discourses of dyslexia

Way of conceiving of identity	Potential dyslexia-related consequence of this concept	Matching discourse of dyslexia
Biological	Brain deficits	Patient
Cognitive experimentalist	Learned helplessness; the search for a reason for difficulties	Student
Experiential	A phenomenological view of the self; seeing own strengths, and trying to fit in with the academy	Hemispherist
Social constructionist	Affiliation to strong beliefs	Campaigner
Psychodynamic	Need for another person to explain who we are; need to be mirrored	Range of discourses of EPs

A focus on the physical brain which characterises the biological view of the self (Toates, 1996) (see Chapter 2) has links with the language used in some dyslexia literature (Hornsby, 1984; Galaburda, 1989) and by EPs such as Peggy's, who talked about her having 'a smaller clip-board' than other students. A biological view of consciousness holds that conscious experience is a property of the physical brain, and that emotions are 'caused' by chemical substances in the brain. From the earliest days of dyslexia research, many have believed that dyslexia is a neurological deficit (Miles and Miles, 1999). The 'hemispherist' discourse is also based upon what amounts to a neurological and thus 'biological' concept. But it has another dimension too.

Central to the cognitive experimentalist view of the self is the search for attribution (Lalljee, 1996). Students who are dyslexic will ask: 'why am I doing badly at school/college?' The process of intrapersonal analysis may result in 'learned helplessness' beliefs, such as attributing academic success to luck or the easiness of the questions (Butkowsky and Willows, 1980). Those who adopt this view of the self may seize upon the IQ/

attainment discrepancy often adduced by EPs as an explanation for students' problems at school. The cognitive experimentalist model of the self (Lalljee, 1996) focuses on the interpretation of events. Someone with a 'student' discourse of dyslexia does not necessarily interpret academic difficulties as implying a fundamental defect in the self, as a 'patient' generally does.

From an experiential standpoint (Stevens, 1996b), the self is understood from a position of subjective experience. Humanistic psychology (Rogers, 1951) accepts the person as s/he is, rather than applying pathologising labels. The 'hemispherist' discourse of dyslexia is self-accepting in its belief that the individual has both strengths and weaknesses. It is also accepting of others, acknowledging that many people are 'left-brained' and that this works well for them. The use of metaphor to conceptualise human experience is widespread and the polar analysis 'left-brained/right-brained' or 'linear/global thinker' is akin to a personal construct (Kelly, 1955).

The concept of discourses of dyslexia is itself a social constructionist approach; discourse analysis proposes that language use actively constructs the world and the self (Wetherell and Maybin, 1996). As suggested in Chapter 2, adoption of the label dyslexic represents affiliation to a belief, or identification with a socially and culturally advocated concept. However, the 'campaigner' discourse of dyslexia, as expressed by Lance, goes further in claiming that academic procedures, particularly academic writing, are not absolutes but social constructions. From this standpoint the disability of dyslexia could be said to be constructed by the academy.

Table 8.4 above might imply that most EPs adopt a psychodynamic perspective on the self but this is not so. However, if we agree with Thomas (1996) that from a psychodynamic standpoint understanding the self requires the help of an 'expert,' the link with the profession of educational psychology becomes plain. Turner (1997:117) is clear that the 'technicalities' of dyslexia assessment 'remain essentially beyond the reach of those who do not have the specialised background'.

The four-level model of dyslexia self-awareness proposed by McLoughlin et al, (1994) and reproduced in Chapter 3 is a fundamentally psychodynamic concept that assumes there can be conscious and unconscious awareness. (McLoughlin is an EP.)

The development of a discourse: the 'campaigner'
Examining the 'campaigners' in more detail will illustrate how evidence for a discourse of dyslexia in informants is built up. The four 'campaigners' are Mel, Lance, Patrick and Aarti. (For brief 'life maps' of informants, see Appendix II. There is a case study of Mel in Appendix III, and a vignette of Lance on page 131.)

General evidence for the discourse

As a teenager, Mel had read about dyslexia and asked to be assessed for it. She said her assessment report raised the awareness of the staff at her school, and she thought this 'did quite a lot to make it easy for other people'. When interviewed, she was in the process of setting up what she called a 'peer support group' for dyslexic students.

Lance described himself as having 'always been politicised'. At Burtonforth University, he soon began to work for the Student Union. Disappointed by the level of dyslexia support available – 'the support I've had, I've had to fight for, largely' – Lance formed what he called a 'Dyslexic Society'. The following quotation exemplifies the 'campaigner' discourse. Lance had just referred to a well-known book on dyslexia, and had been asked what he thought of it:

> I think he's got his point, but, um.... I think he's not dyslexic. I think, with all due respect to people who are not dyslexic, that it's basically: you haven't lived through it. I'm taking it from a political persuasion – I think dyslexia is going to be like gay rights, I think it's going to be like feminism. I think feminism was progressed not by men but by women, and gay rights have been pushed for by homosexuals. I think dyslexia is very close to – is very very similar to homosexuality – we've been discriminated against, we've been persecuted, you can't judge us from our skin.

Patrick had also been involved with a dyslexia support group at his university. He had been motivated to join it because he had been marked down for 'diabolical English'.

Aarti felt that all University staff should be aware of the needs of dyslexic students: 'I'm talking about the IT suite, the library, people at the offices'. She resented having to remind library staff that she was entitled to extended loan times.

Self as a writer

Mel remembered pestering a teacher for spelling information at Junior School because she wanted to 'use English fully'. This feeling persisted at university, where she still refused to paraphrase in order to avoid a word she could not spell: 'It's my English, I want to use it!' In spite of this, she felt that school examinations represented a 'fair fight', because she could receive marks for including key facts.

Aarti on the other hand was angry about what she saw as the unfairness of exams. Her campaigner mentality shows more in her anger and struggle at home than in relationships with institutions. She decided that she had failed her A Levels because of poor essay structuring:

> I got past papers back to like the 1970s, and I did a draft for every possible essay in any different way it could be structured, and learnt them. ... So

when anyone says I'm not bright and I'm not intelligent, the fact that I did that proves that I am.

Lance also re-sat an examination: he had tried five times to improve on his D grade in English Language O Level. Arriving in HE, he had hoped that his English 'would be less of a problem – they'd be wanting my ideas, not grammar, spelling, the likes'. Disappointed to find that this was not the case, he was motivated to form the Dyslexic Society. He believed the academic staff did not know about dyslexia: 'I think I get penalised for not writing linear stuff'.

Patrick could remember the marks he had received for every piece of university work he talked about. He had disputed several marks with his tutors, and on one occasion felt he had scored a point by deliberately using what he called 'jargon' to achieve a higher mark: 'That'll teach the bugger'. However, Patrick was most angered by the aftermath of his formal assessment as dyslexic. He was convinced that he would be offered a viva after his examinations, and disputed his marks, arguing with the course tutor and the moderator: 'I slammed the door and left'. Patrick had not been identified as dyslexic until late in his course, and believed that all students should be screened for dyslexia on admission to Higher Education.

General self-esteem

The 'campaigner' attitude to self-esteem shows itself in a variety of ways. We have seen the efforts the students made to prove their academic worth. Mel had wanted to obtain evidence of her intelligence when she was in her teens, and successfully passed the test for joining Mensa, a UK society for people rated as having high IQs. She promptly announced this to her convent Sixth Form teachers, eager to '....basically look Sister straight in the eye'.

Aarti denied her school any credit for her passing GCSEs, believing it had all been down to her own hard work: 'Round the clock, round the clock I slogged'. Lance also considered the education system unfair, believing that fellow students with less grasp of the subject were gaining higher marks than he just because their essay structure and examination technique were better. He also felt that his campaigning activities might influence tutors: 'I know also – since I've kicked up a fuss, I'm not a favourite person'. Patrick also thought that examinations were unfair, believing that Maths O Level involved too much reading and comprehension and too little mathematics. In terms of his self-esteem, he showed his 'campaigner' approach when he reported negative comments from teachers about his prospects: 'That's a spur, when I think of the words they said about me'.

Notably, these students generally show signs of having combative personalities from an early age. These traits cannot be separated from dyslexia experiences; the literature notes the emotional strain of being dyslexic at school (Osmond, 1993; Edwards, 1994; Miles and Varma, 1995; Riddick, 1996). But without further interviews and study of their families, it cannot be claimed that their 'campaigner' discourse and behaviour was purely due to their dyslexia experience.

Sources of these discourses in informants' lives

The roles of significant others, the media and university publications in presenting definitions of dyslexia were discussed in Chapter 5. As well as EPs, there are other significant people in informants' lives who may influence their discourse of dyslexia, such as:

- **Family members**: Parents may identify themselves as dyslexic, or have other children who are already so identified. Some parents make their own inquiries about the subject, and dyslexic siblings may pass on their views (examples: informants Sally, Phoebe, Eliza, Will, Enid).

- **Teachers**: Learning support teachers feature prominently as providers of information, but tutors on Access courses also play a role (examples: informants Charles, Fenella, Lance, Jemima, Gary, Robert).

- **Other students**, particularly those who are dyslexic themselves (examples: Stephen, Patrick, Harry) and information about dyslexia come upon by accident in the printed and broadcast media (examples: Chuck, Mel, Alice, Ron, Geraldine).

The points in their lives at which the informants came upon the concept of dyslexia varied from their primary schooldays to their forties, but the sources of their images of the nature of dyslexia are likely be as above.

Routes to Higher Education

The routes to Higher Education of the four categories are summarised in Table 8.5 opposite.

In many countries, including the US, UK and Australia, dyslexia is legally recognised as a disability. Awareness of this brings about an overlap between 'patients' and 'campaigners'. The key element of the 'campaigner' discourse is political, not a belief that dyslexic students are no different from their peers. 'Patients' such as Jeremy, who was keen to make sure he was not penalised, and Chuck, who was angry about the invisibility of his 'disability,' thus have something in common with 'campaigners'.

'Students' like Jemima may ask about support arrangements at their admission interview because they have absorbed an IQ/attainment discrepancy discourse of dyslexia and are confident about their intellectual ability. Those who have received several years of learning support, such as Gary, may also have benefited from a boost to their self-esteem as a result.

Table 8.5 : Approaches to University admission

Patient	Student	Hemispherist	Campaigner
Negative self-image:	'Students' tend to have been identified as dyslexic in childhood, and therefore have an expectation of learning support.	Often encouraged by EPs who explain about the hemispheres of the brain.	May have lobbied LEA for support; parents may have pressed for Statement.
Poor self-esteem, academic and social.			
Expectation of rejection by courses and institutions.		Drawn to subjects which have 3D aspects, such as architecture.	May contact University in advance to ask about support.
Expectation of failure in examinations.	May also have had several years of specialist tuition.		
Dyslexia as something to hide.		Tend to be confident about dyslexia at admission interview.	Likely to be well-informed about legislation.
More positive self-image:	Usually had extra time for A Levels.		
Dyslexia as a disability to declare; demand for support arrangements.	May ask about support arrangements at interview.		

'Hemispherists,' such as Eliza and Stephen, who are aware of their cognitive strengths may also be confident at an admission interview. Two of the 'hemispherists' (Robert and Ron) had been engaged in three-dimensional thought in their previous work, but no one was currently studying a subject such as architecture which overtly requires this. The claim about this in Table 8.5 arises from professional experience in HE since 1995. Three of the 'hemispherists' had been identified as dyslexic before admission and one, Rachel, took her EP's report to her interview and asked about the match between her profile and the demands of the course.

Of the 'campaigners', only Mel indicated that she had adopted such a discourse before admission to HE, and only Lance's parents had pressed for him to be assessed and supported at school. As the 'campaigner' discourse is a response to HE experience, admission is not at issue.

Experience of HE once admitted

Table 8.6 on page 126 summarises the experience of university academic life of the students adopting each discourse and their approaches to dealing with it.

It was noticeable that informants who continued to doubt their intellectual ability, such as Enid and Victoria, were all 'patients'. They had all sought, or expressed a preference for, individual learning support tutorials, and were clear that dyslexia was a personal defect. Some 'patients' such as Victoria lacked confidence in their ability to benefit from ICT strategies.

Table 8.6 : University life for the four discourse groups

Patient	Student	Hemispherist	Campaigner
Overall University experience			
Adopts skill deficit model of academic writing: sees problems as within self e.g. poor spelling as a personal defect.	Often reluctant to receive one-to-one support, because of desire to make a fresh start without it.	Enjoys courses and lectures which are set out as diagrams.	Liable to be combative in seeking re-assessment of low grades.
Short-term memory difficulties as something to apologise for.	May see ICT equipment as a route to overcoming all difficulties.	Keen to explore own learning style.	Works to raise lecturers' awareness of dyslexia.
May continue to believe self to be lacking in intelligence.	Will often seek oral assessment instead of essays where possible.	Responds well to alternative forms of assessment such as portfolios.	Founds or attends a support group.
			Makes full use of arrangements such as identity cards as dyslexic.
Coping strategies			
Preference for human support as opposed to technology.	Talking over topics with others e.g. for revision.	Enjoys concept mapping, both on paper and with a computer.	May reject the term 'coping strategies'.
Possible interest in diet and/or drug regimes (but not the present informants).	Full use of word processing and screen readers.	Uses this for note-taking as well as essay planning.	Approach is to claim a 'level playing field' as of right.
Awareness of arrangements such as extra time in examinations as disability facilities.	Often likes amanuensis support in examinations.	Also uses colour and shape.	Gains strength from support of campaigning group members.
		Likes to make information pictorial in her head.	
		Needs to apply information to something concrete.	

'Students' by contrast, such as Alison and Will, were generally very keen on ICT and seemed to be using it successfully. This may be partly due to their greater self-confidence intellectually, although no informant made such a connection overtly. Informants such as Gary, who had received many years of individual support, were determined to manage their courses on their own. Because of their frequent focus on IQ/attainment discrepancy, these informants often preferred oral assessment. They were also aware of the benefits to understanding and memory of discussing course material with fellow students.

If the 'students' hoped for oral assessment in order to avoid writing, the 'hemispherists' sought an alternative form such as the portfolio or project, so they could use maps and diagrams, and avoid linear essays. Whereas 'patients' and 'students' tended to blame difficulties in lectures such as running out of time to copy down information on their own shortcomings, 'hemispherists' often spoke positively about lecturers whose style they liked, such as those who used diagrams and concrete demonstration.

The 'campaigners,' however, reacted promptly to a lecturer they thought was not 'dyslexia-friendly'. But we can see an overlap between these discourses in Victoria, a mature 'patient' who spoke confidently about having reminded her 'Field Chair' several times about 'dyslexia-friendly' delivery. Lance set up a 'Dyslexia Society' and Patrick was active in the support group at his university. Mel has set one up as part of her learning support role in the job she is doing at the time of writing (see Appendix III). Although others such as Jeremy and Stephen deliberately avoided such groups, 'campaigners' may relish the solidarity with peers they offer.

So the informants who had differing discourses of dyslexia coped socially in different ways. 'Patients' worried about memory and either laughed it off or asked for sympathy; 'students' insisted that their social lives were not affected; 'hemispherists' tended to find their faith in this discourse shaken by social problems and sometimes fell back on 'patient' discourse; 'campaigners' did not discuss social difficulties in their interviews except for Mel, who said that her boyfriend needed to be patient with her conversational style.

Vignettes follow of the informants who represent the four discourses.

Vignette 8.1 Fenella, a 'patient'

Fenella was 44 when interviewed, and studying social anthropology. Brought up in France (her mother was French), she had moved to England at the age of 6, and encountered English for the first time. Fenella described her childhood self as small and pretty, with long blonde hair. As she had been frequently ill and unsuccessful at school, her parents apparently decided that her future would be a domestic one, so had not troubled themselves about her academic progress. She remembered teachers calling her lazy and expressing frustration with her inability to comprehend her reading and produce accurate written work.

The only O Level subject Fenella had enjoyed and succeeded in was Art. She enrolled for the A Level, but dropped out and became a window-dresser, feeling 'out of her depth' at school but also in other aspects of her life. After trying to live in Paris, she returned to England and worked in a telephone exchange, where she found the initial training very difficult.

Fenella married at 20 and had two children. After her divorce, she began doing voluntary learning support work at a local primary school. Because most of her friends had degrees, she began seeking a qualification: 'Here I am, feeling this terrible emptiness – there's something wrong with me and something terribly missing in my life'. After passing English GCSE in her mid thirties via an adult literacy class – she described getting to the end of the exam as a major turning-point – she enrolled for an Access course. Her new partner at the time had 'degrees and letters'.

Once on the Access course, she spoke to the tutor about her slow reading, thinking that there was 'something not right' about herself. On being screened for dyslexia by a learning support tutor, Fenella burst into tears because she misunderstood the expression 'specific learning difficulties'. The Access course had links with the local university, and Fenella went to her interview rather anxiously. Once admitted, she found about the DSA from the learning support unit. Her LEA would not accept the Access tutor's screening report, so she paid for an assessment by a local EP, by which time she was 42. This report included her reading and spelling ages, which she found 'just shocking'.

Fenella set up a support group for dyslexic students in her faculty and persuaded the Dean to arrange accommodation for them. After unsatisfactory learning support sessions with a counsellor who wanted to focus on her emotional life rather than the purely academic guidance she was seeking, Fenella graduated with a 2:1.

In 2001, Fenella was working as a dental practice receptionist, which she described as 'not the career I would have chosen if I'd gone to university earlier in life'. She felt her self-esteem was still poor, and did not refer to her dyslexia at work, as it is 'a defect from an employment point of view'.

Vignette 8.2 Gary, a 'student'

Gary was 20 and studying computer science. At his primary school, he had a teacher who recognised dyslexia so he was assessed at the age of seven. This led to many years of withdrawal from class for learning support. Socially confident, Gary had enjoyed his schooldays up to GCSE, and said he had always had a thirst for learning.

By the time he entered the Sixth Form however, Gary was 'sick of work-sheets and little cards'. Nevertheless, he was determined to go to university. He began to feel resentful when he saw other students, for whom it was 'so easy to do well', making little effort while he was 'trying to learn as hard as I can, and it's so difficult'. Gary felt that he had ability in science subjects, although this contrasted with his inaccurate spelling and grammar. He continued to be popular socially, but had to force himself to go in to school. With extra time, he obtained good enough A Level grades for admission to his preferred university.

Some people with a 'student' image of dyslexia make detailed inquiries about learning support arrangements when choosing their university. Gary had no intention of spending any more time with support tutors, but he did indicate dyslexia on the UCAS form. Once at university, Gary declined to go to a support group for dyslexic students: 'I don't really see the need for going along to some society about something which is a mere inconvenience to my life'. He came out as gay, but did not see a parallel with coming out as dyslexic, because 'that is my social life, and my dyslexia affects only my academic life'. He added: 'I find dyslexia a bit of an irritation, but I just get on with my life'.

As a student of computer science, Gary knew how to make good use of ICT to help him. The only support he needed from the University was extra time in exams. He was aware of his own learning style, commenting that learning support tutors had often suggested using a tape recorder whereas he preferred to work visually.

Looking ahead to job applications, Gary was preparing to be open about dyslexia, believing that this would not be seen as a problem in the computer industry, and that his 'degree should speak for itself, when I've finished, really'.

Vignette 8.3 Robert, a 'hemispherist'

Robert was 31 and studying Law. He remembered being slow to learn to read at primary school. He was labelled as lazy and lacking in intelligence, and compensated for this by achieving social and sporting success, although his father tried hard to help him with multiplication tables. This pattern continued at high school, where the contrast between his oral ability and examination results drew down the label 'under-achieving'. Eventually, in his fourth year, the French and Maths teachers told him not to attend their classes any more, on the assumption that his frequent requests to have material repeated amounted to insolence. Regularly called 'exceptionally lazy' in reports, Robert began to feel that he could not prove himself otherwise. He failed almost all the CSEs he took, and enrolled for a City and Guilds photography course.

The portfolio he assembled on that course enabled him to obtain a job producing architectural graphics. He enjoyed that work, but had to wear sunglasses to avoid headaches caused by the combination of fluorescent lights and the whiteness of his drawing board. His employer sent him on a BTEC Building Studies course, but he could not manage its Maths and Physics components. But he succeeded in various jobs with architectural practices partly because, as he said of a building plan: 'I can see it; I can walk through it and I can picture colours, where the lights are, everything '. Another aspect of his employment success was a talent he discovered for painting architectural perspectives, water-colour impressions of prospective buildings.

After a period of self-employment producing such perspectives, Robert became frustrated with the pressures of pursuing clients for payment. Remembering how on the BTEC course he had been interested in the legal aspects of building work. When he was 29, Robert went to the local FE college to inquire about routes to studying Law. He was advised to take an Access course and checked that this would be acceptable for admission to a Law degree.

The Access course tutor suggested that he seek a formal assessment for dyslexia. Robert's parents paid for him to see an EP at a famous university dyslexia unit, where not only did he feel patronised but found the report so full of jargon that it was hard to understand. However, once admitted to his Law degree course, he obtained the DSA and found the computer he bought extremely useful, particularly for voice activated word processing and concept mapping. He became increasingly clear about his preference for focusing on global concepts and for expressing his ideas orally.

Robert described having struggles with telephone numbers, writing cheques and other daily activities, but succeeding with 'conceptual ideas' as opposed to 'factual information'. His metacognitive ability helped him to achieve a 2:2. After a Bar Vocational Course, he is now working as a barrister.

Vignette 8.4 Lance, a 'campaigner'

Lance was 24 and studying politics. His mother had persuaded his school to have him assessed for dyslexia when he was 10. At comprehensive school, his response to academic difficulties had been characterised by anger. He spoke sarcastically about his teachers, particularly about their ignorance of dyslexia. He had also resented not being asked to read aloud in class.

Looking back on his schooldays, Lance recalled being bullied because he was different. He began to find strength in being able to put an argument orally, and took to political debate. He passed four O Levels. He was determined to improve on his grade D in English but although he re-sat it four times he never did.

Lance's parents separated when he was 12, which, he said, 'added to the emotional traumas'. But they paid for a private tutor, who showed him 'spider graphs' and 'bullet plans' for essay writing, and 'how to think holistically about problems'.

Lance was determined to get a degree for career reasons. His A Level results were very mixed: U and N, and a B for General Studies. But he was optimistic about higher education: 'My English would be less of a problem, they'd be wanting my ideas, not grammar, spelling and the likes. I've learnt the reality is, they still want all that'. Lance remarked on the contrast between his ability to talk about a subject and his attainment when writing about it. He resented spending 'twice as much time on essays' as other students, but not receiving good grades. His anger about this only made him more determined. Once elected a Student Union officer, his first campaign focused on the lack of anyone who worked specifically for dyslexic students, although the university had a Disabilities Officer and a Welfare Officer. 'I also found that the knowledge the staff have of dyslexia is none', said Lance. He set up a Dyslexic Society because he wanted 'the support of having a group of dyslexic people around me'. At the time of his interview, he was trying to persuade the university to fund a leader for the group.

'I think dyslexia is very close to homosexuality; we've been discriminated against, we've been persecuted, you can't judge us from our skin ...' Lance's ambition was to be employed as a researcher into the needs of dyslexic students and the best response the higher education community could make to them. Meanwhile, his motto was: 'Dyslexics want the things when they want them, and they want them now'.

Table 8.7 on pages 132/133 shows all the informants, as grouped by discourse of dyslexia.

Table 8.7 : All informants, grouped by their discourse of dyslexia

informant	age	discourse	expert views from	Family dyslexia	Parents' input	Approach to univ.
Arnold	20	patient	various Ts;EP;counsellors	not stated	pressure	not stated
Charles	44	patient	LST; rdg on 'word blindness'	not stated	M typed work	not stated
Jeremy	19	patient	GF; psychologist	not stated	M non-specif	ambitious for career
Chuck	34	patient	EPs; own reading	3 siblings	Took him to EPs	ignorant of demands
Ann	21	patient	EP	not stated	M req'd asst	reluctant
Enid	20	patient	Parents; University psychologist	F; GM	M (= T)	'natural thing to do'
Fenella	44	patient	SNT at College; LS unit	not stated	M read to her	kepg up w frnds;nervous
Victoria	50	patient	D.I. teacher; EP	not stated	not stated	keen but anxious
Peggy	38	patient	EP	not stated	not stated	very anxious
Mel	32	campaigner	Reader's Digest; EP	nieces	M did reading	confident
Aarti	22	campaigner	EP	not stated	not stated	determined
Lance	24	campaigner	LST	not stated	M; M+F=LSTs	determined
Patrick	25	campaigner	EP; other students	not stated	private T 6 yrs	not confident, so HND
Lisa	50	student	S. Hampshire, mags, D's EP	B, D	not stated	'learning bug'
Jemima	20	student	SNT; EP	M (probably)	ETH, spec sch	confident
Phoebe	21	student	3 EPs; M	M	Sent to bdg sch	confident
Alice	37	student	Newspapers; LST (University)	F, B	ETH, emot.	v. keen
Susan	45	student	LSU staff; EP	M = illiterate; 2 Ds	F = reading	very tentative, but keen
Sally	19	student	EP, M	B	M 'all the way'	always going to go

Table 8.7 : All informants, grouped by their discourse of dyslexia (continued)

informant	age	discourse	expert views from	Family dyslexia	Parents' input	Approach to univ.
Harry	27	student	Other student; EP	not stated	non-specif	career interest
Gary	20	student	class T; LSTs	not stated	M = emot. support	always determined
Alison	20	student	EP; Ts; LST	S; M; uncle	ETH, gen enc	'have a go'
Charlotte	21	student	LSU staff; LST	not stated	ETH	keen;ignorant of dyslxia.
Bruce	24	student	EP	B? S? Cousin?	Not stated	det. to leave home
Will	18	student	M's reading; other dyslxic boy	not stated	M req'd asst; ETH	not stated
Eliza	22	hemispherist	EPs, SNT, parents	no	'all along'	didn't expect to go
Geraldine	53	hemispherist	own research + self-analysis	not stated	not stated	not stated
Rachel	20	hemispherist	EP	F	M non-specif	'out' at interview
Stephen	22	hemispherist	D.I.T; M+F read books	not stated	M+F a lot	engineering like F
Adrian	25	hemispherist	EP	not stated	not stated	not stated
Betty	49	no clear discourse	Ds' EP (then went herself)	2 Ds	not stated	wanting to improve self
Robert	31	hemispherist	Access T; EP	not stated	financially	determined
Ron	41	hemispherist	Access T; EP; own research	B	F = help w h'wk	desire to be a nurse

Table 8.7 shows that 69 per cent of informants were formally assessed and identified as dyslexic in the 1990s. This implies two things. Firstly, none of the four discourses can be associated with a particular era, and secondly, since most of those in each discourse group were assessed in the 1990s, the medical view of dyslexia is as strong now as it was 100 years ago.

Only three of the twelve informants who adopted a 'student' discourse of dyslexia were older than 27; most older informants were 'patients' or 'hemispherists'. Erikson (1968) proposes that the developmental tasks of those in their twenties include deciding on an identity focus and repudiating alternatives. Since a key element of the 'student' discourse is that it sees dyslexia as limited to academic issues, the decision to adopt such a view might well indicate the desire to forbid it any influence on other aspects of life.

All but one of the women who were 'students' were aware of other dyslexic people in their families. Indeed, most of the informants who reported having dyslexic relatives were women. This may be because males tend to be less aware than females of family matters. The majority (63 per cent) of those who referred to dyslexic relatives adopted a 'student' discourse, which suggests that family conversations about dyslexia would focus most often on school or university based issues rather than on wider social issues.

Table 8.7 reveals other aspects of the 'student' group. They are markedly the most confident, keen and determined in their attitudes to HE. This may be because the IQ/achievement discrepancy involved in this discourse has indicated to them that they are intelligent. Furthermore, most of the 'student' group were assessed in their teens and earlier and all those who were assessed at primary school became 'students' or 'hemispherists'. This suggests that as time passes and successful strategies increase, medical views give way to more positive models.

All but one of the 'campaigners' were in their twenties, a likely age for political intensity. The four 'campaigners' attended Burtonforth and Axbridge Universities, both in the north, and came from East London, Staffordshire and Merseyside, so no pattern is visible in their regional origins.

There was however one observable North-South divide: no one from Spenceton was a 'hemispherist', and there was only one at Belleville. The EPs seen by the Spenceton and Belleville informants all used IQ/attainment discrepancy models of dyslexia, in some cases with the addition of a neurological approach, and all their clients became 'patients' or 'students'. The latter discourse would have been reinforced by the ideology of the Belleville learning support team at the time. Sixty per cent of Spenceton informants were 'patients', and this may similarly have been reinforced by the learning support tutors, who were mostly psychodynamic counsellors.

Finally, 15 informants (45 per cent) had believed they were unintelligent when they were at school. This group included all but one (85 per cent) of the 'hemispherists', who may have seized upon this discourse to explain their difficulties positively. The rest of those who had thought they were unintelligent during their schooldays were clustered in the 'patient' group (five) and the 'student' group (four). None had become 'campaigners'.

Case studies and comparisons between the discourses

All the informants have been placed in one or other of the discourse sub-groups, except for Betty, whose interview did not reveal any discourse of dyslexia. One representative from each group is described in a case study in Appendix III.

All the informants regarded dyslexia as a given, although they had different views of it. They had accepted the label 'dyslexic', but had also internalised the notion that they were 'different', and that this difference meant that they had problems within themselves. Only Mel spoke of the academy changing its style of learning and teaching so that the concept of dyslexia might be redundant. Even the other 'campaigners' saw the campaign in terms of disability rights.

The four discourses of dyslexia can, however, be paired. 'Patients' and 'students' see their difference as constituting a deficit or defect, whereas 'hemispherists' and 'campaigners' feel some sense of group solidarity, and generally have a more positive view of their own cognitive style. The 'dyslexic' label offers learners an explanation for their experiences (Miles, 1993), but it is hard for these informants to make sense of their overall experience because of the cognitive views they hold.

Apart from the 'campaigners', the students did not make an overtly social analysis of the dyslexia concept or link it to their university's style of learning and teaching. But when 'hemispherists' spoke about appreciating a visual or diagrammatic manner of presentation by lecturers, they were commenting on a social aspect of life for a dyslexic student.

Similarly, from the viewpoint of literacy as a social practice (Barton, 1991; Street and Street, 1991; Hamilton, Barton et al, 1994), all the informants accepted an autonomous model of academic literacy, saying:

- ■ I still find structuring essays very very difficult.

- ■ Some essays I was doing three or four times before I could actually hand it in.

- ■ I can alter my ideas to fit the way they want reports.

- I get my girlfriend to read it through, who changes my English around.

- The very first essay I wrote, the tutor sat and went through it with me, and all I saw was this red pen all over the page.

- That's probably why I feel thick ... I can't do the essays.

Lance (a 'campaigner') was critical, as he had hoped 'they'd be wanting my ideas, not grammar, spelling, the likes – all that. And I've learnt the reality is, they still want that'.

As Gerber *et al* (1992) explain, re-framing needs to start with self-recognition and self-acceptance (see Chapter 1). The person's sense of identity is central. There is a parallel between the identity issues which arise for students labelled dyslexic and those for mature, 'non-traditional' HE students (Pollak, 2001), in that both groups may question their right to be in HE or their ability to cope. Conceptions of dyslexia and of HE are both 'culturally recognised, ideologically shaped representations of reality' (Ivanic, 1998:17). Consequently, the discourses of dyslexia students adopt are likely strongly to affect their ability to re-frame the experience.

The informants who adopt the 'patient' discourse are farthest from being able to do this, believing themselves to be deeply flawed. 'Students' are often a little further on in terms of re-framing, frequently affirming a belief in their own intelligence and saying that dyslexia was simply a problem with academic study (see statements in Table 8.2 above). The downside of such a view is the expectation as expressed by Harry, that in the world of work, dyslexia would seem 'a bigger disability'. 'Hemispherists' are usually considerably further along with re-framing, as Tables 8.3, 8.5 and 8.6 indicate. However, it was a 'campaigner' who had the most positive view of all:

> I don't think I really think of [dyslexia] as impinging on [the rest of my life].
> I tend to take the positive view that it gives me a different perception. (Mel)

It might be expected that students with such varied views of themselves and dyslexia would cope quite differently with HE. The study could then have concluded with recommendations for learning support tailored to the needs of each student, according to the discourse of dyslexia they adopted. Table 8.6 showed that the students did prefer particular strategies but, except for the 'hemispherists', these were attitudes rather than precise methods. The data overall revealed that they all selected their approaches and techniques from the same range, as listed in Figure 8.1 opposite.

These approaches are listed by other authors on dyslexia in HE (Cowen, 1988; Gilroy, 1991; Gilroy and Miles, 1996; Riddick, Farmer *et al* 1997; Cottrell, 1999; Hunter-Carsch and Herrington, 2001). All but the last four strategies are positive independent steps which involve metacognitive self-awareness. 'Avoiding reading' – an attitude not confined to students

---

Figure 8.1 The informants' 'coping strategies'

Tape recording lectures (though no one said this was effective)

Using a PC

Concept mapping

Using colour for essay editing and examination revision

Talking to self and peers

Avoiding reading as much as possible

Selecting modules assessed orally or by coursework

Trying to relate detail to an overall picture

Trying to relate detail to a real-life situation

Asking for copies of OHTs (often on coloured paper)

Making multiple drafts of essays, often by hand

Seeing a learning support tutor

Asking peers to read textbooks aloud and/or proof-read essays

Writing 'I am dyslexic' on examination papers and assignments.

---

labelled dyslexic – may be a positive strategy if it means that information is gathered through audio/video tape or CD ROM (with which screen-reading software may be used). Seeking human support can also be seen as positive, but usually involves acceptance of a degree of failure. If students write 'I am dyslexic' on written work it may appear practical but may suggest that the students regard themselves as defective.

The 'hemispherists' and 'campaigners' have a rather more positive self-concept than 'patients' and 'students' and it is they who show signs of discourse-specific strategies. 'Hemispherists' are, by definition, better at metacognition than 'patients' or 'students', and tend to use their understanding of their cognitive style to devise appropriate study approaches. For example, Robert used his holistic thinking ability to focus on the concepts behind the laws presented in lectures, rather than reading about them; Eliza used colourful concept maps; Rachel sought out three-dimensional anatomy models.

Being a 'campaigner' is itself a strategy for survival in HE. Lance believed that he could better do himself justice with oral assessment, or at least ask that his essays be marked for content, not language. His aim for the student Dyslexia Society was as much to lobby for such provision as to provide mutual support.

That the study strategies are not discourse-specific is because students pursued the same approaches for different reasons. So students who adopt a 'patient' discourse might write 'I am dyslexic' on their work so their disability is recognised, whereas 'campaigners' might do so to raise awareness of the number of dyslexic students at the university, or to claim their 'right' not to be penalised for language errors. This contrast was exemplified by Jeremy and Lance. Or 'patients' might use voice-activated word processing because they believe they need it to compensate for poor typing skills, whereas 'hemispherists' would embrace such technology because they realised that speaking aloud enabled them to maintain a focus on the global concept rather than spelling.

The vignettes above offer a brief overview of students who represent each of the four discourses of dyslexia. The case studies in Appendix III provide fuller pictures of their learning life histories.

Kurnoff's categories of dyslexic HE students

Kurnoff (2000) interviewed 142 dyslexic people in the US, ranging from primary school to university, about their feelings about dyslexia and how they coped with it. The tone of her book is illustrated by this brief passage:

> 'Your child has dyslexia.' Four simple words. Four words loaded with emotion.

Most of Kurnoff's subjects are reported as talking of 'having dyslexia' or being 'learning disabled', but the author is positive about what dyslexic people can achieve, though she takes an essentialist stand-point.

Interestingly, 47 of Kurnoff's respondents were college students, and she divides these into four categories, which she presents as 'themes that best categorise their responses':

- ■ 'conventionalists', who follow the advice of learning support units very closely rather than creating personal strategies, and claim every special assessment arrangement possible

- ■ 'low profilers', who do not disclose that they are dyslexic, associate with learning support units or claim special arrangements

- ■ 'independents', who rely on their own coping strategies and make special arrangements on an informal basis

- ■ 'pragmatists', who 'try to strike a balance between special accommodations and personalised coping strategies'. (*op. cit.* 232)

These categories are divided not by their discourses of dyslexia but by their responses to it. There are however some parallels with the discourses of dyslexia reported here. Kurnoff's 'conventionalists' have in common with the 'student' discourse that some are aware of IQ/attainment discrepancy. But all Kurnoff's categories are 'students' in that they seem to regard dyslexia as entirely an academic matter. Some of her 'pragmatists' sound like 'hemispherists', seeing themselves as looking at the world 'differently' and processing information 'unconventionally' (*ibid,* 242). Some of her 'independents' resemble 'campaigners,' making statements such as 'choose your battles wisely' (*ibid,* 285) and 'advocate for yourself' (*ibid,* 289).

Kurnoff's book is in the West Coast self-help book tradition, with its exhortations to 'dream the impossible dream' and 'feel the fear and do it anyway'.

Summary

This chapter has drawn on the pathway typology proposed in Chapter 5 to show how many of the models of dyslexia that go back 100 years (see Chapter 1) are found in the discourses of dyslexia which influence HE students today. The students may have been exposed to these discourses in childhood, offered by various significant others such as family members and teachers, and by the media and university publications. Most influential of all is the EP, who has the power to identify a person as officially dyslexic. This status means that when the EP's report contrasts the subject with the norm, the student is likely to feel authoritatively – and immutably – labelled as abnormal.

Definitions of dyslexia lead to discourses of it, which in turn affect these people's sense of self and identity. Internalising such discourses shapes their affective and social responses to the label. For those identified before admission to HE, the various discourses are likely to influence their routes to university. When they are identified after admission, their university experiences are modified by the discourse of dyslexia they adopt.

The final chapter sums up the results of the study, discusses the implications and offers some recommendations.

Chapter 9

Conclusion and recommendations

Introduction

This book set out to increase understanding of dyslexia and to produce insights which help Universities to work with dyslexic students. It also contributes to the debates about academic literacy and special educational needs.

This chapter summarises the findings of the research study. It outlines the new account of dyslexia implied by these findings, and links it with models of learning support and academic literacy. It ends with recommendations for the HE sector and for further research.

The definition and experience of dyslexia

- The students saw themselves as different from their peers

- Most saw this difference as a personal problem, as difficulties which lay within themselves

- Their social and academic self-esteem was often poor

- 27 per cent saw dyslexia as a biologically based deficit (the 'patients')

- 36 per cent saw it as an IQ/attainment discrepancy confined mostly to their academic lives (the 'students')

- 24 per cent regarded dyslexia as a matter of cognitive style, with strengths as well as weaknesses (the 'hemispherists')

- 12 per cent of informants viewed themselves as members of a group which needed to engage in a struggle with the academic establishment (the 'campaigners')

- Most of those who had been identified as dyslexic at school adopted the 'student' discourse and had approached University admission confidently

- Those who had not been identified as dyslexic at school had nevertheless seen themselves as 'different' whilst at school. Despite their different discourses of dyslexia, their university experience was quite similar because of the 'difference' they felt. 'Patients' and 'students' tended to see this difference as focused on a defect in themselves, whereas 'hemispherists' and 'campaigners' were more positive about their own strengths and more critical of their universities' learning and teaching approaches.

Students' sense of identity and self-concept (This includes their routes to higher education and academic progress.)

- 27 per cent of the informants had been labelled as lazy at school, and 54 per cent had been called unintelligent

- Dyslexia had often been explained to informants in terms of weakness in their brain functions. Their comments about their own perceived deficiencies sometimes demonstrated a discrepancy between their 'ideal self', 'actual self' and 'ought self' (Singer, 1993). This is exemplified by Alice (see Appendix III), who attributed her mental breakdown to dyslexia

- In spite of the dominant role of EPs in the process of formal identification of dyslexia, not all the informants had been assessed by one

- The experience of formal assessment was similar for most students in two ways: they had been advised that assessment was necessary because they had a problem, and they feared a verdict of 'not dyslexic, just unintelligent'

- EPs' conclusions tended to be either: 'you have a defect and special arrangements will have to be made for you', or: 'you are different from the majority but there are ways in which you can succeed'

- What the informants gleaned from the press and on television about dyslexia supported the deficiency discourse

- Those who approached admission to HE with most confidence overall were the 'students'

- 58 per cent of 'students' stated that members of their families were dyslexic

- 'Patients' tended to lack confidence about admission to HE because their academic self-concept was focused on their deficiencies

- The 'hemispherists' approached HE with more confidence than the 'patients'. They were generally older, so had had more time to enjoy successful work experiences through their self-knowledge

- The 'campaigners' were the youngest group. All but one developed this discourse of dyslexia after admission to HE

- Most of the informants expressed a view of academic life as a struggle. Their 'difference' made them feel they had to work harder than their peers

- Their inconsistent statements related to their self-concepts suggested that it was hard to maintain a positive approach to academic life. Most (apart from the 'students') seemed to approach academic life unconfidently, believing that the cards were stacked against them

- Most informants at times adopted an experiential perspective (Stevens, 1996b). In HE, they were having to construct themselves as students from day to day, and often conceived of this process in absolute terms – 'she is good at essay structure, I am not' (Kelly, 1955)

- From the perspective of life-span psychology (Erikson, 1968), a typical 18 year-old entrant to HE is dealing with the developmental tasks of late adolescence, separating from their family and establishing their own identity. So the experience of being formally identified as dyslexic and receiving a report about their cognitive and academic weaknesses is likely to give them a sense of being flawed. The resultant self-concept depresses their academic self-esteem, and this can even lead to poor social self-esteem too

- One of the formal rituals of adolescence identified by Erikson (1968) is graduation from high school. Mature students who enter HE via Access courses are likely to have left compulsory education with a sense of failure. This may carry over to taking a degree

- The identities of the younger informants were strongly influenced by their families. Many spoke of parents who encouraged them to persevere, paid for private tutors and put pressure on schools to help them. This affected their identity in one of two ways: either 'I have a problem for which I need special help' or 'I am different, but I can do it'.

- The informants were searching for meaningfulness and autonomy. Mature students constitute a new population which may 'present a challenge to the dominant values, practices and discourses of the institution of higher education' (Ivanic, 1998:9) and they may 'feel alienated and devalued within the institution of higher education. Their identities are threatened'. She points out that entry into higher education raises identity issues because it involves a new social context. She describes the writing of an academic essay by someone for whom this is difficult as foregrounding issues of difference and self-presentation. It helps define the boundaries between one identity and another. Ivanic's observation can apply to dyslexic students of any age

■ A few of the informants said that they would have opted for different courses had they not been dyslexic. Others believed it lowered their grades. Students identified as dyslexic have been told that they have a deficient ability to use language, particularly print. HE is centred around written and printed language so language and power are related (Fairclough, 1989). Power in the academy is wielded by those who have facility in conventional academic writing (Street and Street, 1991; Lea and Street, 2000). Nationally, many courses which emphasise non-written assessment, such as Fine Art, are attended by relatively high percentages of dyslexic students (Morgan and Klein, 2000). Many informants spoke of writing repeated drafts of essays and of being highly critical of their own writing ability.

The value of the discourse concept for the students

The label 'dyslexic' offers students an explanation for their 'problems', but their cognitive views made it hard for 'patients' and 'students' to make sense of their overall experience. For example, those such as Victoria who were frustrated by their inability to do themselves justice – as they saw it – in academic assessments attributed this to a defect in their own mental processes. Their frustration and anger prevailed because they accepted both this 'absolute' and the seemingly immutable nature of the academy and its procedures.

Students who overcome their 'difficulties' often do so by re-framing them (Gerber *et al,* 1996). The hemispherists and campaigners showed evidence of this. For example, Eliza said:

> You do things differently, and you do them in different ways, and you have your own ways of doing them, but you'll get there in the end.

A campaigner is likely to reframe by adopting a different view of dyslexia rather than a different view of the self. Mel said:

> I'm not even convinced that dyslexia is going to stay as dyslexia ... somebody will decide that we need all the cognitive styles or whatever, that they're useful and a balanced society is going to get somewhere.

Informants from all four discourse groups were claiming the Disabled Students' Allowance (DSA). This, the principal funding mechanism for learning support for UK home students – though not internationals – by definition involves accepting the label 'disabled'. Both 'patients' and 'students' regard their difference as constituting a defect. 'Patients' such as Chuck have no difficulty with the name of the DSA, as they frequently use the term 'disability' to describe dyslexia. 'Students' (like Susan) may be uncomfortable with the name but regard it as a means to a legitimate end: the levelling of the academic playing field. 'Means to an end' is also espoused by students who adopted the other two discourses. In the case of 'hemi-spherists' (such as Robert), ICT equipment offers an attractive means of working in a manner which suits their cognitive style, such as on-screen concept mapping (also used by Ron) and voice recognition word-proces-sing (used enthusiastically by Robert). 'Campaigners' expressed some-what conflicting views about the DSA. Those such as Aarti who accepted a disability model found it easy to claim it, whereas Lance, who refused to regard himself as defective, took the line: 'I'll claim whatever I can off them, to compensate for the problems they have caused me'.

The value of the discourse concept for the academy

Historically, literature on dyslexia has used a variety of models (see Chapter 1). Since the study presented here was begun, the important report of the NWP (Singleton, 1999) has appeared. It shows tensions be-tween the disability model (dyslexia as a 'condition') and acknowledge-ment of the potential strengths of dyslexic people – perhaps because there were fourteen people on the NWP.

The variety of students in HE today is greater than ever before (Jary and Parker,1998; Preece *et al,* 1998). The number of students identified as dyslexic increases steadily (Singleton and Aisbitt, 2001). Retention of, and attainment by, such students can be improved if universities understand that they regard dyslexia in a range of ways. Even more important is how the academy itself regards dyslexia. Herrington and Hunter-Carsch (2001: 121) observe that:

> We consider that it is not helpful to view dyslexia through a narrow lens of 'in-person' weakness. We prefer a broader framework.

Elements of this proposed framework include taking 'full account of the disabling effects of some ideas embedded in the culture about literacy and intelligence/educability' (*ibid,* 121).

In the 'culture' of HE, how are mainstream learning and teaching concepts linked with the dyslexia-related issues raised by the present study? The concept of a holist-serialist dualism (Pask, 1976) is not new. Manuals for University teachers (Cowan, 1998; Fry *et al,* 1999) frequently enjoin lecturers to take account of the wide range of learning styles of any group of students. Entwistle (1988) refers to the potential contrast between a teacher's habitual mode of information processing and those of students and the study presented here underlines this. But it also demonstrates that dyslexia may be multi-dimensional, but addressing it need not be any more demanding than established good practice.

De Montfort University in Leicester, UK has a 'Vision' of good practice which includes the intention to be a University which promotes inclusion and meets the aspirations of a diverse student body. No doubt the authors of this statement were referring to students from diverse ethnic and socio-economic backgrounds, as well as those admitted via 'non-traditional' academic routes. By focusing on the identity and sense of self of students identified as dyslexic, the study presented here has shown that they are as 'diverse' – and as intensely aware of the fact – as members of any group. And the current system for assessing these students as dyslexic emphasises their sense of difference and, possibly, of deficiency. Yet at the time this research was carried out, many of the students – although not all – succeeded in maintaining some positive academic self-esteem although an essentialist model of dyslexia prevailed in the teaching and educational psychology professions and in university learning support departments. It is likely that exploring their own educational life histories for this study helped their self-esteem.

Although the study focused on students from only four universities in England, it found marked inconsistencies between them in the way dyslexia was identified, learning support provided and academic assessment made. Evidence (Sanderson and Pillai, 2001, Hunter-Carsch and Herrington, 2001) suggests progress has been slow in the UK until the Association of Dyslexia Specialists in Higher Education was founded (Morgan, 2003). My research not only sought to increase understanding of dyslexia, but also aimed to produce insights to help universities to work with students identified as dyslexic. It offers a new way of looking at dyslexia and dyslexic students that moves away from the ubiquitous cognitive emphasis. Much of the literature and the reports by EPs assumes that dyslexia is a unified concept and that readers will agree with the model being used. This study has shown that there is a range of models of dyslexia and that HE students may adopt one of several different models for themselves. The study reveals that in the course of being identified as dyslexic and being exposed to a range of influences, the students developed discourses of dyslexia which included ideas and beliefs regarding its effects and the nature of academic life.

Implications for academic writing

Academic writing was not a specific focus of the research questions, but it clearly has powerful links with identity (Ivanic and Simpson, 1992; Ivanic, 1998). Almost all the students reported struggling with academic writing. It is useful to explore Lea and Street's (2000) three models of student writing in the context of dyslexia (see Chapter 1), because there are links between them and discourses of dyslexia and also with approaches to learning support. Students' sense of self is centrally involved in the writing process, as the literature and research data set out above make clear. This is illustrated in Figure 9.1.

Figure 9.1: Relationship between models of student writing, dyslexia and learning support

Student writing	Dyslexia	Learning support
Study Skills	Medical model	Disability model
Academic socialisation	The different brain	Learning style
Academic literacies	Social model	Analysis of linguistic practices and their social meanings

Lea and Street (2000) describe the 'study skills' model of student writing as viewing problems with student learning as a kind of disorder which requires the student to have treatment. Publications which adopt this model tend to present studying as a matter of technical skill. For instance Williams states that 'studying is a skill, not a body of knowledge' (Williams, 1989: (x)). This assumes that language is primarily a matter of grammar, spelling and punctuation – which are 'autonomous, nonsocial qualities' (Street and Street, 1991:152) – and essay-writing is likewise a set of discrete skills. Students who lack these qualities need to be 'cured'.

The medical model of dyslexia (or the 'patient' discourse) similarly locates any problem as lying within the student. From the earliest references to it (Kussmaul 1878; Berlin 1887; Morgan 1896) to the more recent (Critchley, 1970; Hornsby, 1984; Snowling, 2000), dyslexia has consistently been represented as a biological deficit. The NWP report describes it both as a 'condition' and as a 'syndrome' (Singleton, 1999).

The model of learning support in higher education which equates to the medical discourse of dyslexia is the disability model. Students who need support are seen as having a disability which makes higher education inaccessible to them (Oliver, 1988; Singleton ed., 1999). The funding of learning support in UK higher education is currently arranged, for those who qualify for it, by means of the Disabled Students' Allowance or DSA (DfES, 2004). Many Universities place learning support staff within a Disability Unit or similarly named department; one of the London universities until recently had a 'Dyslexia Clinic'. Information published for dyslexic students which adopts this model often speaks of 'students with dyslexia' as if it were a disease, and informs them of the need for a 'diagnostic assessment'. In the medical model, learning support is an exercise which takes place in isolation, with little or no liaison with a student's course tutors or subject context, even if students would prefer this (Keim *et al,* 1998).

Universities which have re-defined 'study skills' have begun to focus more on student adjustment to learning or interpretation of the task of learning (Lea and Street, 2000). Using this model, Peelo (1994:74) describes a tutor marking an essay as 'a representative of an academic readership', and asserts that 'the finished product must look like what passes for communication within that discipline'. This is what Lea and Street (2000: 34) call 'inculcat[ing] students into a new 'culture,' that of the academy'. The academic socialisation model focuses on the role of a student's learning strategies or style in the process of acculturation into academic discourse. It thus parallels the discourse of dyslexia as a 'difference', or a constitutional developmental pattern of learning which inhibits easy acquisition of fluency in symbolic material. Informants who were 'hemispherists' were identifying with this discourse of dyslexia, and spoke of their learning strategies in terms of 'study skills'.

Traditional university study operates almost entirely through the medium of the written and printed word. On-line courses and materials remain text-dominated. In 1996, the then Higher Education Quality Council in the UK produced a 'paper to stimulate discussion' on the 'attributes of graduate-ness'. This lists:

> ... ancillary qualities that would be expected of a graduate, but which had not previously been regarded as the responsibility of higher education to teach. These ancillary qualities would be likely to include such things as the ability to write in grammatically acceptable and correctly spelt English ... (HEQC, 1996:para. 14)

It states:

> There seem to be irresistible arguments that no-one should graduate who lacks such ancillary skills. (*ibid,* para 15)

This seems to conflict with the Dearing Report's recommendation that there should be increased access for students with disabilities, among which it included dyslexia, combined with the availability of learning support for such students to graduate (Dearing, 1997). The report of the NWP observes that

> A tension still exists between the concerns of quality and of access, and ... this tension is heightened when it comes to participation of students who are likely to have poor literacy skills. (Singleton, 1999:18)

The academic socialisation model of academic literacy treats writing as a 'transparent medium of representation' (Lea and Street, 2000:35), much as the HEQC document does. It thus fails to consider literacies as social practices. Lea and Street assert that under the academic literacies model, student writing and learning are seen neither as matters of skill nor of socialisation. Instead they are viewed as taking place within institutions whose academic practices are founded both on power and on discernible discourses of literacy and knowledge-making. When literacy is seen as a social practice, or rather a variety of social practices, the kind of literacy which is demanded in educational institutions becomes just one variety, albeit one which is accorded supremacy (Street and Street, 1991). In universities which adopt what Street (1984) calls an autonomous model of academic literacy – which seemed to apply to all four of the universities in the present study – students are expected to master a range of linguistic and communicative practices for different settings and purposes. The academic literacies model thus operates at the levels of both epistemology and identity (Brodkey, 1987).

The word 'discipline' certainly applies, if 'correctness' in grammar, spelling, referencing and so on are controlling and potentially discriminatory:

> Insistence on correctness has a regulatory function in that it limits both the possibilities and the desire of many ordinary people to use writing to express their views. (Clark and Ivanic, 1997:215)

The concept of the expression of views also involves identity:

> A student's personal identity – who am I? – may be challenged by the forms of writing required in different disciplines ...., and students may feel threatened and resistant – 'this isn't me'. (Lea and Street, 2000:35)

Lea and Street's proposition, although it applies to all students, whether dyslexic or not, is particularly relevant to those who have been labelled dyslexic and have adopted a 'hemispherist' discourse of dyslexia with its awareness of preferring non-linear thought. Mature students (and indeed younger ones) may be in the process of changing their identity as they try to become members of an academic community, and this may conflict with other aspects of their identity (Ivanic, 1998). Ivanic suggests that most mature students 'are outsiders to the literacies they have to control in order to be successful in higher education' (*ibid*: 68). This self-perception seems to apply to most students identified as dyslexic, and was expressed by most of the students in the present study.

So what discourse of dyslexia matches the academic literacies model of student writing and university study? The head of the Computer Centre for People with Disabilities at the University of Westminster has observed:

> In terms of the social model of disability, I have always regarded the brain functions associated with dyslexia as part of a perfectly normal variation in the population, but the English language as a social factor 'disabling' dyslexics in much the same way as stairs inhibit those in wheelchairs. (Laycock, 2001)

In the study presented here, it was the 'traditional' students who had been admitted via A Levels, who were the most confident espousers of dyslexia as part of the normal spectrum of human brain development – although their confidence was tentative.

Learning support approaches based on an academic literacies stand-point centre on supporting students' self-awareness and sense of identity. All students need some metacognition – thinking about how they think, learning about how they learn – in order to succeed, but those who differ from the mainstream need particular understanding of their own cognitive style (Krupska and Klein, 1995; Given and Reid, 1999). This differs from the 'academic socialisation' model, which involves concepts such as 'deep' and 'surface' learning, in the analysis of the university as a site of discourse and power. Ramsden and Entwistle (1981) found that university departments perceived as 'allowing freedom in learning' had students with 'an orientation towards personal meaning in their studies'. Wankowski (Raaheim et al, 1991:109) advocates a 'feeling of mutuality in the social transaction of learning' and 'the feeling of approval and recognition from another human being' (ibid, 117).

Learning support tutors who are aware of the academic literacies debate can encourage students to maintain a sense of self in their writing even while obeying the conventions of their subject (Creme and Lea, 1997). This can be supported by developing their critical language awareness (Clark, 1992). The model of learning support adopted by dyslexia tutors at many UK universities involves listening to students' ideas and working towards a way of putting them into an essay which feels right for them, acknowledging the validity of their natural sense of these ideas as a two or three dimensional pattern, and the way the hegemony of standard academic practice shoe-horns them into a linear order. Staff working with such students require counselling skills. They need to let students know that they have been heard and understood. Counselling skills can also facilitate students' private challenges to the disability model of dyslexia, even though under the present UK system they have to accept it publicly in order to obtain funding for learning support via the DSA (DfES, 2004).

Students' experiences of learning support can be very variable (Sanderson and Pillai, 2001). It carries a great deal of emotional content. As Peelo (1994) points out, the first task is often to confront the issue that special arrangements such as extra time in examinations may feel like 'cheating'. Examining learning styles and time management on a one-to-one basis inevitably raises issues about domestic life and this needs sensitive treatment (Raaheim et al, 1991). A mature student may have children to look after as well as a job to cope with, and as the type of brain currently labelled 'dyslexic' runs in families, a child might have also been identified as dyslexic.

Morgan and Klein (2000) suggest that students' self-esteem can be markedly improved by helping them to see how much their previous teachers contributed to their educational failures. The interview process for my study facilitated this for some informants and can form a valuable part of early individual learning support work.

Under a social model, learning support tutors aim to help students to accept themselves as they are, what they can do and what it is not worth trying to do. This may be particularly successful when the support tutor identifies herself as dyslexic, as we saw at both Belleville and Axbridge Universities – the students could identify with the tutors.

Ways in which lecturers can help dyslexic students are summarised from a disability perspective in the report of the NWP (Singleton, 1999). The present book suggests that since most informants clearly took a cognitive view of dyslexia, and from what they said or implied suggested that they would find reframing their self-concepts and view of dyslexia difficult, it is useful to adopt a social constructionist view of dyslexia. This allows for a match between dyslexia and models of academic writing and learning support.

Recommendations
The informants in the present study recommended the following to the academy:

1. All students should be screened for dyslexia on admission
2. The student library card should carry electronic identification as dyslexic
3. All lecturers should be informed of which students are dyslexic
4. All staff, including support staff, should have professional development about dyslexia
5. Information such as computer suite instructions should be provided in audio format
6. Study skills advice should be on floppy disk or CD
7. Lectures should be well structured and their structure made very clear, ideally with diagrams
8. Technology such as CD ROMs should be used to provide plenty of practice questions and glossaries of terms
9. Provide full lecture hand-outs, with space for annotation
10. Make greater use of assessed presentation and discussion.

The first four of these points focus on dyslexic students as different; they invite the university to seek out and emphasise this difference. The others, however, are inclusive of a range of learning styles, so amount to no more than good practice. They do have cost implications, but this may arguably be offset by improved retention and better student results (Cottrell, 2001).

The following recommendations emerge directly from the study:

A) Discourses of dyslexia should be questioned and reappraised

The data do not suggest discourse-specific pedagogical responses. Most of the 2 per cent of UK HE students formally identified as dyslexic in 2000 (Singleton and Aisbitt, 2001) probably see themselves as academically flawed, and in many cases medically so. Consequently some HEIs (for example Kingston and Sunderland Universities) are adding dyslexia policy statements to the disability statements required by the DDA. This is considered the appropriate place for such statements since dyslexia is legally defined as a disability. The study presented here suggests that universities should move away from this model towards a genuinely inclusive policy for students with 'different' approaches to learning.

Awareness of discourses of dyslexia would potentially empower students, helping them to question the ways they are described in assessment reports. Such awareness would also assist their successful metacognition, which is an essential skill for all students (Hunter-Carsch, 2001).

Awareness of discourses of dyslexia would strengthen the work of learning support tutors. Paying close attention to students' own accounts is a key prerequisite for learning support. A learning support tutor has the job of integrating the cognitive, affective and social dimensions and facilitating the students' analysis of their own discourse of dyslexia. Re-framing of the dyslexia concept by students involves them in noting how it is socially constructed. Cognitive approaches are insufficient, and academic guidance should also address affective and social aspects of dyslexia. After all, 'the process of learning is emotional' (Peelo, 2000a:5).

Herrington and Hunter-Carsch (2001:121) admirably sum up the case for a revision of the discourses of dyslexia currently operating in the HE sector:

> In summary, we consider that it is not helpful to view dyslexia through a narrow lens of 'in-person' weakness. We prefer a broader framework which:
>
> ■ draws on research from many disciplines and traditions
>
> ■ reflects an integrated holistic view of the learners and deeper models of the mind
>
> ■ takes full account of the disabling effects of some ideas embedded in the culture about literacy and intelligence/educability
>
> ■ adopts a more open-minded and exploratory approach to unravelling the broader parameters of thinking and learning styles of this kind.

B) Physiological aspects such as vision must be taken into account

A third of informants to the study reported the effects of Meares-Irlen syndrome. Induction and/or key skills screening exercises should include awareness-raising material about visual disturbances, because many students assume that everyone sees things in the same way, so do not mention it. There should be staff in HEIs who can screen students for coloured overlays, and the overlays should be provided. Information about local specialist optometrists should be available. Staff development about visual perception difficulties should use the computer package which simulates their effects and demonstrates ways of making course materials accessible (Beacham and Szumko, 2005).

C) Funding for learning support

Although the study did not set out to investigate funding, it has shown that the current UK learning support system in HE upholds an essentialist view of dyslexia. The remedial response of learning support departments experiencing funding pressures is typical of the students' experience, confirming their sense of 'otherness'. And claiming DSA funding – which universities insist that dyslexic students must do – involves not only accepting the label 'dyslexic' but also linking it with disability. As many disabled people would point out, this is not automatically negative, but for a dyslexic student it may seem like yet another label.

The DfES should reconsider the funding approach to learning support. Currently, dyslexic students are identified as disabled and those who do not qualify for the label because they cannot demonstrate an IQ/attainment discrepancy (Herrington, 2001b) are penalised. Providing funding on an individual basis is not an efficient way of distributing resources. Loans of assistive technology would be greatly preferable.

D) Discourses of academic literacy should be questioned and re-appraised

Many of the informants struggled to be writers. If literacy practices are situated, 'academic literacy' becomes one variety among many. Most HEIs probably adopt an autonomous model of student literacy (Street and Street, 1991) and assume that concepts such as 'argument', 'structure' and 'clarity' in writing are not only givens, but essential. Once this assumption is questioned, and the variety of literacy practices which diverse students bring with them into HE is accepted and welcomed, the concept of 'deficits' and 'difficulties' can be challenged.

The portfolio is often proposed as a flexible alternative to the essay (Winter, 2000). But an overall synthesis of the content must be specified, or it may lack academic rigour. Winter – who is not writing about dyslexia – suggests what he calls the 'patchwork text' (ibid), a coursework format in which various types of writing are built up during a course, including analytical commentary. This approach takes account of the author's voice and perspective, thus meeting the need for students to feel a sense of ownership of their writing (Benson *et al,* 1994). Learning and teaching approaches which are helpful to dyslexic students are often put forward as potentially beneficial to all students (Singleton, 1999; Morgan and Klein, 2000; Cottrell, 2001). In the case of 'patchwork text', an approach beneficial to all brings with it advantages for dyslexic students.

Academic literacy is much more than writing. Although many adults identified as dyslexic are efficient readers, most find reading a laborious way of obtaining information, as has been shown here. Yet traditional HEIs still base their requirements on the assumption that their students – of Humanities or Social Sciences at least – must be able to assimilate information by reading and express their ideas by essay-writing, often under time pressure in examinations. We saw that informants often avoided reading, and knew they read less efficiently than their peers. At the very least, key texts and sections of the work should be identified (Cottrell, 2001). Information can also be given in audio format, on video-tape and on CD, which allows students to use screen-reading software.

Just as literacy can be understood in society as a set of social practices, with different literacies correlated with different areas of life (Barton and Hamilton, 1998), so academic literacy too can be construed in more than one way. Regarding academic literacy as a social practice helps to integrate the cognitive, affective and social aspects of academic study.

'It should at least be possible to make explicit the language, literacy and cognitive paradigms in use in each discipline' (Herrington and Hunter-Carsch, 2001:125). Aspects of courses should be made explicit, such as the basic knowledge and performance or skill levels required, how the course will be assessed and what alternative forms of assessment are feasible (Cottrell, 2001).

The key assessment criteria for a course should also be made explicit. Is writing style an essential learning outcome? Lecturers can find accommodating learning difference challenging because it calls upon them to re-visit learning outcomes and assessment. A 'remedial' model of dyslexia is easier for lecturers to respond to as the 'problem' rests with the defective student and not the course. As the Code of Practice of the Special Educational Needs and Disability Act (SENDA) (HMSO, 2001) makes clear, there are limits to what can be accommodated; for example, a journalism course is entitled to decline a place to an applicant who cannot write grammatically correct English at speed. Accommodating learning difference does not mean that any student is entitled to take any course. But making admissions and marking criteria wholly explicit is beneficial to all (Cottrell, 2001).

E) Models of learning support should be questioned and re-appraised

Figure 9.1 set out a way of looking at the relationship between models of student writing, dyslexia and learning support. The first three of the proposals made by informants (see page 151) are based on an essentialist model of dyslexia. Item 4 might read 'staff development work focused on the range of student cognitive styles'. Other recommendations by the students such as numbers 7 and 9 are simply good professional practice and if lecturers learn more about the variety of learning styles they would satisfy the last one. Dyslexia remains a legally recognised disability, and the terms of the DDA Part Four – and similar legislation in the US and Australia – mean that HEIs are obliged to follow recommendations 6 and 8.

Most UK HEIs, including the four in the sample, treat dyslexia as a special need requiring special provision. This disempowers both the student – as having a 'defect' – and the lecturer as not being a 'specialist' in this disability. It also means that dyslexia support is seen as the province of a separate department (Student Services, the Learning Development Centre) so not the responsibility of the lecturers.

Shifting this responsibility requires re-visiting the learning outcomes of courses. To ensure genuine inclusivity, this process should include determining whether rapid reading and linear essay-writing are essential for each course. In other words, Faculties would do well to review their models of academic literacy in the interests of student retention.

Meanwhile, many students, whether or not they are identified as dyslexic, will need academic guidance. The universities attended by this cohort took an essentialist view of dyslexia, locating it as a problem for and within the student. An analytical and holistic approach to academic guidance (Herrington, 2001b) is needed, so that students identified as dyslexic are actively engaged in 'dialogue about their styles of thinking, learning and writing' (*ibid,* 173) and can discuss which discourse of dyslexia they adopt.

Herrington and Hunter-Carsch (2001:127) propose that the development of policies and practices relating to teaching and learning support involves:

- recognising learning diversity

- allocating continuing professional development time to allow teachers to advance their ... knowledge and skills in relation to ... learning difference ...

Development of a positive learning environment, although challenging for the institution, can improve student self-awareness and attainment (Pillai, 2003).

The social model of physical disability (Oliver, 1988) does not propose that a disabled person is physically indistinguishable from an able-bodied person. A social constructionist model of dyslexia does not deny that there is a recognisable type of brain, which is currently labelled 'dyslexic'. But the spirit of the DDA Part Four (HMSO, 2001) is clear: educational institutions shall not, by their practices, disable students who cannot access their courses by conventional means. This legislation differentiates between a 'special educational need' and a 'disability'. But it also endorses the general practice of universities to construe dyslexia as a disability and locate provision for dyslexic students within a disability unit.

F) Reframing the concept of dyslexia

We have advocated that academic literacy be regarded as a social practice, to help integrate the cognitive, affective and social aspects of academic study. This might mean that certain students need not be identified as dyslexic. Rice and Brooks (2004:87) observe:

> The most urgent topic for revision is the concept of dyslexia itself, not least because it has in effect been commandeered in order to invest un-successful learners with responsibility for the shortcomings of their teachers.

Rice and Brooks suggest that the label dyslexic is potentially stigmatising:

> After the first awareness campaign ... dyslexics appeared to become the butt of a spate of cruel jokes. We should not be surprised if the word 'dyslexic' eventually goes the way of 'spastic' and for much the same reason. Science and the world of literacy teaching and learning might be no poorer if it did.

However, Rice and Brooks centre their definition of dyslexia on 'the alpha-betic principle'. Herrington (2001a) posits that a focus on literacy in relation to dyslexia distracts from awareness of its non-literacy parameters such as alternative patterns of perceiving, thinking and learning (Davis, 1995; West, 1997). The 'hemispherists' show that re-framing the dyslexia concept in that way could benefit students identified as dyslexic. If universities do so it may well enrich the curriculum for all students (Herrington and Hunter-Carsch, 2001).

Herrington observes that 'much of the suffering endured by dyslexic adults stems from 'how [their] difficulties are, *or have been*, viewed by others' (Herrington, 2001b:170, my emphasis). This resonates with the present study's findings regarding discourses of dyslexia, and with the discussion of social construction. The social element of the triangle of cognitive, affective and social factors includes social construction and thus identity. The disability aspect of dyslexia is perhaps socially constructed (Barnes and Mercer, 1996).

In the psychosocial perspective on dyslexia (Hunter-Carsch, 2001) the relationship between cognitive and affective factors within it are recog-nised (Vail, 2001). Students in the present study reported feeling misunderstood by significant people in their lives, from family and peers to teachers and tutors, and understood how the emotions evoked affected their ability to learn.

Cottrell (2001) points out that issues associated with dyslexic students, such as copying quickly from OHPs, note-taking skills and concentration, can arise for all students. They may 'lack the knowledge base which is necessary to distinguish the 'gist' or the key points of a lecture or text' (*ibid,* 233), and those who are doing long hours of paid work or looking after dependents may drift off in lectures. 'What helps a dyslexic student in such circumstances tends also to serve a wide range of students who have not been identified as having a particular need. Often the help required is little more than good practice in teaching' (*ibid,* 233), such as giving an overview of a topic at the beginning – particularly in diagrammatic form – and providing 'gapped' handouts. Students would have welcomed the application of the old adage: 'If he can't learn in the way you teach, teach him in the way he learns'.

G) Routes to university

Some course leaders have what Cottrell (2001:235) calls 'an antiquated notion' of what a typical student should be like, rather than realistic aware-ness of the students themselves. Students' expectations will be closer to those of the course tutors if the admissions, performance and assessment criteria are explicit. This is true for all students but may be particularly important for those labelled dyslexic. Many of our informants arrived at university without knowing what to expect, or with mistaken assumptions. Students on Access courses often expect the level of learning support in FE – generally a frequent individual tutorial – to be maintained. Bridging courses are helpful, provided either in FE or by universities, and should be widely extended.

Before entering HE, 'learning disabled' students could ask themselves 'is college right for me?' (Citro, 2001). Pisha and Ruzic (2001) urge a potential student to 'learn as much as you can about yourself as a learner'. With the hegemony of the autonomous model of academic writing in HE and the current disability model of dyslexia in mind, it is useful that they add:

> ... you are going to have to work much harder than many of your peers who do not share your individual array of strengths, weaknesses, bless-ings and curses. Get down, get a grip, get used to it, and get a clear picture of reality. (*ibid,* 141)

I hope that ultimately students will no longer face the dispiriting prospect of being labelled dyslexic or learning disabled.

Recommendations for further research

Students identified as dyslexic have a great deal of information to offer the HE sector, as this book has shown. But their voices are seldom heard. A much larger study is needed, that covers the various kinds of university. If this is centred on the cognitive, affective and social aspects of life there for 'dyslexic' students and if it involves both academics and students, further insights would be gained into:

■ the way such students think and learn

■ the emotional aspects of being labelled and of studying in HE

■ what it is like to be assessed, both for dyslexia and academically

■ developing alternative approaches to learning and teaching in universities.

The present study was confined to students who had been formally identified as dyslexic and had sought Student Services or Learning Support. It would be revealing also to investigate students who choose not to seek identification or learning support. And what of the universities' models of academic writing and learning support, particularly in the light of the inclusivity and widening participation agenda?

Afterword

The research reported here has shown that the learning life histories of students who regard themselves as dyslexic can throw light on the experience of dyslexia in HE today. Dyslexia has been shown to be more than a disability and to be part of the learning and teaching, inclusivity and widening participation agendas.

Jary and Parker (1998:21) see 'graduateness' (HEQC, 1996) as a potential barrier to expansion and widening participation, and cite 'academic oligarchy' as a vested interest that is set against social demand for HE. Although writing about a broad inclusivity agenda, their views apply to dyslexic students. Dyslexia, whether defined as a neuropsychological condition or as part of the natural spectrum of human brain development, confronts academic autonomy and oligarchy.

This research suggests that the 'disability' of dyslexia is largely socially constructed. As Ann's remarks about memory (see page 100) imply, there is more to this pattern of brain functioning than academic study alone. However, academic study aspects involve the other area with which we see dyslexia to be linked, namely academic literacies (Street, 1984, 1991, 1994; Lea and Street, 2000; Herrington, 2001b). Their own identity as writers is important for students. Lea and Street (2000) conclude that the very notion of a learning support unit implies that students lack skills, and ignores their interaction with institutional practices. They ask whether knowledge is 'transferred', or 'constructed through writing practices' (Lea and Street, 2000:45). These issues

> are located in relations of power and authority and are not simply reducible to the skills and competences required for entry to, and success within, the academic community. (*ibid,* 45)

Reading and writing will eventually come to be seen as the skills of a medieval clerk (West, 1997). As technology advances it will change the cognitive make-up of dyslexic people from apparent deficit to advantage. Meanwhile, a good many people are struggling to find a sense of identity as students in higher education. Many are 'mature', of 'non-traditional' background or dyslexic, and some are all three – like most of the mature students in this study. Re-framing learning difficulties/dyslexia requires the individual to 'reinterpret ... the learning disability experience in a more productive and positive manner' (Gerber *et al,* 1996:98). What is also required is reframing by the universities so that they move away from labelling their students as having a 'problem' to seeing any 'problem' as for the institution to resolve:

> In response to the widening access to further and higher education, all teachers need to re-evaluate their approach to teaching to accommodate larger numbers of students with a wider range of individual needs (Morgan and Klein, 2000:137).

These sentiments are supported by Singleton *et al* (2001:5):

> Dyslexia support is an equal opportunities issue. Dyslexic students ... need access to the learning methods that will enable them to use unorthodox learning approaches. ... A level playing field should be provided.

What constitutes 'level' and how this might be achieved are still contested. With its range of examples of students identified as dyslexic, this book contributes to the debate.

Appendix I

Informants' descriptions of their experiences

These extracts have been selected because they are typical of the way each person spoke, and because they exemplify what they talked about: their school experiences, being assessed as dyslexic and their experience of teaching and learning at university. Above all, these extracts exemplify aspects of the four discourses of dyslexia set out in this book. The informants are grouped according to the discourse which they adopted.

'Patients'

Ann

A: First of all I went and saw the Special Needs person and she said my main problem was I couldn't hear sounds, so when you said a word and I tried to write it down I couldn't get the fundamental letters together, I couldn't hear the sound, as you said the 'mm' for mouse and that lot I just couldn't hear it at all. Erm, and then about half a year later she said, you know, 'I got you this appointment with this guy'. But he kept missing his appointments so she'd left when I'd finally got my appointment in the next year when I had this new teacher.

D: And this was an EP?

A: This was an EP and he did an IQ test on me, and a reading test, and a spelling test, erm, analysed the results and said 'Right, you can have 25 per cent extra time'. Which was the main reason; we weren't really doing it for anything else, you know, we just went for it for extra time for my exams.

D: Mmm.

A: Er, also with the taking notes in the lectures I sat next to girl in Zoology that wrote beautiful writing so teacher's dictate and I would copy her. Erm, Chemistry fortunately, the spelling of the chemistry teacher wasn't wonderful so she'd go slow enough for me to write it down and Maths there's no writing in it. Whereas here I have a terrible problem trying to get notes, so it's a bit of a pain.

D: Mmm.

A: She put me, she said, 'Right, I want you to sit next to Jo 'cos she's got neat writing'. So they were quite good in that sense.

D: They were weren't they, yes. Erm, so you still didn't regard yourself as dyslexic, then?

A: Erm, not until I got the test. I knew my spelling was bad, but as, you see, you don't know how anybody else thinks, or anything like that, I forget everything and I can't spell. Well, that's just a problem trait, you know, everybody's got their things they're not very good at.

D: Yes. Absolutely, yes.

A: It's not until recently, you know, that you realise how bad you actually are. Now you know that there's some reason for it. You don't realise how bad you actually are until everybody, or else you, you know, especially if you don't have, you know, that little tight-knit group of friends that you used to have, you've got a wide range of friends that don't know all your problems and ins and outs –

D: Yeah.

A: – and they, yeah, they're a bit miffed as if you liked ... or they just count you as being unintelligent because when you are speaking a sentence you can't remember that word that you want to fit in. I think that's my main problem, is remembering words and how they sound. Because you are trying to picture them in your mind so that you can speak them out loud, but you just can't get that damn word. I think that's the main problem, is getting words as opposed to writing backwards and forwards.

Arnold

A: When I was a sophomore at high school, about 15, it started to really bring me down. I was always frustrated, I was always returning things late, I was always having trouble with writing and math and things and I was always ... because what you produce, if you are not at a certain level of like proper production, you're put into a lower track. It's what I guess the American education is, tracking.

D: Hm, yeah, yes.

A: I remember there were these series of dinners where I would just sit there after dinner. They'd ask me how school was going. We'd talk and suddenly I would just start crying because I was so ... I was getting so angry. I was feeling so trapped within what my ... within something that had been created.

D: Yeah.

A: Going back, I know it wasn't me. It wasn't, but I remember it was how I was feeling about myself and just like ... I used to use the expression, I felt I got trapped in a bubble. I felt like I ... I would just cry. It was just like, what is going on? I don't know what is – I don't know what was going on. I would sit there and my parents were, my parents would get upset because they didn't know what to say, you know? To them it was a mystery, what to do, you know, and I was, I was put into more of a learning, a learning, a learning centre. That's was it was called, the learning centre.

D: Right. So you arrived at high school with a file on you already -

A: Right.

D: And the modifications and all that?

A: Yeah. The modifications, the individual education plan, my plan.

D: Were you the only one?

A: No, there was, again there was an extensive network of students.

D: Right.

A: There were two classrooms in the high school, one for ... which, looking back, for more accelerated learning disabled students, the other one for very remedial, and basically the one for the remedial was kind of a place for them to feel even more worthless.

D: Oh, yes.

A: Even though it helped them out. And there was another room that just let them go wild and really didn't help anyone. But the one I was in, we got help when we wanted it and the aim was for us to like be very, to advocate for ourselves things but I remember the feeling was that it was not ... I needed help in how to craft my ideas, the paper, how do I ... and that didn't come until my senior, my last year of Coll- , my last year of high school.

D: But at that point, though, when you first went to high school ...

A: Yeah.

D: You knew that you were intelligent then, that you'd been put in this –

A: Well, I don't know .... no, because, again, because ... I guess I didn't start to claim ... My reaction to feeling so depressed about it was to react, was to like, I don't know, to create a positive image, to like nationalise myself or something like ... somehow ... except that what I'm going to create isn't better than anything, you know, it's – yeah, other people have done this but they haven't ... I've ... they've never done it like me, you know?

D: Hm.

A: But I wasn't very forthright up until last year. It was like I didn't view my own fate, I didn't view my own ability as significant because I was always trapped, I guess, in a very self-defeating cycle because I wouldn't turn things in.

D: Hm.

A: I wouldn't be able to do math, I wouldn't be able to do something, I'd always get lower grades. I was realising that I was in a lower track of schooling and I was becoming frustrating because I wanted to be in higher tracks with other people because I felt ... I just was ... I was embarrassed about being where I was, and that just built up and built up until, I think, you know, and then it would just ... I wasn't getting help, you know?

D: Yeah, yeah. So you had these dinners with your parents when you were frustrated: were they able to tune in to what was happening for you?

A: Um, it's interesting: My father, whenever he would see me get down, he being himself, I don't know what caused it but he was always wanting to give advice and my mother was always one to identify with. She would create comfort for me by helping to, you know, identifying her problems with mine.

D: Hm.

A: My father would always be, like, you know, 'we've always told you, you've just got to believe in yourself', which is comp- it doesn't make any sense until you can actually be at a stage where you can be like, you know, where I can be up on stage and you can do it.

D: Hm.

A: And, and, yeah, and part of the other thing was that because I wasn't finishing things and because I wasn't able to, you know, I would get like, 'oh, it could have been an A but it's a D' and so it's like ... My father really described it really well that I had been ... because of what I was producing and how it was being produced and the time it was taking, I was creating more and more like a negative self-image. This is my own idea. Just because I was, the feedback I was getting with all these negative ...

Charles (1)

C: There are times when I write and for some unknown reason I will write an 'a' when I'm thinking about a 'z' or something else, and I don't know why.

D: Oh, hm.

C: I think I told you about my famous one where I wanted to write Croydon and I actually wrote Groydon because the Y and the G, for some unknown reason, got mixed up inside my mind. Why they did it I haven't a clue. And I sat there and eventually you turn around and say, 'what a prat'. The amount of times I write an envelope and have to throw it away because I've made a mistake.

D: Hm.

C: This is the beauty of the computer. You make a mistake, you can actually delete it and alter it. And again, that's why I like the pencil. You can actually rub it out and change it.

Charles (2)

D: So you went to see _____, the EP, at the suggestion of the Learning Support Unit, did you? To help you get the DSA.

C: Um, well, J (*learning support tutor*) reckons that there seemed to be some form of dyslexia there but I had overcome some of it. As she suggested that I actually went and looked outside of the university to actually be quantified because she's ... because ... at that point I was in quite a desperate state, you know?

D: Yes.

C: Mentally I was drained and, you know. It really was quite an unpleasant experience.

D: So you weren't really... You weren't feeling strong enough to be told what your spelling and reading age were, really?

C: That didn't worry me. That didn't worry me at all. It was just nice to actually, for somebody to turn around and say ... I said to her, 'this is what I'm feeling, this is what I'm going through', and by being tested it actually came back that 'this is why you're feeling that way', which was rather nice, you know?

D: Yeah.

C: It's like having permanent headaches and you actually say to yourself, 'why am I getting these permanent headaches? It either is because you need glasses or because I had this learning difficulty I was under a considerable amount of stress.

D: Yes.

C: And, as you know, I was very stressed out at times.

D: Yes. But did you feel that N (EP) handled you alright then?

C: I got on very well with N. I like N, yes.

D: Hm, that's good.

C: It was nice actually, because there she was, a lady of, let's say, indeterminate age but a very confident, very warm personality who you could actually ... I found it was very easy to communicate with her. There was no, there was no ... It was very difficult just to appear outside somebody's front door and say, you know, 'test me', but she made it very comfortable and very easy to be able to do that and to be able to communicate with her.

Chuck

C: I think dyslexia should be described as suffering, as in that it's er- the physical manifestations are bad, basically are bad wiring of parts of the brain, and subsequently it can be connected to a physical disability. And it's a good way of explaining to someone who doesn't know, to describe dyslexia as a bad, or a badly wired part of the brain, and using the language of computers, they find it easier to understand.

D: Do you find that explanation personally acceptable? Can you accept that?

C: I think it's – it can explain, at basic level it can explain a, fairly simply to some-one who understands; if they have any idea of computers, they can understand that a badly wired computer doesn't work properly.

D: Yeah, OK.

C: On a higher level, if you get a badly written piece of software, or memory, parts of a computer that, say, a more intellectual person can understand, then if the everyday or short-term memory of the computer is wrong, the program doesn't work; so again, they can understand, you know, if they've had ex-perience of computers going wrong as a result of different parts of the pro-gram or the software not working; so I think it's a good analogy for people who understand computers.

D: But what about, um, how do you feel that relates to your own basic intel-ligence, if there is such a thing – how do you see your own brain power?

C: Um, well, I mean, the IQ test etc. they talk about, when they fragment the sub-jects and you can score, I scored very highly in some subjects and very low in others, and um I don't know how that relates, but I feel that I'm intelligent- I'm not stupid, I can see things clearly. I also feel that I tend to understand, um, the underlying principles of a particular point or the ramifications of- I mean, er, the implications of particular points, I feel that I can pick up quicker than most people.

Enid (1)

D: What image of dyslexia did you have?

E: Um, I didn't know any other dyslexic people. Um, I just knew I – the reason why I had difficulty spelling was because I was dyslexic. I'm not seriously dyslexic; it was just –

D: Right. Your parents explained it to you, then –

E: Yes.

D: What I was. And how did they put it across to you?

E: Um, well my father is also dyslexic, and so is my grandmother. The thing is, my grandmother has never admitted she's dyslexic, so she wasn't in the picture at all. My father said he'd always had difficulty spelling, and he said the only thing you can do is to start memorising it, writing out five times, and –

D: Yes. And does that work for you, writing –

E: Yes, it does.

D: Right. So he passed on to you some of his strategies?

E: Yeah. And of course my mother was an English teacher, English as a foreign language, and so she basically – by this stage, my parents were divorced, so what was happening is I was getting one and then the other.

D: Right. But were the two different kinds of input that you got from them, were they complementary?

E: My mother was – my father wasn't so strict (*laughs*).

D: Yes, what, she made you work at set times, and –

E: Yeah, I found – well she made me work at er French more than English. Um I would get fed up and bored with having to learn how to spell and things like that, so I wouldn't bother. So I would have – I've always had bad spelling on my report (*laughs*).

D: Yes, er OK. But they presumably explained to you that it wasn't to do with intelligence?

E: Yeah, they made that very very clear.

D: Right. So, when you were starting up on GCSE, your image of dyslexia was that it was a memory difficulty, but it wasn't to do with intelligence?

E: Yeah.

Enid (2)

D: So how do you define dyslexia, then?

E: Um, as a memory problem. Well actually as – not necessarily a memory problem but as actually seeing it – as getting the information into your head, sort of thing.

D: Yes. Um what are you like with essay structuring?

E: Er, I have to be very very careful with it. It's the essay structure, rather than actually writing the essay, which takes me longer.

D: How do you get round that?

E: Um, I set it out very very clearly. You know, I'll do my plan first, and I will do a very very detailed plan, even in my exams.

D: How have you learnt to do that? Have you taught yourself to do it?

E: Well I started off learning how to do a brainstorm and a spider diagram, but I don't use that as much any more. Like it depends what the essay's on. If it's a complicated subject, I will brainstorm.

D: Was that from Learning Support here?

E: Uh uh, no, that was from our English teacher at GCSE; she taught us all to do that.

D: Great. Have you had any learning support here?

E: No. I don't need it (*laughs*).

D: No, you've got all the strategies already.

E: Yeah. I think my marks are good enough to not require it. Nowadays, I don't need to brainstorm any more; usually I've got a pretty good idea about the subject, if I do enough reading. Um so you don't need to brainstorm.

D: OK. Um, but the memory aspects are still a problem.

E: Um, yeah; well, memory in everyday-life terms, I've learnt to write myself notes; and now I'm actually better than most people (*laughs*), because I combat it. Um –

D: Where to be at a certain time?

E: Yeah. The memory doesn't cause me problems. I know it could cause me problems but it doesn't cause me problems because I've figured out ways of combating it. It's things like er, I've just done a course on statistics, and I had to get everyone else to check my calculations because I can do something like, with 292 I'll write it out 929 or tap it into the computer wrong. Um, or I'll miss something out. So my calculations always took twice the time everyone else took it, but I always came out with a better result, because I was more careful.

D: Yes. You have to spend longer than many students on everything, presumably.

E: Um, my essays, I told you I wrote them out 4 times; I couldn't hand an essay in that I hadn't written out several times.

D: You still do that now?

E: Yeah. Because er trying to get my English in an understandable method, sort of get my paragraphs short and concise sort of thing –

D: But this is you working on this alone still, then, isn't it?

E: Yes.

D: You can look at a sentence or a paragraph and think 'this isn't right', and –

E: I read it out loud to myself first.

D: Do you think when you have your own computer you won't write things out so often?

E: Um, I don't like the computer for writing essays, because I prefer being able to write something, then read it out, and a computer that types it all the same, it looks like it's a final draft. Um, I just don't feel comfortable with it, and also I can't type, but I'm getting better. But, it's just –

D: Oh yeah.

E: It's on the screen; I hate that screen (*laughs*). If it came out as handwriting, it'd be fine (*laughs*).

Fenella (1)

D: When did you first, when did anyone suggest you might be dyslexic? Did you discover about the existence of dyslexia?

F: No, I didn't know anything about it really.

D: But when did, when you got to university then?

F: No, no, it was ... Once I'd got safely ensconced on my access course then I went to the group tutor and said, 'I'm a bit worried because I'm quite a slow reader and I do feel that there's something not quite right, you know, because I'm very, very slow'. It's hard because I'd never really told anybody before because it's like the beginning of actually opening up to all this stuff, you know?

D: Yes, yes.

F: That I'd been kind of, I'd been keeping to myself for a very long time, thinking that I was abnormal, that there was something drastically not right, but not knowing what it was. I didn't really know about dyslexia.

D: You'd never read about dyslexia in the paper or ...?

F: I had, I think I had but I don't really think I'd ever ... It hadn't got anything to do with me.

D: Oh, of course.

F: It never ever. Actually, I know: a friend assumed I was dyslexic because I was very close friends with her and I told her, you know, she knew that I was a slow reader and this, that and the other. And one day she called me dyslexic. She said, 'oh, because you're dyslexic, aren't you?' and I said, 'I'm not dyslexic!' [*laughter*]

D: Yes.

F: 'No, no, no. I never said I was dyslexic. No, of course I'm not' You know, I just didn't ... and I was really shocked. It was really funny.

D: So that was the end of that. Did she backtrack then?

F: Yes, she said, 'oh, I'm sorry'. I think then I thought ...

D: You'd pursue that?

F: Oh, you know, I suppose, you know, maybe, maybe I have got a touch of dyslexia. I don't know. I said, 'I don't know, I don't know. I've never ... no idea'. I've never been called dyslexic at school. Nobody ever did anything about my difficulties all the time I was at school. Not a thing.

D: That conversation with your friend, did that influence you in some way to go and see the course tutor then?

F: Um, I don't know. I think ... I can't remember when that conversation occurred, whether I was already on the Access course or not. No, I think that was before, way before I was doing the Access course. I think possibly just talking about education and stuff and talking about what I'd like to do.

D: Hm, right.

F: But what was holding me back all the time, that feeling that it's ridiculous a person like me thinking of doing something like that when I knew there was something wrong with me. Do you know what I mean?

D: Yes, yes.

F: But it was when I was, once I was ensconced and I told the tutor – and I think she thought, well, you know, lots of people are slow readers – but she, and she didn't pick ... and she said, you know, a problem with the projects, the first sort of month or two's work that we'd done, she couldn't see anything to suggest that I was but suggested that I go and see someone at studies skills and ... It was my dyslexic friend who knew she was dyslexic, V, who was also on the access course, who ... just everything I said she could relate to.

D: Hm.

F: And she said, 'Obviously you've got to see somebody who knows what they're talking about. As a dyslexic person, I think you may well be dyslexic'. In a way, although it was scary, it was almost ... I felt, at last, there's a reason why I've had all these emotions about my ability and why I'm so slow at reading and why I could seem so silly at times.

Fenella (2)

F: I got this report which I found devastating. Absolutely. It knocked me for six, I tell you.

D: Yes.

F: I almost thought, well, I might as well give up now. Indeed, I felt very defeatist. That's something I remember actually as a child, always being accused of having a defeatist attitude, and I suppose it's because everything such a struggle that I didn't believe I could do anything.

D: Hm, hm.

F: I think my daughter was away at the time. I think she'd gone to visit her father or something, and I was on my own and I received this and I found it shocking, really shocking.

D: Yes. So what was the most shocking thing about it?

F: I think, you know, when I actually went to have the test, I actually thought there was a possibility that she'd say, well, I'm sorry dear but you're not dyslexic, you're not all there, you're not quite as bright as you think you are, sort of thing. When she actually did say that yes, I have to tell you that you're dyslexic, I kind of ... there was a bit of me that was saying 'Oh, thank God', you know.

D: Yes.

F: There's a concrete ...

D: She told you that before you left, did she?

F: Yes, but that she was sending me a full report.

D: Yes, so that was ... the actual live session with her was alright then?

F: Well, it was but there was this bit of me that was saying, 'thank God, I am dyslexic' and then thinking, 'oh shit, I'm dyslexic'.

D: Yes, of course, yes.

F: But there was this kind of relief that, well, you're not bananas, you know?

D: Yes, yes.

F: There is a reason why you're like you are, and it kind of, I don't know, it did sort of ... Even having the test and everything, when she was questioning me and what have you, it did actually, things were beginning to fall into place. I did actually realise that I did have this process. She was asking me about the numbers and everything, going backwards. I was actually ... she was asking me to repeat numbers backwards. I'd have to visualise them on the blank wall.

D: Right, and did you look up at the ...?

F: I wasn't aware I was doing it until she was saying, that's amazing, the way you did that, the fact that you can recall those. And I sort of had to analyse how I was doing it. I analysed how I was doing it. There I was, trying to get the best marks in anything that she was testing me on. Do you know what I mean?

D: Hm, hm. Yes. So the shocking thing about this report was the spelling age and reading age, was it, mainly?

F: I think, yeah. I think the comprehension and stuff, yeah. It was horrific to see those ages down and I was reading about this person who was me, an adult, you know?

D: Hm, hm, hm.

F: How old was I? Thirty-nine, forty?

D: Forty-two, yeah.

F: Um, it's just shocking. I already felt that a fish out of water at university and here I am in a grown-up world, a world that I never thought I'd get to because although I wanted to, it's really all beyond me, and who the hell do I think I am, you know, sort of doing this, and to see those ages, it just threw me back into that frightening world that I was in as a child. It's like I'd put myself in that situation in a way again that I'd so wanted to escape at sixteen.

Jeremy

D: What about reading?

J: I never read. I mean that's –

D: You still weren't reading.

J: I, I used to, I wanted to try; actually when I, my Dad joined this, buy five books and you get so many, one of those things. And I actually asked them to get me a few books, because I was always very paranoid, everyone was talking about – when it's like filling in your UCAS form, if they say like 'if you put reading you state that you've got some books', or whatever, and I've never read. It was never seen as – I mean my parents never really pointed it out to me. I just never read; so I tried to read um – what was it? – *Silence of the Lambs* was the first book I tried to read. I'd seen the film, so I figured if I've seen the film, at least I know what's going on, so I can't get lost in the book'. Because I used to lose concentration; but I got probably as far as Chapter 5, and then I just – it wasn't following through, it wasn't like I was getting into it; it was just another page and another – I was reading for the sake of reading.

D: Yeah. What book was that?

J: That was *Silence of the Lambs*.

D: Oh yes, right. Do you find when you've read a page that you can't remember what was on it?

J: Um, it was getting that – it was getting to say half-way through a chapter, and I was thinking of the story, what had happened two pages back; I wouldn't – there was no – I couldn't take it into my mind, I couldn't follow the story, although I'd seen the story, seen the film, that was the whole – that's the reason why I did it. That was my first, because I was the movie when it came out, on video. And I read the book, but I still couldn't follow the book; I couldn't under-stand what was going on. So I could read the pages, I could read the whole page, no problem.

D: So was that – that must have been a bit of a shock to you, then.

J: Um, it was a shock, but it was expected, because I'd always had that trouble when I was – I expected it, not like, I mean – I expected it. My mother – I can't remember actually telling my parents, I never said 'I'm not going to read this book any more', going up in my room. And it was, it wasn't a overall shock to me that I couldn't follow it, because I never – I wanted to, I really actually wanted to read the book. Just to say I'd read a book; I mean, when I was younger, I used to read the little 10-page books which – that's not a problem, I mean it's not a book, is it? But I couldn't do that. And then I actually moved book to another story, which was called 'Rush', the book was; that book was about Police officers and drugs, drug agency. But again, that, I mean I just didn't get any – , I read a few chapters, skipping a few pages just to, because I wanted to read a book, that was my ultimate goal. But then I thought 'I'm just reading it page after page, I can't, you can't, no-one can ask, if anyone asked me a question, I've got absolutely no idea what I've just read'. So I said that was that for books. But I did try; it was actually, I knew I hadn't read it, because everyone was, everyone at the school was, if they had free time to spare, some, they'd just get a book out, or they'd read a book, or people would just be going through novel after novel. And I, I never did; I couldn't read – I mean I could read it, but – I never really had trouble with the words, reading it, but it never went into my head, so I never followed the story. So I just kicked it on the head, sort of thing.

Peggy

D: How would you describe dyslexia? It is very different for different people, isn't it, but for you then, what are the main aspects of it?

P: Um, well in being asked, one of the first things I would say is it's different for other people, all I can do is describe my own, I mean that's, if someone was asking me, yeah, that's – I would. Um, I would say that I do what most people do: I misread things, um, I get sentences sort of with various tenses of things – not so much er I do it in speaking, but I do it much more in writing. And, I really do mis-spell the most obvious words and I can't recognise that it's mis-spelt, even if there's sort of you know two words next to each other, the same word spelt differently, somehow I don't see it. My eye seems to run over it so quickly, it just doesn't [feel] it. Memory is a dreadful problem, and that's part of it, that's part of mis-reading and mis-writing things, because my memory's bad. Um, I think everybody has that, but it's worse, it's worse. It's very frus-trating, it's constant – you don't just have bad moments at it – it's all the time (slight laugh). Everybody has bad days, where they've sort of written a load of garbage, or you know have read something and gone off on a tangent because they haven't read it right, haven't understood it because they've again just haven't read it correctly. Everyone does that, but when you do it all the time, like every time you pick up a book you're ready to do it, as it were, wait for it, and you've got to sort of actually work round it; it's a lot of work just to do the slightest thing. Like it doesn't come naturally to just read, or write a letter. I've actually got to try and put all those faults aside, actually concentrate on the faults, to not do them, to write or read something, and that's a constant effort, it's not the same process that I think other people go through by just auto-matically reading or writing something; it's all an effort, therefore it constantly comes out all wrong (*laughs*).

D: So, it sounds as though you're saying that for you, dyslexia is mainly a question of difficulties with reading and writing.....

P: Well I think that's how it manifests itself...

D: Yes. If you were not doing a degree course, how would being dyslexic affect your life?

P: Um... well basic everyday things that you sort of need your memory for, like going shopping; I can't have a list [in my head], I've got to write it down. If I've got two or three calls to make in town, I've got to write down the places I'm going to, or I shall go right by them. Um, you know, I mean people can usually remember that they're going to go to the post office, then they've got to call at the butcher's, then they're going to go to the library. I can set off and I'll miss the library, or miss the post office. I just walk right by because I don't re-member even in actions step by step things that I'm doing.

D: Have you been like that all your life?

P: Yeah. So I've sort of had to get very organised to know what I'm doing, stay very calm, concentrate on one thing at a time. But.... I can cope with that, and I think everyone's a bit like that. But um, I do feel it's worse. So my sort of dyslexia is just this memory problem.

D: Yes. And yet, are you aware of ways in which your thinking style is stronger than other people's?

P: Um.... yes, I think I'm better than most people at seeing how to do it, broader, more far-reaching concepts, I can see a whole pattern in um, can't think of an example... For example, if I go back to when I actually ran a company, I can see how it all works out, how it integrates, how one depends on the other, what all the mechanisms are, what all the relationships are, how things actually work, in that sort of way, but I'm asked to look at the phone book – you know, it's the little things. I mean I think I'm probably better at applying like a lateral thought, is one way of putting it, as I'm trying to describe it, you know which is more than just the 'ah, but what if?' question, it's the 'ah, but what if', but in saying that, actually seeing things from um, it's so hard to describe, I can just see the sort of the broader concepts of things, whatever it is you give to me, yeah? But don't ask me to write it down (*laughs*).

D: So, how do you feel about people or articles and books that present dyslexia as some kind of a medical problem, not exactly a disease, but a weakness?

P: I mean again that's getting onto people's ideas, the sort of stigma which um...I mean I can remember J (EP) explaining to me that really what I have, probably physiologically, is a smaller clip-board than anyone else, which I think is a nice way of putting it, and I think yes, I can accept that, um, yes and it probably is a physiological thing, yes?

D: Yes, that does seem to be one of the theories, yes.

P: Um, that is one way of putting it and one way of thinking of it, and once you know and accept that, why get any more upset about it than if you take five or size seven shoes? I mean, to me...

D: Yes. So, to continue wit the computer analogy then, you may have a smaller clip-board than some people, but what other software have you got, or hardware even?

P: (*Laughing*) Um.....I think a lot more sort of, I can apply myself to problems and work them out. I can go into a complete unknown program and work it out, take time, and with very little information and trial and error and think about it and work things out – actually working a problem out – then I will arrive with information and knowledge that I'll never ever forget and I can go on and use further. But if you just pin something on my clipboard, like I read a chapter, it's not going to stay there, I know it's not! (*laughs*) That's the difference, and I think if I actually work with knowledge, I do something with it... So now what I do, is any work I do do, I try and do something with it, to make it stay as it were, to actually feed it in, to make a program out of it rather than just pin it on a board, which is how I find most learning happens – you're just continually just lodging stuff on a clip-board that at some point will get filed somewhere – but with me it doesn't, it falls off (*laughs*), yeah, whereas if I don't put it on that clipboard, if I actually do something with it.....Now I find that is an asset that other people don't have, because they get given information and they don't know what to do with it, they just know how to put it on a clip-board and hold it. So I would say that is an asset, a very subtle one, but very good.

D: Yeah. So, dyslexia is an individual difference of style, isn't it? Like as you say, different size shoes. And yet, when it's heard of at all, it tends to be presented as a disability. It is classed with disabilities, isn't it? Um, what would you say to a University lecturer who claimed that dyslexic people were not entitled to do a degree?

P: Um, I would say that if I knew enough about him I would find a reason for him not to do a degree (*laughs*). There's always a reason; everybody is good or bad at something. He may have what I may call something of a disability, i.e. not getting on with people, or... It's rude enough to say that somebody suffering dyslexia should not do a degree, when somebody like that should not do a degree. You know, it's um...

D: And yet, given the way Universities are run at the moment, you have to prove what you know by doing exams, writing essays or dissertations, in other words doing lots of things that dyslexics are not good at.

P: And I suppose really the answer would be, go and do some vocational degree, or some ...., but then that academically is sort of considered sort of less, less of an attainment, which is very unfair.

D: If you had a free choice of how to present your knowledge, how would you like to do it – to prove that you had understood all the stuff you'd done in your degree?

P: I think, um, it's very restricting just written work, it's very restricting. I think that's one skill and only one, and everything seems to be channelled into that, er... There are far more ways of expressing yourself, of putting over ideas, of learning, you know, giving or receiving education than writing and reading. I don't think you can do without them, but I think other things should be able to back it up. I think you know more should be made of verbal communication, because at the end of the day you know, you do your degree, you go to get a job, what's one of the first things you do? You go to an interview, and yet there's very little put on communication skills and verbal skills.

Victoria

V: I mean, I have trouble – I don't know what everybody else feels, thinks of here (*points to head*), but I – I don't know, I haven't – my thinking process are bizarre. Do you understand what I'm trying to say? I don't know what you, what you see up here in your own head. Getting very deep, this, isn't it?

D: No it's very interesting, because it's the whole crux here, really.

V: I don't know what – I mean I've said this to G; I said 'what do other people think and feel up here?' She looked at me as if I'd completely gone out I think. But I don't know – I have trouble focusing, up here; I don't mean visually. Does that make sense to you?

D: Go on, please, yes.

V: I can't get things into order. There's no order up here; it's like spaghetti junction.

D: Right. But sometimes it does click.

V: Sometimes it clicks.

D: What does it feel like when it clicks? What's the difference?

V: I know why I can see where I'm going. I can see the road ahead. Instead of loads of blind turns everywhere, suddenly I can see the road ahead, there's signs telling me where to go. Does that make sense? With an essay at the end of the day, I might eventually know exactly what I'm going for. But I can't – that doesn't happen until I've got through God knows how many pads of A4, and tears, and books have been slung. But that's the frustration that comes with this affliction, if you like.

D: Yes.

V: I mean the frustration is horrendous; I don't know whether anybody else has mentioned this on tape, but the frustration of it!

D: And the hours, the extra hours that –

V: The extra hours, and sometimes at the end of the extra hours you've got nothing from it. That is what's so soul-destroying. That's why you give up.

D: Yes. Er, so, you've got your essay topic, and you've done some reading –

V: Hopefully, yes.

D: – and you've been to some lectures, and you've read the title and lots of ideas come into your head –

V: No ideas come at all. Ideas don't come until I start writing.

D: OK. You look at the essay title –

V: And I think, 'God what do I do with this?', yes.

D: – and nothing comes. So what do you do then?

V: Panic! I mean I do mean sheer panic. Panic. Put it away, have a wobbly, um, get the wretched thing out again the next day, have another wobbly, um, and then very slowly it can all start to sink in, bit by bit. 'Ah' I think when I'm busy with something else, 'I recall that I read that in so-and-so, and that relates back to so-and-so'; and I think, 'why the dickens couldn't I have done that two weeks ago?'

D: So the ideas about the title, or whatever it is, have to mature in your head –

V: Yes.

D: – without you even being aware of it?

V: Yes.

D: Things are going on?

V: Yes. But I haven't realised, but that is actually right.

D: Right, so you just have to think for a bit about the title, and then leave it –

V: Yes.

D: – and your processes will eventually –

V: Yes.

D: Now, when the thoughts do come to you, what are you doing at the time? Are you thinking about something else when it, when the answer comes to you?

V: Well, anything could be happening really. I could even be reading something in the paper, and I think 'ah, interesting!'

D: Yeah. So what do you do then, when these ideas begin to suddenly come to you? Do you write them down?

V: I write them down, and promptly lose the piece of paper, yes.

D: Right. But you write them – what form do you write then in?

V: Longhand. Is that what you mean?

D: Yeah, and do you write them sort of one line under the other?

V: Yes.

D: Do you write them in blocks, or –

V: No. One line under the other.

D: – not diagonally along.

V: Or really if I've got any sense, I brainstorm them of course, but I haven't got any sense when I do things in a hurry.

D: Right. And, yeah, so you've got your essay, you've got some thoughts to do with the essay – do you find that once that process has begun, and you start to understand the question more and more –

V: No, I might forget everything I've thought about. That's another dreadful probability.

D: Yes.

V: Which does happen, actually, and that's when the frustration sets in, and the anger.

D: You knew you had an idea –

V: Yeah, and it's gone. And I can look it up, and I think 'God, what the hell have I written here?' And often what you've written, you can't (a) remember having written it, or (b) what it relates to.

D: Yeah.

V: And you think, 'God, what essay was that to do with?' You know. And this has happened, because we were given four assignments in one week. It was a nightmare. It was a nightmare! I didn't know what was what, and in the end I just had to have a folder for each, and a pad of A4 for each essay, that was the only way I could do it.

D: To keep them separate.

V: Keep everything separate.

D: Yeah.

V: I even put them on my computer, and that was a disaster; they all ran into each other. You can't do things in a hurry, that's another great problem. And one thing at a time, I'm afraid.

The 'Students'

Alice

D: But out of your whole life, you've put yourself through hundreds of courses, haven't you?

A: I worked it out, and since, post-compulsory education I've done 11 years of additional study, and five of those have been full-time and six part-time. Huh – and I'm now looking at the Doctorate! (*laughs*) And I think I shouldn't!

D: Goodness me. Yes.

A: But you see I, I've been doing very well on the MA, I've been getting A grades on my work, written assignment work; and how I got tested: when I had the interview to do the MA at the end of the Cert. Ed, the course tutor interviewed me. He'd taught a module, and he said you know, 'without doubt you can have a place, but do you have any worries?' And I said 'yeah, I'm worried about my reading element, because I can't read very well'. And then I said um – 'well, I know what – I think I'm dyslexic', and he said 'oh don't be ridiculous, absolutely, there's no way you can be dyslexic'.

D: 'Look, you've done all these courses'.

A: (*laughs*) You've done all these courses! And I said 'I think I do have a problem', and he said 'OK, I'm going to make it a requirement, as a personal objective, that you get tested, but it's not a requirement to come on the course'. And someone had written 'only an HND' across the top of my form for the entry; and he said 'isn't it strange what one word can do?' And he said 'how do you feel about that?' And of course again it hit everything; it's always been 'only', and not quite enough, you know. And so, I didn't want to go and get tested at all, because I've always avoided it, because I was aware you could go and get these things done; and I had once or twice asked about it privately. And um suddenly here it was; he was saying 'I want you to be', so um – he told me I could ring the Student Services, so I did, and they just went through this very basic checklist. And I said 'oh I need something a bit more scientific than that', and he said 'well we can't do anything, you'll need to see an EP'. So I did, I got in touch, and they wanted something like £189; and of course, working part-time, I don't have that sort of money, particularly for something I didn't want to do. Anyway, so I told him I couldn't afford it, and they said 'well we'll give you a bursary'. I had to suggest how much I would pay, and fill out – there were nine pages of comments about your finances, and –

D: To get the bursary?

A: Yes. And I thought 'oh they won't give it to me anyway, so I'm not going to get it', and I said I'd pay £25 towards it. They wrote back and said they'd do it, and it was all fixed up. So I had – I was just reduced to tears when I did it. It was so emotional for me, because it was bringing back things like you did on the 11+, things that I just, they hurt me to try and do. Um, it was horrid.

D: I know how it is, yeah.

A: So I did that, I got tested in May of last year, yeah, and the guy – I brought the report along if you want to have a look.

D: Yes, please.

A: And the guy said 'on a continuum of 10 being severely dyslexic, you're about 7, but your coping strategies are such that you managed about 5, and you're well compensated', you know. And I think I do, but I do find it very hard, very very hard.

D: What was the name of the person who did it?

A: R.

D: Oh yes, I've heard of him. Did he relate to you well as a person?

A: Oh yeah, he was excellent, excellent.

D: Only the report is – did you agree with what he's put in the report?

A: I didn't understand what he put in the report, to be honest, because it's quite – he uses technical terms, I think, and things like that – he explained what he was going to say, he explained it, but I think what he didn't take on board, and I think it's partly my fault because I don't always reveal how I really feel about things, I'm very good at masking things, was that I, I always felt that because I hadn't been well, with these stomach problems, and that once I was well, all the learning difficulties would go away. So here he was, really telling me they would never go away, you know. And so it was suddenly 'well, even if I get really well, I'm never going to able to read any better, and I'm never going to be able to find my way, and –' and the impact of that was quite – there was no follow-up with it – it was almost like 'here you are', three hours of testing, and then 'oh yes, you are dyslexic and you are', you know, and I think he felt that 'well you've achieved so much already, why, you know, it can't really upset you very much', in a sense. Do you know what I mean?

D: Yeah, yeah.

A: Whereas it did; it was very upsetting.

Alison (1)

D: So your mum said to the school, 'my daughters', or you anyway, 'may be dyslexic', and they said 'no, no, there's no such thing'.

A: Yeah. I think she definitely suggested it, but it came out later; it was mentioned later, or – for some reason it came up, and I think it was discussions while I was doing my GCSEs, because it was then suggested by a teacher who – I was in the same year as her daughter. Her daughter had been diagnosed as dyslexic, and she noticed the signs in me.

D: Ah.

A: And because she knew, and she was quite – I suppose she was good friends with the, in the school, with lots of the teachers, and she actually pushed to get me tested for dyslexia before my exams, so that I could get extra time.

D: So she was, this woman was actually teaching at the school –

A: Yes, teaching at the school; she did art, and she had taught me for art, and her daughter was the same age as me and in the same form as myself.

D: But when you started secondary school, did you think you were dyslexic, or had you any mental picture of what that meant?

A: I didn't – no, I hadn't. I'd heard of dyslexia, and it wasn't until later that I had any idea what it was, but I knew that it was a reason for having bad English skills, yet still remaining quite bright at the same time. Um, but it was – the word had floated around for a while; I think teachers had mentioned it in front of me and stuff, but um there's always stuff in the media about it at different times. I'd heard, but it didn't twig that it was, that was what I'd got, though I did suspect. And when they said 'we want you to have a test to see if you're dyslexic', it seemed quite natural to me that it was going to come up and say I was dyslexic. There didn't seem any reason why it shouldn't.

Alison (2)

D: So we've established that you don't see dyslexia as coming under the heading of disability.

A: No, I don't.

D: So what is it to you? If someone who's never heard of it said 'what do you mean by dyslexia?', what would you say?

A: I'd say that it means that I have problems with spelling and reading, er and really things like it extends to me for things like co-ordination. Um, but I am as intelligent as anybody else on my course. But it's very much a case of high intelligence but low reading abilities, and it's short- and it – when they say 'short-term memory is a problem', boy, do I know it! Short-term memory is a huge problem for me. The amount of times I've been told off for forgetting to turn a radiator off. Just before, my Dad told me two minutes before to turn it off before I left the room; or take the dogs round for a pee whilst they're out doing the shopping, poor dogs, or feed them, even! (*laughs*) I forget things like the moment they're said to me – the other day, somebody told me about some nice cough mixture or something, that's very cheap and really good for clearing throats, and I went downstairs repeating the name of this thing, and I got into the staff room five minutes later: I couldn't remember the name. I forget people's names. Less – I remember names by association with someone that I know with the same name. Otherwise, particularly new ones, particularly new pronunciations I've never heard before, I forget the pronunciation, very

177

quickly. Always walking up the stairs, getting to the top of the stairs, and think: 'now why was I going up the stairs?' Always.

D: I know what that's like, yes. So, it spreads out into – the short-term memory thing affects general everyday life, doesn't it?

A: Oh yeah, mmm.

D: Yeah.

A: It affects my work as well; if I don't get down that moment a point that I've just thought of, I forget it, it's gone until maybe some time later I'll suddenly think 'ah yes, I meant to do that, I meant to write this'. I have to get it out straight away, otherwise it goes.

D: You do use a tape recorder, do you?

A: Er, I did do, but it's getting round to listening back to it, and I hate the sound of my own voice. I tried it once, doing it for an essay, and my mark actually went down, because I very quickly verbally get off my explanation but it wasn't actually good enough for a written essay.

D: Hmm. What about tape recording lectures?

A: Er, I tried it at one time, and I actually managed to um listen back, and I did it particularly in History. But it's actually then finding the time and the inclination to listen back to it.

D: It's a chore, isn't it?

A: Yeah. If I could be relaxing at that point, or something – no, do a piece of coursework! (*laughs*) Not an easy thing to do, specially seeing as the tape will be two hours long, you know.

D: Have you tried having a notebook in your handbag? For example, if someone says about a cough mixture or something.

A: Yeah, I have my diary I carry all the time. It's got note bits at the back, and I always write things down. And that day, I didn't have my diary on me, or I didn't get it out I think. And I always – I generally speaking write as much down as – take notes, get things, write it down, like 'don't go away, let me write that number down'.

D: Yes. So you get through a lot of – is this a kind of Filofax diary?

A: It's a, it's just an ordinary quite big diary. It's about that big, spiral bound. It's really brilliant, it's got notes bits at the back. I'm really not looking forward to losing it. It was a Christmas present last year, and I've got to make sure I get another one, otherwise I won't be able to live without it.

D: Have you got your timetable in there, and your –

A: Um, my timetable I carry around for about the first two weeks, and then I remember all of it. I remember that quite quickly, my timetable, so I don't need to carry that. But, if it's appointments, unless I write it down I get myself double-booked. Always do that one. Er, I have to have my diary to check against appointments because I don't relate – say, someone will say, 'right, next Thursday', I won't relate that to a date, so I have to have my diary for that reason.

D: Yeah, I do as well, yes. Um, do you use your diary to plan your academic life? Like, 'I've got such-and-such a thing to give in here'?

A: Yes, yeah. I put the course – if I can get all the course-work deadlines in, it's really helpful.

Bruce

R: Um, I remember lots of sort of, 'about the universe', books, um er there was, I think probably an American book called um *Tell me why?*, and it was like an encyclopaedia. Um there was *Still more tell me why.* And *Still more tell me why.* Um, so I had books like this, and I was probably bought a lot of those books. And I would imagine that um – I know that when we were back in um Scotland, um they had a book club, *The Chip Club*, and it was usually something non-fictional, or an Asterix book or something, that would be what I would go for. Um, so until um the last couple of years, I haven't really read for pleasure. I've read non-fiction, and it's I think, I think I just um, in some ways I'd like to think the interest was stimulated by the books I'm reading. Um, but I read them. That's actually another memory: I was having a laugh with someone a couple of days ago, er it was er yes taking me a week to read a commando comic! (*laughs*) I read books really slowly.

D: Yes. So when you were a boy, it actually took you a long time to read a commando comic?

R: Yeah, I would have thought it did, actually; I mean I suppose because, you know we'd pitch tents, we'd got lots of space, so you'd pitch tents and things – this was in the good old days when kids went out to play, you know – big cliffs and a raging sea, but yeah you still go out to play. Um, so yeah I guess er I was slow at reading comics and things like that.

D: What the other kids noticed even at that age, I mean they –

R: I probably noticed; or maybe I'd noticed in the past; because I think I guess the way the measure of time is you'd lend them out, and people would want them back (*laughs*), or they'd give them back before you'd finished them; so I assumed they were reading faster er than me. But whether it actually took me a week, I don't know; maybe I just have a short attention span.

D: Uh huh. Right – another thing. Was that an issue for you at that age?

R: Attention span?

D: Having a short attention span.

R: It seems to be an issue for me just now, because I really need to crack on with my work. I don't know whether that's personality; and that's a discussion really, isn't it, is er, is my attention span um linked to the fact that I get fatigued because I'm putting a lot of effort into my reading and putting sentences together –

D: Yeah.

R: – um and keeping up with it, or is it because I'm in essence a um, a, an extrovert that gets um distracted from a task quicker, and using some sort of personality trait –

D: Yes, chicken and egg, isn't it? Yeah, that's interesting, that.

R: Um, I don't know, I don't know. Um, I wonder, I mean and that's another theme, the having a bit of dyslexia is um, if you're looking for negative experiences, is after a few negative experiences, I decided to 'sod them; the way I'm going to beat you bastards is by doing better'. I mean not that I probably went and studied and stayed in for years and years, but I thought 'I'll show you'. And that's been my attitude, is to play it down because it's the best way to deal with it, I've decided. Um so I wouldn't, I wouldn't like to get into the mode of making an excuse of the dyslexia, by saying 'I have a short attention span because I actually have to put more effort into reading and having to re-read things, and having to um, you know, look through another process to correct errors'. Um, I'll be quite say it's because I'm lazy (*laughs*). But er maybe, I don't know.

Charlotte

C: So I left for university, arrived on the campus, erm, eczema overtook me; I looked like I'd been in ten rounds with Mike Tyson. I had eczema all over my face and I'm sure you know what it's like if you're going to anywhere new, where you're going to meet new people

D: Yes.

C: – you want to look your best; so when you've got your face which is flaking everywhere, it's not really the best impression you want to give.

D: And it was from the stress and tension of –

C: Yeah, I was petrified.

D: – starting a Degree, yeah, yeah.

C: Yeah. So, erm, everything seemed to be going okay. It was my School course which actually pointed out the dyslexia. What actually happened was, I handed in my very very first essay.

D: Mmm.

C: Now the School course was called 'Are We Returning to Morality in the 1990s?' We were talking about spirituality and the teaching of religious education in schools. Erm, we did a chapter from *Folk Devils* and – Folk Devils and Moral Panics perhaps – it was something like that and the whole thing just went over my head and I just thought 'Oh my God, I'm drowning!'

D: Yeah.

C: First essay came back and I've never seen so much red pen in my whole life.

D: Mmm.

C: Erm, she just said 'This is not the standard that we expect at university', erm, 'I don't know what this is here', erm, 'Do something about it'.

D: Mmm, mmm.

C: So I went to my personal tutor; my personal tutor just said 'I don't know what to do about it, Charlotte'. And, so that was at the beginning of October. Erm, more essays came back, erm, and they were just, well they didn't go down too well. Erm, spelling was picked up on terribly; grammar I was just slaughtered for. Erm, I didn't know what was going on until one day I walked into the school office and P just turned around and said to me 'Have you ever thought you could be dyslexic?'

D: Mmm.

C: And I just thought that was the biggest joke out and because also, but it was also like, 'Well, maybe'. Because it was, like, 'At least I know I am not stupid'. Because I just thought, I thought 'Oh my God, what's going on?' Erm, I felt really bad. I was just like you know 'I can see it now, I'm going to be chucked out' –

D: Yeah.

C: – 'going to be sent home'. You know, the whole fame of going to university, especially with my circle of friends would have been, well I would have gone back with my tail between my legs feeling very very sorry for myself.

D: Mmm, mmm.

C: So, I went to the Counselling and Psychotherapy Unit and, and said 'I need a Dyslexia Test. I've been told to come here, you're the people to talk to'.

D: Yeah.

C: And the day before my nineteen –, the day after nineteenth birthday, so this was the 22nd of November, erm, I had a Dyslexia Test with M.

D: M did it?

C: Yeah.

D: Oh he did the Bangor test did he?

C: Yeah. But before I had a session, like there was a previous session when I thought I was having the dyslexia test

D: Mmm.

C: – that's before my birthday, erm, but we basically just went through my, my history, my personal history with the attack and things like that and other things –

D: Yeah.

C: – which, you know.

D: Yeah.

C: Erm, and so we went through that and then I had this dyslexia test and I was sitting in this room, I thought this was piss easy. I was just like, erm, he was asking me these questions and I was having major problems with the Maths, I always remember having major problems with the Maths questions, but with the, er, Bangor test, number sequences and left and right, 'You point with your right hand to my left knee'.

D: All that, yeah.

C: I thought were just the easiest things since sliced bread.

D: Yeah.

C: Er, I literally thought he was having a joke. So when he said 'I'm pleased to tell you that you're dyslexic', it was very odd to hear 'I'm pleased to tell you', 'You've turned out positive and you are dyslexic'. It was just like, half of me was quite chuffed, cos I thought 'Right, well, I'm dyslexic; there's something wrong, but I am not stupid and thick and dumb, and I'm sure there's some miracle cure somewhere out there'.

Gary (1)

D: Did you ask about Learning Support?

G: Oh, I didn't. I didn't even go to see – in fact, it was only – the University contacted me, that I was dyslexic.

D: Because you'd put it on the UCAS form?

G: Yeah, and they'd also had the report sent on.

D: Right. OK.

G: What have you; so it was only the fact that they knew; I would not have even mentioned it. In fact there's a, um a society, a Dyslexia Society, which I get letters from from time to time, which I didn't sign up for and which I have no intention of going to. But I still get letters from it, because the University's put my name and my address down for me. But I mean I have simply no intention of going to ... I see no point in going along and there's a group of dyslexic people there. I mean, what does it matter really? I make my friends because they're my friends, and if they're dyslexic or if they're not dyslexic, it's just not something that I consider; and I don't really see the need for going along to some society about something which is a mere inconvenience to my life! (*laughs*)

Gary (2)

D: What got you going on reading?

G: Um, I liked fantasy adventure things, and um, and my Dad reads all the time, as does my Mum actually – but he tends to read loads of fantasy adventure things like that – and I, I suppose first, I just liked – he gave me a description of one of the stories, and what it was like. And it was part of a trilogy er by Douglas Adams.

D: Oh yes, yes. Didn't he write 'Hitch-hiker's guide to the galaxy'?

G: Yeah, yeah, and what-have-you. And um I really liked it – I didn't actually read those books, but I really liked what he was telling me, and I watched a couple of films. And then there was these other books by David Eddings, that um, that had always been on my bookshelves for quite some time, and um the ten books all in a long row, and it was all very nice books, with all nice covers and what-have-you. And um, so I asked him about those, and he described the story of those, and I would really like them, so I decided to have a go. And I picked one up, and um, and I read the prologue; and it was a pain, and I put it down for three months. And then I picked it up again, and I carried on going through it, and I thought 'give it a bit more of a shot'. And um so I tried a bit more; and er I read the first chapter, I think; and it took me about two hours, but I enjoyed it, it was a nice good story, and I was 'Oh, that's quite good'. And so the next night I read another chapter; and um I started to get into the story. And um, the story grabbed me, which is quite lucky, because it might not have done, and if it hadn't have done I probably wouldn't have read on. But it grabbed me very quickly; and then I started reading more and more of this book. And like, I'd read in the day-time; if I was at home, I could read like three chapters. And I would read more, because I was dying to get onto the next bit of the story; it was really irritating that I was holding back, and I would read more and more. But then I'd get a headache, because I'd read for three chapters, which was the surest thing in the world that would give me a head-ache; there just wasn't the ability to stop it. And um, but I would still have a go, and think 'perhaps I can just squeeze a little bit more before it starts to hurt'. (*Laughs*)

D: Did you get blurring of the print?

G: No, never.

D: Er, or glare: does the, do the lines seem to flash against the white paper?

G: No.

D: You just get the headache from –

G: I would think it's from the concentration.

D: – staring at it, yeah. Ever move a ruler down the page?

G: I sometimes move the bookmark down the page, um, actually I do that quite often as I'm reading down it; sometimes I don't, but sometimes I do. I'm used to sitting in front of a computer as well all day, and so I'm used to looking at text everywhere.

D: Um, yeah.

A: It's quite easy to stare at a page of text and not read a word of it; that is so simple just to – you're looking at a page of text, and all it is, is a jumble of letters, and you think 'right, I've got to start from the beginning', and you go away, look at the first word and off you go.

D: Do you sometimes read to the bottom of a page, and realise you haven't taken any of it in?

A: Oh, all the time. If I reach the end of a line – by the time I've got to the end of a line, I've forgotten the start of it.

Harry

A: The only other thing was, I was keen to get my grant cheque. It was the end of the first year, and there was a little sign on the wall saying 'if you can read this, maybe you should consider, or think about dyslexia' or something. And I read it, and I thought 'well, I can read it'. I read it loads of times, and thought 'well what's wrong with it?' And I realised 'you' was spelt the other way round; it was 'YUO'. And there was another little spelling mistake. And er it wasn't till I'd read it four or five times, I thought 'oh there's spelling mistakes in it, just switched round'. That's it. I get the message.

D: I've never seen that poster. OK, so you thought 'oh yes'.

A: And er I just like talked to my friend. And think when I'm curious – so 'maybe I am'.

D: Yes. So you could face the thought of being assessed, anyway.

A: Yeah.

D: So you came here and did you see – you saw C then?

A: Yeah, initially, and um I was referred to Dr R who did the test.

D: Right. And that's quite gruelling, isn't it?

A: Um yeah. Well it was OK. I think it just comes down to the fact that I kind of – the spelling test meant thinking, you know these are tricky words, and you know 'is it double l here' and – the rest of the test was OK. The spelling test was the worst.

D: The spelling was the only thing that was really bad?

A: Well not the only thing that was bad; it was just when you actually sit the test, you participate in all the various little bits, and it all seems OK. And then he brings the spelling test and you think 'I don't like these words'.

D: So did he see you in just one long session, or two?

A: It was two one-hour sessions.

D: Two sessions, yeah. And then, at the end of the second session, did you say to him 'am I dyslexic or not?' or did you just wait for him to write –

A: No, at the end of the, I think the end of the first session, he said he was a bit, he was not sure, he'd have to go and look at them. But he said it wasn't a bad case of dyslexia. It was after the second – I think it was after he'd looked at the first set of tests and after the second er hour's session, he said that um my spellings were certainly below what you'd expect an undergraduate to be at, with all the kind of education you'd had before. Um I think he described it as 'developmental dyslexia' in the report.

D: Yes. That's opposed to 'acquired', which would be the result of a blow to the head or something. Er, yeah; so how did the report strike you? Did it seem fair?

A: Um, yeah, it was – mainly the report er mentioned the tests, and mentioned the standard deviations away from the normal um results. And they were – although it was, they were quite scary because they were like four standard deviations away from the norm in the spelling test and the test on the phonemes. I was quite worried, although the margin of variance wasn't that big, four standard deviations that was quite a lot. But other parts of the test was quite, been OK really. So I thought it was fair.

D: Yes. What has being achieved – being assessed achieved for you?

A: Um, well, it was a little bit of relief I suppose; like there is some kind of problem. But um you've still got to get down and do the work. I think it's one where there's no kind of 'cure'; you're no different; it's just 'oh you are dyslexic', and you come out and you think 'well, it can't all be bad', so you've still got to carry on exactly the same.

Jemima

D: Your parents got you a tutor?

J: Yeah.

D: And what was that person like?

J: She was lovely – I had, erm, I had two when I was at junior school. I had one who was really lovely, she was a special dyslexic teacher and she was really really good and I learnt a lot with her, she taught me how to, sort of, plan essays and write how I would feel comfortable in writing. And then I changed to another one who wasn't the special dyslexic one and erm, she just didn't understand and erm, I don't think she ever thought I was dyslexic, she just thought I was stupid and that's how I didn't gain anything from being with her at all.

D: Right. But by then you knew you weren't stupid.

J: Yeah. But I don't think she actually believed in dyslexia, herself, so I don't think, she just thought that I was a slow learner, or not very intelligent.(*laughs*)

D: Right. But the first one, you described her as a dyslexia teacher.

J: Yeah, she was –

D: – so you knew about this thing called dyslexia by then?

J: Erm, yeah, cos erm, I had, awful problems seeing when I was younger, I couldn't see, I had problems with my eyes, I don't know what it was but I had to have a patch over one eye-

D: Oh yes.

J: – and so, erm, and then it originated from there that I had to go and see different people and that's when I was diagnosed as dyslexic. I was about nine or something.

D: Ah-huh. Erm, and what were you told that dyslexic meant?

J: Erm, that I had, well I knew it was, I thought it was, like, mainly problems with my eyesight and not being able to read or spell, erm, but nobody actually sat down and explained it to me.

D: Er, did your parents know what it meant, either?

J: Erm –

D: Had they come across it?

J: Not properly – my mum has, erm, very severe spelling problems though, I think, she has never being diagnosed as dyslexic, but she thinks maybe it's originated from there.

D: Mmm.

J: Erm, but I don't think that they've, up until, only when I was like diagnosed as being dyslexic did they actually realise that there was, erm, this thing around.

Lisa

L: Well, erm, I took a year out last year for personal reasons. Erm, my mum died and my dad needed extra help and I thought 'Well, I can't cope with everything'. Erm, and then I thought 'Well, I've done really well in the practical assignments, erm, but my exams are letting me down. Erm, I'm not being fair to myself; if I could get diagnosed as dyslexic I could get extra time in exams'. Er, and I think for the first time I actually was bothered about what grade of degree I might get.

D: Mmm. Yes, yeah.

L: I mean...when I first came, the actual degree at the end of the day was irrelevant, it was just the study that I enjoyed and wanted to do.

D: Yeah. But your sights kind of go up and up don't they?

L: Yes, and I thought 'Well, you know, if you are going to do yourself justice and you're entitled to extra time in the exams then why not get it'.

D: Mmm.

L: So I thought for the final year I'd try and get the extra time. So that was when I came to see –

D: Yes. And she sent you to Dr R?

L: Yes.

D: Who did the assessment?

L: Yes, he did an assessment.

D: Right. And what did you think of what he wrote?

L: Er (pause) I thought...I was very interested in the tests that he did. I was interested that he said, er, that some things I had scored very highly on and some things I hadn't.

D: Yes.

L: Er, he, he highlighted things which I hadn't sort of recognised in myself that I, er, some of the tests he did...well, there was one test in particular where I was just one off 100per cent, and he said if I got that I would have been the first person to do it.

D: Yeah. Mmm.

L: But he didn't really pick up on, er, the possible tracking problem or eye-related problem which I think I have got but I still haven't had it diagnosed. Erm, I was just pleased that he'd said yes I was dyslexic.

D: Yes, of course, yeah.

L: And that I was entitled to extra time; I got what I wanted out of it, so –

D: Yes. Sure. Yeah. Mmm.

L: He did also lend me a filter, a coloured filter, er, to put on reading, which I found helpful; trouble is I keep losing it. Er, but I was fascinated the way it lifts words off the page for me.

D: Yes. Well, you do definitely need a specialist eye test, really now.

L: Yes.

D: But he wouldn't have lent that to you unless you'd talked about the visual effects that you get when you are reading. So –

L: Yes.

D: – did he raise that subject or did you do it?

L: Erm, well, I remember telling him about seeing the credits on the television that flashed rather than scrolled.

D: Ah yes. Right, yes.

L: Erm, I might have told him that my daughter had got a tracking problem.

D: Yes, right.

L: Er, I can remember telling him that I felt that there was something that I still wasn't getting to grips with, erm, and I think it...it was very much a last minute idea, was to try these coloured films.

Phoebe

F: Um, I don't really know what [GCSE grades] I thought I was going to get. I always used to, I think I always used to fob it off, saying I hadn't worked hard enough or something like that. Er, I don't know, I don't know what I thought I was going to get.

D: All the time you also regarded yourself as dyslexic presumably, didn't you, because you talked to your mother about it?

F: Yeah. Yeah, that was always in the back of my mind. But then again, it, it's a kind of excuse isn't it, when I don't think it should be.

D: No, that's true.

F: Cos if you sit there and feel sorry for yourself, 'oh I'm dyslexic, I can't do it', um I mean, as you know, it's not directed, you know, to intelligence is it, so –

D: No, not at all.

F: – I don't think that's really a feasible excuse.

D: But can you remember talking to your mother about what it was like for her, to be dyslexic?

F: Er, yeah, she had a very difficult time with it, because she was one of the first people to sort of be diagnosed. And of course – so before she was, it was like she was stupid you know kind of thing, and um also the other thing was um she wanted to be a nurse, and she was accepted onto quite a few courses, she was going to go to St Thomas'. They found out she was dyslexic and turned round and said 'no, you can't join us'. So, I mean that – she's, that's always been a sort of massive stigma to her. But it's upset her a lot because she's, that's what she's always wanted to do; I think even now, if she could turn back time, I think she'd still want to be a nurse.

D: Yeah. How old were you when she told you those sort of things?

F: Er, probably about 15 or so. So she's quite negative about it, because nobody's ever helped her; um, and er I think she's probably actually worse than me.

D: So she, perhaps she didn't expect anyone to help you, then?

F: Er, probably not, no. Because I think – what I think is, I think it's very difficult for somebody to, who's not dyslexic to try and teach somebody who is, because they don't know. I mean – do you know what I mean?

D: Hmm, yeah. It's a great advantage, isn't it, to have a teacher who really knows what you're seeing things like, or, yeah, sure. But can you remember talking to your Mum about how she coped with her problems?

F: She said that she used – she said 'to survive, we've just got to be different; just got to go about things a different way'. Although I don't think that's my theory; I like to sort of go with the flow, so to speak. But she's subsequently, I mean she'd very sort of self-confident now and loud and that kind of thing, whereas I probably tend to be a bit more reserved, serious.

Sally

D: So, did you feel that he [the EP] understood you?

S: Erm, yeah. I think so. I was actually quite surprised, I mean, with the reading, I was just, always slow at it, and then when he did the test with, er, where you have to read, like, a page and then put it down. Like you have to read it aloud and he'll ask you questions, and I was just sitting there going, 'Oh, come on, you've just read this page, how can you not remember?' I couldn't for the life of me remember what I'd just read and I thought, 'Well, that's why in multiple choice I have to read it three or four times', and for other things as well.

D: Yes.

S: It made things a lot more clear in the end.

D: Yes. Erm, did you agree with what he wrote in this report?

S: Er, yeah. Actually, I haven't read it for quite a long time, I don't think I ever thought –

D: But, did he tell you at the time, did he talk to you about what he thought, or did he say 'You'll have to wait until I think about it and present my report to you'?

S: No, he, erm, well, he said for the reading especially, he said that he probably would recommend extra time and, er, he outlined what he thought, briefly, what I had difficulties with, and then he said 'I'll follow it up with a report. Send it on to you'.

D: Right, okay. Erm, it says here that he put revision technique notes in with it.

S: Yeah.

D: Was that any use to you?

S: Er, –

D: Or was that stuff you were doing already?

S: I don't know. I can't remember if I read it, to be quite honest with you.

D: Okay. Right but this report served the purpose of getting you the extra time anyway?

S: Yeah.

D: For the A-Levels. Erm, and it confirmed to you your high IQ because you knew anyway, didn't you?

S: Well, I didn't before this test, no.

D: Ah, OK.

S: I think my mum had told me, but, you know how it is, you don't think, you just think 'You're just saying that because you're my mum', sort of thing. She always says 'You're very intelligent' and you're like 'You've got to say that'.

D: Yes. Yeah. So –

S: So I was, er wasn't really surprised at that.

D: Yes. So, you got the extra time and you've got bearable grades in your A-Levels, but did you feel they reflected your real ability?

S: Well, I got a B in Maths, erm, that was a lot to do with, 50per cent of it, the actual mark, was small tests and coursework. So, that helped a lot.

D: Yes.

S: Erm, so, but then I got a D in History and Economics and I, History I thought 'Okay, fair enough, there is so much to learn for that, so many facts' I mean, I loved History, I still do, but, it's just, it wasn't really the subject that I should have taken. But I don't regret taking it, because I did enjoy it, it was a good two years. But when it came down to learning everything and remembering everything it was a very hard subject to take.

D: Yes.

S: Very hard.

D: Were there any teachers that stand out in the sixth form, as being good or bad?

S: Er, in the sixth form, (pause) I don't know. I think they were pretty average. Erm, Mr F, he was my History teacher, and he did realise that, my mum had told him I was dyslexic, and he used to, he did circle my spellings but he used to write the correct one on top of it, rather than just say, 'That's wrong, that's wrong', and he never used to penalise me for them, and he always used to, erm, sort of help me plan the essays and so he was good, he did try and help a lot. Erm, but, I don't know. Economics, she was, Miss W was aware that I was dyslexic but I don't think she really understood it. Because I'd try and explain. She'd say that she could never understand why I couldn't do well in my essays, in comparison to when I talked in class, or whatever. And I would be 'Well, that's because of my dyslexia'. and she'd be, like, 'Oh right', and sort of think 'She's just not revising', sort of thing.

Susan

S: Then I went on to see J (*learning support organiser*) who was....I shall never forget that day as long as I live, because just speaking to her, erm, she seemed to be so aware of the difficulties I had... and what I was going through, and she said 'Do you want to be assessed?' and I said 'Well, part of me does and part of me doesn't.'

D: Mmm.

S: Because if they say 'You have got no problem' how do I account for, for the way I feel? Erm, it would be taking away a sort of crutch I've had... So, er, I felt quite emotional about that and she said 'Well, I can ask you some questions and things... and I can sort of assess roughly...whether you are dyslexic or not, would that help?' And I said, 'Yeah, it might reassure me.' And so she asked me some silly questions like, er, 'What colour is Thursday?' and things like that.

D: Ah, yes.

S: And things about balance, erm, because I was doing Yoga at the time and found it very difficult to stand on one foot. I said 'No, my balance is not very good.' Definitely. I have to lean on a wall to do Yoga and things like that.

D: Yes, yes.

S: And gave me lots of advice about using coloured acetate for photocopying, which cut down on my headaches, and all sorts of helpful things and, and she was saying, 'You know, it isn't really a disability, as such, it's just a different way of your brain copes with things. It's because we're forcing it to do something it shouldn't be doing.'

D: Mmm.

S: Just thinking differences really...whatever that word is.

D: Right, yeah.

S: And that was encouraging and I began to feel better about things and not feel so thick.

D: So, yeah, she then wrote you a recommendation for the exam office then, did she?

S: Well, no, I had to go and see a psychologist... Er, her name escapes me, but she was ever so nice... very encouraging.

D: It was J you saw, wasn't it?

S: No, Er...

D: It wasn't?

S: No, the name would, if somebody said it I would remember immediately.

D: P.

S: That's it. Yes, she was very nice.

D: Right, erm, but, so when you saw P you were, er, forty something by then weren't you?

S: Mmm, yes.

D: It was only a couple of years ago...

S: Yes.

D: And you were forty three or something...

S: Yes.

D: Right, and it was the first time you had been formally fully assessed.

S: Yes.

D: Yeah, so you had the whole works didn't you, the Wechsler intelligence scale...

S: Yes, yes.

D: Yeah. Now, that's a pretty exhausting experience isn't it?

S: It was, but she, she was very relaxed. It...I...I didn't feel pressurised, erm, yes, she was very encouraging, you know... I didn't feel I was being tested, I felt I was being helped.

D: Right. And you got a long report on all that...

S: Mmm, yes.

D: And I think what I am most interested in is how the report struck you. Did you recognise yourself in it?

S: Yes, erm, because P went over it before I left in some way. Erm, for instance, the...the retaining, erm, numbers and things... She was explaining about all these different things and what it meant and how, how it all worked that when I got it, it, it was roughly what she had said, erm, it did help.

D: Mmm.

S: It made me realise that my problems were not intellectual I suppose is the right word but they were actually practical learning difficulties, things that I'd managed to overcome. Sometimes and other times I couldn't and er, I, I'd already, obviously was very aware that my verbal skills were very good, and that I was quite fluent at reading and so on, so that didn't come as a surprise, erm, but it is nice to know that the manual dexterity, for instance and things like that were also there, that were holding me back.

Will

D: You thought, 'Why am I good at maths and science and I can't do this?'

W: Yeah. I mean I thought that up until – well, up until I was fifteen. I mean my Mum pressed the school to keep checking, 'check if he's dyslexic', whatever, but the school didn't act on that.

D: Ah. So your Mum had heard of dyslexia?

W: Yeah. Erm, my Mum ... my Mum's ... one of my Mum's best friends is, erm, works ... my Mum works in a special school and my Mum's ... but she was only a nursery nurse in the sort of special school so – but her ... one of the women she works with, her son was dyslexic and he was diagnosed whilst he was in the infants, so she'd heard of it.

D: Ah, right. So, your Mum thought it was probably – it applied to you?

W: I was actually tested in the juniors as well, but – and they said 'Well, we know he's good at science, we know he's good at maths, we know he's good at visual coordination, but he can't write properly'. And they said, 'We'll check him in the high school'. But they didn't check in the high school either, properly.

D: Ah-huh. Who was this person who tested you in the juniors?

W: Erm, it was some, I think, EP.

D: Yeah. And with the whole ... it was a long session?

W: Yeah, well, it seemed a long time – it was probably about half an hour.

D: Yeah, it does seem a little bit like that. But it wasn't a whole, sort of, intelligence test thing like you must have had later?

W: No, I don't think so.

D: Right. So you'd heard of dyslexia when you were, what, eight or nine?

W: Well, maybe not when I was eight or nine, I think when I was about twelve or thirteen, I started thinking, 'Well, there has got to be something '.

D: Right. Your mother had heard of it before that –

W: Yeah.

D: But she didn't discuss it with you?

W: Erm, well, I mean, they used to ask me why I wasn't very good and things like that –

D: Yeah, yeah.

W: – but, I don't know. I mean a lot...most of the teachers used to just say 'He's lazy, can't be bothered doing the work'.

D: Yes. How did you feel about that?

W: It made me pretty mad.

D: Yes. Yeah. You didn't believe it; you didn't come to believe that you were actually not bothering?

W: No, I mean I always felt that I was trying.

D: Yeah.

W: And I knew that, I knew what I was trying to do, sort of thing, but every time I started writing garbage came out, the wrong to what I thought it should come out.

D: So, how did your feelings come out? I mean, did you used to play up in class or –

W: Erm, I never used to... I think I'd just start daydreaming or something like that, my attention would just disappear from the subject as soon as the teacher said, 'Why aren't you working? Why aren't you working?'

D: Yes, yes.

W: I mean, after a bit you just like think 'I can't be bothered doing this because –

D: It's completely beyond me?

W: Yeah.

D: Yes. So it looked like not bothering?

W: Yeah, but the rest of the class had, say, progressed past a certain stage and I would be left behind.

D: Yes.

W: And the teacher would be like pressing the rest of the class and trying to drag me along with them, sort of thing.

The 'Hemispherists'

Adrian (1)

D: So who was it then, somebody at B ... somebody at B Uni who said you might be dyslexic, was it then?

A: Erm, no, it was actually a friend of mine who was doing a Masters in Human Computer Interaction.

D: Oh, yeah.

A: Er, I was sitting down doing maths one day and he said 'You've got such a strange way of doing something.'

D: Ah-ha, yeah.

A: And he literally, he'd done A-Level Psychology...

D: Yeah.

A: And he was doing Psychology then. And, erm, we sat down and talk, talked about semantic episodes...

D: Yes.

A: And things along this line and erm, I sat down and read his memory book, like how the memory actually works...

D: Ah, yes.

A: I was like 'Hang on a second'...

D: 'Sounds like me, this.' Yes.

A: 'What's this dyslexia?'

D: Yes.

A: And he went, 'Ah, that's so and so' and I said 'Yeah, but doesn't that sound familiar.' He said 'Yeah, but then I am as well.'

D: Yeah.

A: And it's like you're low...you're not as much as...I do this and this but does this make us...

D: Yeah.

A: We had to define... In ourselves...What we thought dyslexia was.

D: Right.

A: So I went along to this woman and erm, just up in...

D: What, what woman?

A: H. I've actually got my dyslexia report, still...

D: Right.

A: If you want to have a look at it?

D: Yes, yes please, that would be interesting, yeah. So, how did you get to the woman in H?

A: Er, went in and talked to the Learning Support Unit and they booked me up, with this lady in H, not H...

D: No.

A: She's out by the –.

D: J.

A: That's the lady.

D: Yeah, yeah.

A: You go in a room and, er, a child's room. It's just the sky with a painted tree in the corner and things like this.

D: Very delightful, yes.

A: It's like I am in a dyslexic house, I love it.

Adrian (2)

D: So, you were saying that somebody there said, 'Well, you could go and see this woman and be assessed if you want'.

A: And see what happens.

D: Right, and was the report enlightening?

A: Oh, yeah, blew me away, blew me away!

D: In, in a good way, or a bad way?

A: Literally. Well she blew me away when I was there. It was like the words, she'd read out, like big words and go slow and she'd speed up and speed up and speed up and there would be smaller and smaller and smaller amounts of text, I'd be like 'ffff' and I was getting into it, sort of thing...

D: Mmm.

A: Really getting into it because I knew it was a test.

D: Yes.

A: And it's just a bit too much. Erm, and she was timing me which is the worst one because I can hear the seconds going down. Erm...

D: Yes, yes.

A: And I was working on that but – she said 'Right, okay, what can you remember?' 'fffff', and she was like 'Grand, grand, okay, okay.' Nowhere through did you know if you were doing good or bad, at all...

D: No.

A: Which was nice, because it didn't prejudge anything...

D: Yes.

A: Or let me prejudge anything and then it came to the pictures and it's like a dog and a car and woman and a car with a lead and silly things, and when it came to that she said I got it back to front, and I'm like, 'That's completely impossible, that is the right way round, do you understand why it's that way round?' and she said, 'Yes, but this is why it is this way round.' It's like 'No, that's impossible, because if that is that way round why is she in the car when she is doing that?' And she was like 'Yeah, that's actually quite possible.' And it's like 'I don't understand it.'

D: Mmm.

A: And she said 'No, but it's round for this reason.' She gave me some really technical reason...

D: Mmm.

A: That was a load of hock, really. But, erm, she said 'Alright, now we'll put your scores on this,' like a line, she said 'If you got a line you're normal'. And then mine were just like the Himalayas, so it was just like 'ffff' – 'What does that mean?' She said 'You're dyslexic.' 'Oh, grand. What does that mean? I don't understand.'

D: Right. Well, that's interesting. So, you, you actually said that to her, did you?

A: What's that?

D: What does it mean? What does dyslexic mean?

A: Yeah. I wanted to know what her definition was.

D: Right and...

A: Not what mine was or what the book said.

D: What did you think of her definition?

A: Hock, again.

D: Yes.

A: It was like, 'No, this is a bit, you can say what you want but that doesn't fit me.' And then a year later I was travelling the Internet and they said 'Oh we've discovered twenty-five types of dyslexia.' And it's like, 'Well, what are you on about?'

Eliza

E: I went to one of her, her study skills things, and dyslexia had not ceased to be an issue for me, but it was something that I dealt with myself, and for a long time I hadn't been used to other people around me saying 'dyslexia, dyslexia'. And so I went to one of G's things, and everyone just sat there for an hour, and said about the experiences they had had, about teachers yelling at them and stuff like that, and I just couldn't cope with it; and I thought 'what a load of bullshit, these people are not learning anything, they're just moping'; and now I think I see that, you know, they needed to get it out because they obviously hadn't discussed it with anybody else, and they needed more like a counselling session; but for me, it just drove me crazy, and I just left. And I didn't get back in contact with G until this year. But I did use dyslexia for its concessions, for its extra time, um for the photocopy card that you get, and stuff like that – so I used it for its advantages, but I didn't go to any of the support systems.

D: You've had extra time on your exams as well?

E: Yeah. So I've used it, but I haven't – I've benefited from it, but I haven't given anything to it. So I feel a bit bad about that, but it just put me off so much in my first year, just the way everyone was rabbiting on about 'the teacher made me do this, and the teacher made me do that', and I was like 'just cope with it, guys, you know, move on to the next stage', but obviously they weren't ready to move on to the next stage.

D: No; they needed to get that out and share that, and realise that there were others who'd had the same experiences –

E: Exactly. But I'd passed that.

D: – as a base to build the group on, but you had passed that, yes.

E: So I couldn't accept that people were like that. But um, this term I've done the – because in your final year you're allowed to do basic modules, and this is a basic module, so I thought 'well, this would be the ideal thing to be doing', and so I did it. Um, and, I mean, it's brought dyslexia back into my life in sort of a sleeping way, because it hadn't, it was again something you know that I'd sort of dealt with quite well inside, but, we did – this class very much taught me that dyslexia is part of my life, as opposed to part of my academic learning. Like, it's not – when I leave here, when I leave academic learning, I'm not gonna leave dyslexia.

D: So you went to the study skills course?

E: Oh yes; it's like, all the learning skills things that she does, that you usually just go to, she's running it as a whole module. So you get the study skills, you get the um learning styles, and you get this grammar component.

D: OK, great; um, and that's been worth doing?

E: Um, it's – yeah, I mean it's perhaps brought awareness more than anything else, because everyone was talking about you know the coping strategies that they've learned, about how they have to write lists, and they have to write, um, how to spell all the different numbers on the inside of their cheque book because they can spell them, but they can't spell them under pressure, and all these things. And I've just found that um perhaps almost unknowingly I've done all these coping strategies – you know I've 'been there, done that', and, but they're just putting a label to it and bringing it out, sort of thing.

D: Yes.

E: And also – the one thing that I enjoyed very much was the different learning styles, and the left-hand brain and the right-hand brain, the alternative learning style sort of thing, with the mind maps and using colours and stuff like that, which really is the only thing that I found useful and interesting enough.

Geraldine (1)

G: The dyslexia is a disability; your thinking strengths are not.

D: Right.

G: But yes. The language confusion that is not automatic – to me that feels like a disability. Yes and I think it is a disability. I think it's a totally unnecessary disability; that if people appreciated the differences, I mean, the chap I hope to work with next summer brought his, erm, school report with him that went all the way through his secondary school. He was really willing. Brilliant report as to how nice he was and everything; 'must try better on his written work', 'must take heed of the comments that are made', and, you know, and if people only knew 'Hey, hang on, this chap's likeable, willing, what's going wrong? We must investigate this and see what we can do to try something else to help him'.

Geraldine (2)

D: We were talking about your model of dyslexia –

G: Yeah.

D: – and you were saying it feels like a definite disability.

G: Mmm.

D: How do you react to the Thomas West type of line about gifted, famous –

G: Oh, I think, I also, to say it's a disability is not to be contradicting people who say we've got these gifts, because yes, I think the gifts are definitely there and because those gifts weren't recognised, erm, I mean, I think, what I think happens is that as you were saying, you learnt that you're an auditory person and not a visual person.

D: Mmm.

G: Now if all your teaching, all your learning was done in a visual way you'd be struggling.

D: Mmm, mmm.

G: So what I think it is, is very much like the left-handed person and the right-handed person. If you try and make a dyslexic person learn in a way that is inappropriate for them, that is, if you don't understand their gifts and use those, then language is learnt in a muddle and becomes non- automatic. So I have no problem with dyslexia both being a disability that has been acquired through inappropriate learning and it's because of gifts that are not being appreciated.

D: Yes. But, some dyslexic people get the false impression that when it is determined that they are dyslexic therefore they must be gifted in some other way, and they can be disappointed.

G: Erm, well –

D: I mean, everyone's got relative strengths, relative strengths and weaknesses, but that's not the same as being gifted in some way.

G: No. It isn't.

D: Or automatically having a brilliant three-dimensional imaging ability.

G: No. I have no visual three-dimensional capacity at all.

D: No, but there is this idea around that if you are dyslexic you must have that somewhere –

G: Yeah.

D: – and you've only got to discover it.

G: Yes. No, I don't think that's true.

Rachel

D: What would you say if you met a young person who was still at school, who said 'I'm dyslexic and I don't think I will be able to go to university, cos I'll never cope'.

R: I'll probably say bollocks.

D: Yes.

R: No, I would just say, I'd say, 'Well, it's natural to think that but you might as well give it a try because you are only young once'. And my sister has always said to me, she said 'You've got to work so long, you might as well go and have a laugh at university for a few years'. And I've picked the wrong course. But no, she said, you know 'You might as well, you're all entitled to it, they can turn you down. But, you know, go and see, you can always leave, there's no shame if you leave university, if you can't cope'. But there's ways they'll help you. There is. I'd just say that, that it's worth a try anything's worth a try.

D: Yeah.

R: At least you can say you've been there, cos you might think for the rest of your life, you might think 'Ohh, I wished I'd tried'. There's no need being...you got to...and the thing is the more people that go that are dyslexic the more people are going to recognise it and they're not going to think you're stupid. Cos when you say that you're at university, and something comes up about how you're dyslexic like it's one of your mates and you go 'Oh, my God'.

D: Yeah.

R: But it's like telling people that it's OK.

D: Yes, OK. Now, just another sort of hypothetical question: if you were in a pub, say, tonight and the word dyslexic was mentioned and someone you'd met in the pub, some new friend, new acquaintance said 'Oh I've never heard of dyslexia, what is it?' What would you say to them?

R: What would I say?

D: How would you describe dyslexia?

R: How would I describe it? I could give them the Latin meaning.

D: Yes.

R: I'd probably say, I'd say it just means that you learn in a different way. And that certain, the normal way can make things difficult and it just takes, sometimes, a little bit longer, but there is ways of, you know. I'd just kind of say it doesn't mean there's any different intelligence. I'd probably say 'I'm more superior'. No, I just, I got told it's cos your brain, you just think a different way, you just, you just think differently and you just have problems with spelling and reading, you just, and that's it really, I suppose; and sometimes, we're not all practical I'd probably say.

D: Mmm. Right.

R: It's dead hard to describe it though, cos it just means, dyslexic, it means difficulty doesn't it in, erm, is it reading or writing?

D: Well with the lexicon, yeah, everything, both really. But is it more than that? You were talking about the way you learn, and the way you think.

R: It's sequencing essays though I find, I'm finding problems with sequencing.

D: Yes. But it sounds as though the OT Department is doing pretty well. Do you agree with that? You're pleased with –

R: Yeah. They could change Anatomy. I think they could make Anatomy a bit, cos I have been to see and ask my teacher and said, you know, 'You're going too quick'. And she goes 'Well, if you can't keep up then you shouldn't be on the course'. But she is just a really old lady and she's really sweet, she's my personal tutor and she's a sweetie, she's really lovely but I don't think she realises. It sounds really awful for her to be an OT and everything but I don't think she realises, but apart from that everyone else is, they are pretty okay.

D: So, how would you like the Anatomy to be taught, if you could redesign the –

R: Redesign it? The thing is though, she said 'You could go for extra lessons', but if you don't get it in the first place you feel thick when she asks you questions you don't understand. But everybody feels the same. The Anatomy is not taught very well I don't think, it's just so rushed and there's not enough time. Maybe – she draws diagrams but they're 2D and it's done so quickly. Maybe if we did more dissection, cos we go to see it, but it's done that quick, but maybe, if you actually had to dissect the arm yourself and saw the layers, I know it would take a lot longer, but that would be a really good way, cos it's 3D. Or maybe get those models, let us all have a model each, and you learn.

Robert (1)

R: If someone said to me beforehand, like 'oh he's dyslexic', I'd have thought like 'is he writing you know just pages and pages of drivel', kind of thing, non-sensical stuff.

D: Yeah. Um, what are you like with spoken information? I mean can you, can you take in someone's phone number and write it down –

R: No, not phone numbers. I mean um when I moved um it took me about, I think about 12 months before I knew my phone number. Because it – it's always an incredibly embarrassing thing. It's very small, but – you'd speak to somebody on the phone, and they'd go 'oh yeah, well give me your phone number and I'll phone you back'. And you go (*pause*) 'er, no that's OK, I'll phone you'. I just could never remember; and in the end I used to have it written down next to the phone.

D: Yes. That's the sort of strategy that people do, yeah. What about writing cheques, and things where you have to spell numbers?

R: Yeah, I always get – well, quite often get them mixed-up, yes. And you get people you know getting a right cob on with you, and thinking 'what are you trying to do here, pass a bad cheque?' It might be like for, I don't know, £82 or something, and you try and write you know 28 or something. Or 3s, I often write 3s backwards, you know, things like that.

D: Yes; and what do you say when people say 'are you –'

R: I used to just say 'oh I'm really sorry', kind of thing, but now I just say 'I'm sorry, like I'm dyslexic and I do that all the time'. And they go 'oh yeah, weirdo', but it doesn't bother me now.

D: Yeah. It's much easier when you can be just up-front about it.

R: Yeah, I just tell everyone, you know. Because all the lads here take the mickey out of me, because you know I go and sit my exams in a separate room because I get a bit more time; and they call it the incontinence room, because it's where all the people go who freak out in exams, you know.

Robert (2)

R: I was doing um Politics, Early History, which was renaissance to reformation, and Social Psychology (*Access course*). And it was during the Social Psychology that the lecturer said to me, 'have you ever been assessed?' blah blah blah. That was the link.

D: Yes, ah; and how did you react when he said that?

R: Um, initially I kind of said you know 'don't be stupid' like; I couldn't have got this far and it wouldn't have been picked up. I just did not think it was possible to get to nearly 30 without someone saying to you somewhere down the line, 'look have you ever, you know, or you may be dyslexic' or whatever. But um, anyway the long and the short of it was, she said 'I think you ought to go and see your doctor and try and get an assessment'. So I went to my doctor, and my doctor said 'don't be bloody stupid, you couldn't have got to this age without –' So I went back and told her, and said 'yeah, I told you, even my doctor says', you know. And she said 'no', she said, 'you must go and be assessed, simply because you will – I know that you'll need the extra time, in exams'. And so I was chatting to my Mum and Dad about it; I didn't have any money at the time; so my Dad said well, if you want, you know, go and – I'll pay for you to go and get assessed. So I was kind of – the more I learnt about it, the more it began to recognise.

D: Ah – so how did this learning about it take place?

R: Er, mainly through the lecturer, who began to explain to me what it was, and what the common symptoms of it were. And she introduced me to a dyslexic student that was there; and when I spoke to her, I suddenly realised that there was many many things that, you know –

D: The pattern of things.

R: Yeah, even to the point of, you know, someone telling you to go left and you turn right, when you're driving down the road and things like that. Um, it was just little things like that really that suddenly began to click, and I thought 'oh shit, maybe I'd better go and get assessed'.

Ron

R: (*on Access course*) I didn't like the essay; I hated writing it, I had a hell of a problem with it. And deadlines came up, and I had one – this was – we had exams in June, and this was May, and in the end I just said 'sod it' and put this piece of work in. I forgot to put it through the spell-check, and it came back, and she said 'well, what's going on here? This isn't your normal standard. Well what's gone wrong?' And I just pulled this word out of my head, that 'oh I must be a bit dyslexic' sort of thing, 'always had a problem with spelling', and I think I got a bit angry, because she said 'fair enough, settle down, we'll talk about it again' sort of thing.

D: Yes.

R: And I came back the next week and said to her 'look, there's got to be some-thing wrong here. I can't be this thick. I don't have a problem anywhere else. Why have I got a problem with this? Is it dyslexia, whatever dyslexia is? And she said 'what are you saying? Are you saying that you want a test?' And I said 'Oh shit, I suppose I am, really' (*laughs*). And she said 'right, fair enough, I'll see what I can do'. The next week I had an appointment with someone I'd never met before, who was the support tutor for the college. Er, I walked – she was in an office. I walked part the door I think 4 times before I actually walked through the door. Er, and I can remember sitting there on this chair doing these silly little tests, which she was very supportive about, and literally there was sweat running down between my shoulder-blades. I was well wound up. Um, and we did all these silly little tests, one of which was 'can you read this book?' or this passage in this book. And er she said 'you're a bit, when you read out loud you're a bit um stop-start, you're not very smooth', and then she said, 'take this piece of acetate, this blue stuff on, does that make it any easier?' and it was like somebody had switched the light on in the room! I thought 'this is amazing! What's happened?' you know. And so we went through all these different colours, and I came up with the blue one. So I was carrying these little plastic sheets around, and I found out I have a problem with black on white, especially bright white. So that caused me a problem; fluorescent lights also cause me a problem, um, which gives me headaches and what have you – at least they do when I'm not wearing my glasses. So um we talked over what I could do and what I couldn't do and all the rest of it, and she suggested an Access course.

So um I went home and talked it over with my wife. She wasn't too happy at the thought of me giving up work for a year, but in the end she said 'well look, you know, if you've got to do it, you've got to do it', so I had all the psychological assessments done, and believe it or not, I got 15 minutes extra for every hour of the English and maths exams. But the psychological assessment for that didn't actually come through until – the exam was at 2 o'clock in the afternoon, and they got the assessment from the psychologist at 9 o'clock in the morning (*laughs*). The support tutor went to the psychologist and picked up the report, brought it back to college and faxed the exam board, so that I could actually get the time in the afternoon. It was that close, you know?

D: Yeah. Golly.

R: Um, but I did both the English and Maths, and Maths was causing me an awful problem, um, because I hadn't had the support. But, I went into it, and I got my calculator out, and I didn't need the fifteen minutes. And I came out with a C. The only thing I had a problem with was algebra. I still can't get my mind round algebra.

Stephen

D: What would you like them (the university) to be doing that they aren't doing?

S: I don't really know, really, because I feel I'm not really that badly affected by dyslexia, that's my sort of opinion. Because I find I did quite well in the – I'm not doing too badly on the course; I seem to keep up with all the lectures, and so I feel I'm all right in myself about things. But I'd like to – I think the main thing that I would do is educate the staff and other people about it, because like everyone's, doesn't really have a clue; they think 'oh, how's it going?' Are you capable, you know, 'are you cured yet?' and stuff like that.

D: Right, OK. So, let's imagine then that you've been asked to speak, that there's a room full of lecturers who've come on a staff development course about dyslexic students, and you've been asked to speak about 'what is dyslexia?' What would you say to them?

S: I wouldn't know how to start really. I'd try and like – people asking things – you can't, I can't really explain it, because like there's like reading problems and things like that, but it's not really that, and they don't seem to understand like you can't learn it that way, but you can learn it this way. They don't seem to be able to see that. So I don't know how – I just wouldn't know how to put it into words, really. I don't know if – maybe the more diagrammatic it is, I find it easier to remember, which is quite good – like as I say, in the Geology Department they're quite good with the diagrams and flowing into things, the sort of system. And examples probably as well, I always find that helps; but I don't really know how I'd advise a lecturer or lecturers; I don't really know what's best for them. It doesn't seem too bad, what the Geology lot are doing.

D: Right. Um, so, you said something just now about, something about being taught the way that is best for you, being presented the best way. Um, does that mean that you don't – you don't regard it as a kind of illness any more?

S: I've never really regarded it as an illness. I thought 'it's just like something you're born with, and you have to adapt round it'.

D: Yeah. Um, have you come across any ideas about different types of brain?

S: I've heard of a few things; I haven't really sort of paid much like – when I was young, my Mum and Dad got quite into all the books and stuff; because I don't read books at all really, because it takes me too long, I've never sort of got into the book concept, I've never really looked at it. But I've heard theories about, hemispheres are larger, and I don't know really what's what and what's not.

D: Yeah. Does it interest you to look into –

S: Everything, I'd like to sort of find out more. I find, yeah, I find I've got definitely more of the – I find I've got really good spatial and visual skills; or not everyone that I know is quite as observant as I am – I notice things that a lot of people don't. But, I find that the education system is just narrowed along one little line. Like all your other skills – I find – I used to quite like art-work and all that stuff; because I didn't choose that line, it's gone, it's blocked out because I just don't do it any more. And like I find that it's very, all a very narrow and one-track system.

The 'Campaigners'

Aarti

A: The lecturers are very good, they're always asking how I'm getting on, if I am struggling in my work, they will say, 'look, do you need an extension?' Stuff like that.

D: Good. Are they doing that as a result of B's (EP) report being circulated, or were they doing it anyway?

A: They're doing it as a result of B's report.

D: Great. So, as soon as their awareness was raised a small amount, they started responding?

A: Yeah.

D: Well, that's very good. So, the other things you've got – you've got extra time in the library, have you? Can you have books out for longer?

A: Yes, I can. But I've had to go in and ask for that; it should be automatically on the record.

D: Yes.

A: Things like that should automatically be on your record, so when you enrol, it says dyslexia, so when you enrol for your library card, they get the information. It should be on the card when you write it down: 'are you dyslexic?' Because we need extra time. There are days when I go in and they say 'fines', and I say 'but I've been allowed to have it for longer'.

D: They don't all know.

A: No. And just silly things, like er, I wanted to go into the IT suite, you know, and I couldn't do something on the computer, so I went over to him and I said, 'look, you know I'm dyslexic so I need to use the computer, but I don't know what to do, help!' and he goes, 'oh, there's a booklet over there, read it and that'll tell you what to do'. I've just said I'm dyslexic and he's told me to, he's just told me that it's written on the first page of the booklet! Now lucky for him, I can read, very well; what about if it's been someone who was a very very poor reader? For him to turn round and say, you know, for someone to say, 'look, I'm dyslexic, help', and he says 'go and read a book', was a bit pathetic.

D: Yes, yes. A lot more awareness needed.

A: Not just academic staff; I mean other University staff: I'm talking about the IT suite, the library, people at the offices; it needs to be made aware of.

D: Would you like the instructions for using the computer on a cassette? You could sit with a Walkman on in front of the thing, and a voice would say 'do this' –

A: Do that, do the other- that's what should be there. Or even come over and help, show me – I mean, I look at it once and I'll know what to do again.

Lance

L: Starting from the second year, I've started to have migraines. I think that's probably the stress of the campaign, and also the stress caused by people at University not giving me the support and facilities, and me running around, and..... I have to admit at times I've also been rather depressed etc about the situation. I'd say, one thing if you're going to set up a dyslexic unit, one thing you need is a trained counsellor.

D: Yes, absolutely. There's a counselling service though, isn't there, the sort of general one?

L: There is, yes, but I've never used it, for the simple reason I don't know how good it is, and also since I've worked with people, I feel very awkward going and saying 'can you counsel me', because I'd probably be going and seeing them and trying to improve the facilities etc. So I set up a Dyslexic Society, really for other people that are dyslexic. Unfortunately, I haven't yet found – I'm probably going to be meeting those people, so I'm in a situation where –

D: Yes, you'd rather meet them as that than as a client. Yes, OK. So, you call it the Dyslexia Society?

L: The Student Dyslexia Society.

D: How many members have you got?

L: Um, on the books we had about um 18 or so. We've had the problem of giving information. People come to the meetings and say 'we think we might be dyslexic, what can you do?' I give them the list of facilities, money etc. They don't join – they just toddle off and use the information etc. So the Society's.... Originally I set it up at (the other university in the city) and this place (Burton-forth). The one at (the other university) has just stagnated, because basically people here were wanting to help and do things, but at the other place basically they're just wanting the information without doing any of the work. I think any organisation supporting dyslexics probably comes across that situation. You need the support groups, I think it's important. I think I learnt more from the support of having a group of dyslexic people around me. I was suffering from migraines – I don't know if they were connected to dyslexia. The migraines might have been – I might be allergic to certain colours, like on the computer screen. I've done some reading around dyslexia , and I've heard about the coloured specs. And there are other things: shared feelings and problems at school.

D: Yes. What do you do at the meetings, then?

L: Basically it was a group of dyslexics talking, also giving advice. It was meant to be more, but it never got to that stage, because basically I just didn't have the time to run it singly, and I'm now hopefully going to use whatever information I've got on this dissertation, to try and persuade for some money to get a full-time officer to run those things and the likes.

Mel (1)

D: Yes. So, yeah, you've said a lot of things that show that you know, you know yourself pretty well. About your character, your personality and your cognitive style.

M: Some of it is because of what I want to do; I'm consciously assessing what I do and relating it to other dyslexics. Having dyslexic nieces, you tend to be aware of where we're similar, where we're different, and how completely different you can be, while still being dyslexic.

D: Yes, sure. But dyslexia is obviously – it's a very central thing in your life, isn't it.

M: Yes.

D: You want your work to be focused around it in future?

M: I think I quite like being dyslexic. I think it doesn't bother me to a point where I – I actually found it odd being in a module that was all dyslexics, and eventually I think came to the conclusion that I rather liked having the excuse of doing things differently because I was dyslexic (*laughs*). But I found a room full of them was rather off-putting. Did find it a little odd being also addressed as a group: 'dyslexics find this, dyslexics find that', and by the third week, I was sick of being told 'dyslexics anything'. We would have done sort of fine!

Mel (2)

M: But I'm not even convinced that dyslexia is going to stay as dyslexia.

D: Ah, yes.

M: Um, delving into the psychology, I fear is sort of – they won't let you use it as a sort of blanket term, rather split it down 'acquired dyslexia' and 'developmental dyslexia'. If you start doing that, which I think is reasonable because you bring in confusions and other effects that might be due to, say, accidents, I'm then not sure that within developmental dyslexia, how much of a blanket term it's become to cover a family of problems perhaps, rather than being uniformly just 'dyslexia'.

D: It is, isn't it.

M: Mmm. I feel that – probably there are some quite distinct sub-groups.

D: Yeah.

M: But I don't know whether it would be beneficial – because is the point of the exercise to say that we ought to be more accepting of different styles, so does it really matter that there's three styles or four styles or five styles within dyslexia, do you need to do it?

D: Right, yeah.

M: If you're going to teach everybody, right-brained and left-brained, a sort of approach that you call on all the senses, make it multi-media, is that something that works exclusively, just for dyslexics, or isn't it a thing which everybody does better with? So in a way, if you dealt with that, would you be making the issue of being dyslexic almost redundant?

Patrick

P: Well the placement is a year out in industry. Um, I went to Nuclear Electric, which in hindsight did do a lot for me, but also it was a big mistake because it was the wrong company. I went – well, no, it was right company, wrong department I went to work in. The thing about that, we had to produce monthly reports for the senior manager, that's the head of the whole department, and um I kept submitting it again and again and again, and then there was one of them I got sent back to me because of the English in it.

D: So it was the English rearing its head again?

P: Yeah. It was the – I was going 'hang on, what's wrong here?' And um –

D: What didn't they like about them? Was it the spelling?

P: Spelling, and the grammar, that was another thing, I got that back. So um I really did not like that when I got it back, so basic- that one was, I can re-member that being rushed, and I didn't have time to sort of put it through a spell-checker; that was basically, 'God! Human', and then every one was OK after that, I didn't get any sent back, although there were probably still spelling mistakes in it. And um, I did that; that year was OK, and I had a placement report, and that was like War and Peace, it was ridiculously large. My place-ment tutor came up, and I gave it to her and said 'look, can you have a read over this? Can you just check this over for me? You know, what I've done so far?' And um, this –

D: Sorry to interrupt you – you'd written this placement report?

P: Yeah.

D: You had written a very long one?

P: I'd written a very long one.

D: Putting all your feelings about it?

P: Yeah, everything. It was everything I felt about my time there. Um, I gave the placement report to her, and um she came back, and was saying like er 'yeah, I can – so you've got loads of spelling mistakes here, took me a long time'. I said 'yeah, well' – that's when I told my placement tutor, who later on referred me to dyslexia, 'well, I did get told once that I might be dyslexic', and she basically agreed with me at that stage. But nothing was done at that stage. So I did that, um, I handed it in, and I thought, 'yeah, I've got a good job in there', I thought yeah, and it was like, the thing about it, there was reward for it, for the best one and so I thought, 'well, I stand –' I thought I'd done a good job. And like the guy that got it, I mean all he had was like he had flashy graphics in the middle of the thing, and it wasn't one half the size that I'd done; I thought I'd done a really good piece of work, and I'd put a lot of research into it. I was – you know, I can remember I asked somebody from PR department to give me some stuff, stuff off them I put that in; I related it all, and I did tons of research work on it, and – yeah, I didn't get any feedback on that, so I didn't know whether it was, the English was that bad on it or not; I still don't know. So I thought, 'move on'. Yeah, the main thing was, again you moved on.

And then, it was the final year, and we started the project, and the project was where the problems began. Um, the project was to do with the effectiveness of computers and the like – well, of software in Higher Education, and I decided to look at all aspects to do with using computers in education. Total packages you should teach, um, and, you know how you could use computing in teaching non- sort of like accounts and stuff like that. And um I decided to use a different department; I used the business school, because I knew about the business school because that's where I did the previous degree, and I had friends there, so it was a double-edged sword. So um, that was where I put, I put an incredible amount of research in. Again, every single day was up and down from where I was and that – sometimes two or three times a day, to arrange interviews with course leaders and different lecturers, to arrange questionnaires to be dumped out, to arrange collection.

D: A lot of organisation.

P: So, I mean I was doing all this, and um the planning behind it went well, um, and um I submitted it, you know, submitted part of it, yeah I submitted it, and um I was in one day, during the break period, you know when you were revising, and A called me in and said 'can you sit down, I want to say something to you'. I thought, 'oh shit, what have I done wrong?' And then, I got this spiel um: 'well, you know, I know you've done a good job, and I want to see you get the good – the mark you deserve, that's why I want you to get this um assessment. So the first step is to get an interview'. So, I went off and er got an interview, and um the interview went OK and he said, 'basically they'll either reach a stage where they might have formed an assessment', or basically I'd have to pay for it. So basically what happened was I got, I had that during the exams, the worry of whether I was going to have to, you know what was going to happen. My first two exams I cocked up basically because of that. It made me a lot more conscious; I was sort of in an exam, I was ner-, going 'hang on, I've done this wrong, I've done that wrong', and it did cock up the exams. And it was like after the second exam, I got a letter through, I got the assessment, the University was going to pay. So I went off, got the assessment –

D: When you saw B here?

P: That's B – he put the letter in, and I thought well, I'm going to get a viva. Certainly going to have a look at it. Comes the day of the vivas er, I didn't get one. I thought, 'hang on, what's going on here?' Went in to get my results, got the results, got a 2:1. I thought 'great'. Got the breakdown results, not so great! The two exam results: I got 50per cent in the first exam, I was expecting to get 60; I got 64 in the second exam which I cocked up. Um, previously, in the course-works, I got 84 and 72, so I should have got close to the 70s, so I wasn't too happy about that. Then the project: 50. I went: 'hang on'. This didn't tally up; I go, 'hang on, no, no, no'. I was expecting something 60 at least, the amount of work I put in. I go, 'this is not right', you know. I ran out, fuming and I slammed the door. You know, I can remember her saying 'you got a good 2:1', but I said 'well that depends on your point of view', and I slammed the door shut and left, because I was very sort of gutted. And um I was going to see- I was really mad, I thought, calm myself down, go and see the project supervisor, and she was out. I saw my moderator, and the moderator said 'well your research work was good, nothing wrong, it was excellent, there was nothing wrong with it', he said ' it was your English was diabolical'. And he said 'I'm sorry we put you through so much hassle'. And it ended up um, they weren't going to bother pushing the case for the project, because I wasn't going to move up a classification.

D: You feel it was because you were assessed too late?

P: It was too late. If I'd got assessed beforehand, I think I would have been more relaxed in the first two exams, I think I would have done better in them. Because I had that thing on my mind, it didn't work out.

D: So what should have been in place, in your opinion, for you to have been assessed earlier? How should it have been organised?

P: Um, really I think basically there should be some kind of um, when people come into Higher Education, there should be some kind of, maybe a test or something. Not an entrance exam; you know, you're- you've got that place, you've got, you've got the A Levels, you've earned the right to get a place, but to say, this is basically just a little test to see if you've got dyslexia, just a simple test, just a screen, screen them, and then from there you can say well OK we're going to make allowances for you, because people are still getting through the net, I think that's it, and – you know, I've since then seen the project supervisor, and I get on well with her now. But at the time, I did have a bit of a grudge, and I realised it wasn't my fault. It wasn't her fault; it was just politics.

Appendix II

Brief 'life maps' of each informant

Aarti – age at interview: 22
From a British Asian family. Second language was Punjabi.

Brought up in London. Described her primary school as 'a complete nightmare from beginning to end', partly because there were hardly any other Asian children. Enjoyed secondary school because it was more racially mixed. Passed all her GCSEs with grades A to C, but believed this was the result of her hard work, not the school's input.

Moved to a sixth form college for A Level Law, Economics and Maths. Failed them all. Obtained past papers and prepared draft answers. Passed re-sits.

Angered by suggestions that her difficulties with English were caused by its being her second language because it was her first.

Went to university to take Media Studies and Drama. Spent the first year thinking that she was not intelligent enough to be there. New head of year suggested that she be assessed for dyslexia.

Obtained the DSA and felt that the computer was a great help, but still angry about the low level of dyslexia awareness at her university.

Adrian – age at interview: 25
Went to several different primary schools in London and Essex.

Placed in special classes. Unstable home life after his mother left his father and struggled to support her two sons.

Passed several CSEs. Enrolled for A Level Biology and History, but failed them.

Worked as a computer technician. Tried an ONC course in computing.

Married; son born.

Enrolled at Belleville for a foundation course in electrical engineering.

Referred himself to learning support unit, and was assessed by an EP.

At time of interview, was taking a 'year out' doing telephone sales in the day and self-employed computer construction in the evenings.

Alice – age at interview: 37

Stated that both her parents and her three siblings were dyslexic.

Struggled with reading and spelling at local primary school, but always felt keen to acquire knowledge and was praised for trying hard.

Given extra Maths at comprehensive school.

Joined drama group, but could not remember the scripts.

Passed four CSEs, and O Level English at the third attempt.

Tried to take four O Levels and three A Levels in sixth form.

Abandoned that and took Business Studies at an FE college; completed OND and HND, including personnel work, with many hours of study.

Interviews for personnel jobs; felt humiliated by personality and aptitude tests, particularly Maths.

Took short-hand and typing course, and then Institute of Personnel Management two year part-time course. Trying to prove that she was not stupid.

Avoided relationships with men because of her poor self-esteem.

Became a company personnel manager at 27, had a nervous breakdown from the strain.

After a period in hospital, took City & Guilds 730 followed by a Cert Ed in adult education.

Interviewed for an MA in adult education, the course leader suggested that she see an EP for dyslexia assessment.

Took what she called an 'extra year' to complete her MA dissertation, which *only missed a distinction by a fraction*.

Married a dyslexic man and became a freelance personnel and training consultant. She also enrolled on a creative writing course.

Alison – age at interview: 20

Disliked school from the start, particularly spelling.

Parents took her and her younger sister to a private tutor.

Began to enjoy Maths and practical activities, but nothing involving spelling.

Received 'special needs' spelling support at secondary school, but moved to another town after one year.

Not identified as needing extra help until fourth year. Given more spelling rule work.

Teacher whose daughter had been identified as dyslexic 'noticed the signs' in Alison. Assessed by EP.

Passed 5 GCSEs with extra time. Undertook a re-sit year, in order to be admitted to a sixth form which demanded '5 Cs and above'.

Enrolled for A Level History, partly because a teacher had advised her not to, Art with Art History and Computing. Anxious about coping with the work, but her parents were keen for her to go to University.

Passed them all, with low grades. Enrolled for degree in Computing.

Ann – age at interview: 21

Described herself as 'wilful' at Primary School.

Disliked writing from the start.

Invented story of books by using the illustrations.

Did very well in Maths.

Placed in 'remedial' spelling group at 11.

Failed English Language and Literature GCSEs.

Mother asked for her to be assessed for dyslexia, but was refused.

Chose science A Levels (at a College of Technology) because she wanted to go into medicine.

Zoology teacher referred her for dyslexia screening, which was negative.

Assessed by EP before A Levels and given 25per cent extra time. IQ 135 (but her sister's was 145 and she still felt a failure).

Enjoyed watching operations during medical foundation course.

Gave up biochemistry because of the burden of learning formulae; changed to Zoology.

Would have liked to be a Doctor, but believed that dyslexia would prevent her from passing the examinations.

Enjoyed dissection and drawing, because it involved three-dimensional structure.

Enjoyed using her computer, particularly the spell-checker, but continued to feel stupid because of her oral word-finding difficulty.

Left with a 2:1 and took a PGCE in secondary science, for which she wrote a dissertation on 'specific learning difficulties'.

Arnold – (American, on 'year abroad' programme) age at interview: 20

Disliked school from the start.

Placed in 'special ed' class in first and second grade.

Suspended from school in sixth grade for failure to hand in work.

Labelled 'learning disabled' in seventh grade after first EP's assessment.

Tension with parents over homework.

Bullied at school and got into fights, and confrontations with teachers.

Had regular sessions with an educational therapist.

Saw himself as defective all through compulsory education.

Did not read a book with independent enjoyment until aged 14.

Kept back a year at 14.

Parents could not understand why he cried in the evenings.

Success in athletics, art and science practicals.

Discovered ability in creative writing, through visualisation.

Learning support teacher showed him concept mapping.

Did poorly in SATs but accepted by a university which welcomed dyslexic students.

Tape recorded lectures and listened to books on tape.

Disliked the linearity of academic writing.

Taught English as a second language.

Considering becoming a kindergarten teacher.

Returned to US and graduated in Political Anthropology; by 2001 he was involved in political activism for disabled people. Published an autobiographical chapter in a book about the life histories of 'people with learning disabilities' (Rodis, 2001), in which he identified himself with 'the disabled classes' but proposed a re-conceptualisation of the term.

Betty – age at interview: 49

Went to a 'pretty strict' Church of England girls' primary school in North London. Given extra reading with the Headteacher.

Failed the 11+. Moved to Welwyn Garden City and went to a mixed secondary modern school there. Left school at 15 with no examination passes. Worked for a pharmaceutical company which offered her day release for a shorthand and typing course.

After 3 years, wanted to do something more rewarding and sat entrance test for nursing training. Became an SRN.

Married during the training and had a child. Eventually worked as a nurse after the children were older. Went to local college to take GCSEs. Then Open University short courses in sociology and psychology.

Daughters assessed for dyslexia; recognised her own processes in the reports. Had herself assessed by the same (DI) EP.

Enrolled for DipHE in Midwifery, but found it too hard. At time of interview, she was on a DipHE in Community Care, Health Visiting strand.

Bruce – age at interview: 24

Went to a small primary school in Scotland. Given speech therapy. Moved to Hong Kong from ages 6 to 8. On return to Scotland, given 'remedial' spelling and hand-writing sessions at school.

Excelled in Art and Sciences at secondary school, but always showed a discrepancy between his oral ability and written work.

Assessed by EP at 16 and given extra time in examinations. Became interested in psychology through this and his sister's work as a psychiatric nurse.

Took first degree in Psychology; course included some Biology and Chemistry. Chose an increasing number of biology options, and became focused on para-sitology. Referred himself for re-assessment for dyslexia in final year and received extra time for his finals.

Accepted for a full-time PhD in parasitology. Graduated and remained at the research institute.

Charles – age at interview: 44

Went to a convent school at 5.

Struggled with reading, writing and multiplication tables; preferred 'mechanical objects' from the start.

Feigned sickness to avoid spelling tests.

Contrasted with more able cousin of the same age.

Kept back a year and passed 11 plus.

Caned several times at secondary school, for bad work.

Started truanting.

Moved to a different town at 14 and was happier at a Grammar School, but continued to believe himself to be unintelligent.

Enjoyed woodwork and began to read for pleasure, albeit slowly.

Kept back a year again.

Began to fear making mistakes and to dislike examinations.

Became aware of a contrast between his difficulties with words and his ability to visualise in three dimensions. Achieved success in Art.

Failed all his O Levels, and failed again in re-sits.

Took a building course at a Technical College.

Became a salesman for a mechanical engineering firm.

Enrolled for part-time Building Surveying degree at age 40.

Wrote essays in pencil and his mother typed them out.

Suffered from examination phobia.

Learning support tutor suggested he might be dyslexic.

Assessed for dyslexia for the first time at age 43; not keen on the label because he saw it as meaning he was defective.

Graduated with a 2:2 and would have liked to start an MSc, but returned to self-employment as a surveyor.

In 2001, Charles was still living with his parents at the age of 51. He said that he still found dyslexia 'very frustrating' in that he could not write well by hand, but had to rely on his computer. He felt that dyslexia had prevented him from fulfilling his childhood dream of becoming an architect, even though he felt he had talents in terms of spatial awareness. Charles' discourse of dyslexia seemed to have moved from 'patient' to 'student'; he said he was open with people about dyslexia, and described it to them as *'problems with spelling but an IQ of over 120'*.

Charlotte – age at interview: 21

Attended a small village primary school until 10. Her parents separated during that period, but she recalled no problems at school, except that she was 'never a great reader'.

Dreaded reading aloud at secondary school, but shone at Drama and Art. Good relationships with teachers generally.

Took GCSE French and German; enjoyed the 'pictorial' teaching style.

Deputy Head told her she would never get into University.

Parents found her a private tutor for Maths.

Then BTEC National Diploma in Business and Finance. Started A Level French as well, but dropped out.

Assaulted by a man when she was 17. This changed her career plan from business to joining the Police or going into social work. Looked for degree courses in Social Policy.

Difficult interview at Spenceton, but accepted.

Suffered from eczema in first semester. Written work given low grades. Course administrator suggested she might be dyslexic. Referred herself for assessment. Appreciated support from two dyslexic women in the learning support unit.

Graduated with a 2:2. Worked in the student union shop, and later at the Rural Community Council in the county town where she lived.

Chuck – age at interview: 34

Went to Steiner School.

Assessed by a range of experts and psychologists.

Said to have most of the main difficulties associated with dyslexia to a severe degree.

Saw dyslexia issues as similar to those faced by the physically handicapped and victims of racial prejudice.

Worked as a builder until enrolling for foundation course in mechanical and manufacturing engineering (after taking GCSEs in Maths and Physics at a Tertiary College).

Unwilling to seek special examination arrangements, as he wanted to be on equal terms with other students.

Repeated the foundation year while following an additional Maths course and an Open University computing course.

Unclear as to whether he completed the degree, as he moved house and did not keep in touch.

Eliza – age at interview: 22

Canadian. Enjoyed kindergarten, but struggled at school as soon as reading and writing began. Teachers expressed concern about the contrast between her 'brightness' and her reading/writing.

Taken by parents for a physical check-up. Developed school phobia. Taken to psychologist by parents and identified as dyslexic.

Private tutor employed weekly for about three years.

Moved to a special school for dyslexic children for two years.

Accepted by a mainstream boarding school at age 15; met two other dyslexic students there. Enjoyed singing, drama and pottery.

Failed preliminary SATs. Predicted grade point average very low, so did not apply to university.

Enrolled for a cookery course in the UK. Then found that her grades were good, so applied for Hotel Management degrees (also in UK, because she believed that British universities were better for dyslexic students).

Graduated in Hotel and Catering Management and obtained a job in London.

Enid – age at interview: 20

Went to five different primary schools in Africa, China and England.

Reached China at 10 and managed Maths for the first time because of the rote learning approach.

Labelled 'lazy' at all her schools before China.

Her parents were both graduates and teachers. They tried to have her assessed.

Returned to England at 13 unable to spell.

Successful at Art; passed 9 GCSEs.

A Level Art, English and History.

Enjoyed oral discussion and choral singing.

Chose Archaeology as a degree: practical history.

Did not indicate dyslexia on UCAS form; still not formally assessed.

Started being penalised for spelling, so referred herself for dyslexia assessment.

Wrote essays out by hand four times before typing them out.

Graduated with a 2:1 and went on to a PhD in archaeology. She wrote: *'Finally I have the freedom to express myself through the type of writing that I am best at, no exams getting in the way. It is also visual based research. I am analysing archaeological artefacts and this requires you to notice things rather than spend all my time reading other people's work'.*

By 2001, Enid had a small child and was still working on her PhD. She did not talk about dyslexia to anyone; she felt it affected her *'in a day-to-day way'* but not academically.

Fenella – age at interview: 44

Mother French; moved to England when she was 6 and had to speak and read English for the first time.

Physically frail and treated as unintelligent; felt that her parents had no academic aspirations for her.

Took five O Levels; failed Maths, English language and literature but 'sailed through' Art and French.

Gave up A Level Art and became a window-dresser.

Then worked in a GPO telephone exchange.

Married; did temporary work as a telephonist via an agency, but could only manage switchboards of the type she had been trained on.

Had two children; divorced and lived with the children.

Enjoyed reading to them. Did voluntary work in a school with special needs children, and took cleaning jobs.

Her friends had degrees; felt that there was 'something enormous lacking' in her life, educationally.

Went to adult literacy classes; passed English GCSE.

Then passed City & Guilds Community Care course.

Joined Access course and discussed her language difficulties with the tutor. Fellow student assumed she was dyslexic.

Screened by learning support tutor. Shocked by the expression 'specific learning difficulties'.

Took degree in Social Anthropology. Struggled with first year, and referred herself for EP's assessment.

Graduated with a 2:1. In 2001, she was working as a dental receptionist/administrator. She was avoiding mentioning dyslexia in case she was blamed for wrongly filed papers. Fenella felt that dyslexia was 'still a major part of (her) identity' and that she still had poor self-esteem because of it, which affected her personal relationships.

Gary – age at interview: 20

Brought up in Sheffield. Stayed with the same primary school teacher for several years. Referred by her for dyslexia assessment at age 7.

Given intensive extra teaching hours. Did not read for pleasure until he was 17.

ETH continued at secondary school, but he began to dislike worksheets, the extra work and frequent testing being dyslexic involved him in, and the fact that much of the curriculum was 'taught on paper'.

Re-assessed before GCSEs and given extra time. Did well in sciences and Maths; passed all the 9 he took.

Took A Level Maths, Physics and Computing. Wanted to do them without help from learning support staff. Disliked the whole experience, but was determined to go to University.

Grades were not very good (apart from Computing) but was offered a place at University; he believed that his being dyslexic caused the University to be flexible. Enrolled for Computer Science.

Harry – age at interview: 27

Brought up in Sheffield. Parents had done no post-compulsory education.

Happy at school; enjoyed Maths and sport, but found English difficult.

'Drifted' on to A Level Maths, Physics, Chemistry and General Studies.

Left with two Cs and two Ds and became an accountant. Seconded for a foundation degree course in accountancy. Failed the examinations in spite of repeated attempts.

At time of interview, had read only two books.

Decided to abandon accountancy and take a degree in Economics.

His work was returned with much red ink, but his grades were average.

During his first year, a friend was identified as dyslexic and described the indicators; Harry began to wonder about himself.

Referred himself for assessment after reading a poster on campus about dyslexia. Internal psychologist's reported included standard deviations from the 'norm' which worried him, but he appreciated extra time in examinations, extended library loans and computer via the DSA.

Asked his housemates to check his English.

Outcome of degree: 2:1.

Jemima – age at interview: 20

Went to private primary school for girls. Labelled stupid and lazy. Her speech was somewhat unintelligible until she was 6.

Assessed as dyslexic at 9. Wore an eye patch for reading.

Parents found her a private tutor for English.

Transferred to private secondary school; withdrawn from class for extra English.

Enjoyed cookery, textiles, biology practicals (and woodwork at home).

Started to read about biology because of her interest. Parents read with her every night, and paid for another private tutor to see her at school (using the Dyslexia Institute method).

Passed 10 GCSEs (with extra time), although the school had told her parents she would fail them all.

Moved to private dyslexia special school for sixth form. Dyslexia assessment updated.

A Level CDT and Textiles, and 'Diploma of Vocational Education' in Health Care.

Keen on occupational therapy (partly because her parents were a nurse and a doctor). Moved to a 'crammer' at 18 and took three A Levels in year: Sociology at Work, Pure Sociology and Biology (the latter with individual teaching).

Enrolled for occupational therapy degree. No classes specified, but she was told hers was 'the equivalent of a 2:1'. Worked at Rampton (a secure mental health hospital) for a few months, then became a locum occupational therapist from her parents' home. Subsequently went away 'travelling', with the intention to be away for 20 months.

Jeremy – age at interview: 19

Good at Maths and Science, so thought to be 'lazy' at English.

Could not remember content when reading fiction, so gave it up.

Achieved A Levels, but struggled with 'wordy' examination questions.

Self-referred at university for dyslexia assessment at instigation of girlfriend.

Anxious to avoid using dyslexia as an excuse for bad work.

Self-conscious about inclusion of dyslexia in employment references.

Graduated with a 2:1 in Biochemistry.

Failed the 'verbal analysis' element in psychometric tests for a post with a pharmaceutical company. Offered a job by a chemical company before he graduated, as a technical advisor. Then became a salesman for the same company. Promoted to Account Manager for a large area in 2000, and bought a flat in London. Ceased to regard dyslexia as a defect or an obstacle.

Lance – age at interview: 24

Brought up in Liverpool.

Bullied at primary school because of his stammer and accent.

Assessed for dyslexia at age 10 and saw a private tutor for two years.

Placed in high sets for most subjects at comprehensive school, but taken out of French and placed in a remedial English group.

Passed four GCSEs but failed English several times.

Took A Levels; failed Maths and Physics, but passed Economics and General Studies.

Enrolled for an HND in manufacturing management; passed minimally. Was involved in the student union as a 'student affairs officer'. Decided that he liked politics. Enrolled for degree in Politics and Urban Studies.

Set up a student Dyslexia Society.

Planned to take a PGCE and try to become a learning support teacher.

Lisa – age at interview: 50

Went to an independent primary school, and independent boarding secondary school after failing the 11+.

Struggled with reading and spelling but did well in Art. Wanted to be an architect, but realised that A Levels would be too hard for her; also received parental pressure to marry young and be a housewife.

Parents decided she should go into floristry, but take a secretarial course first. Liked shorthand because of its logic, but did not complete the course.

After she taken floristry training in London, her parents bought her a flower shop (at age 19).

Saw Susan Hampshire talking about being dyslexic on television.

Married at 23 and had two daughters. Could not read to them.

Recognised herself in difficulties her daughter was having at school, and again when the girl was assessed for dyslexia and eye tracking problems.

Divorced at 46. Took O Levels, including English, then a Joint Matriculation examination for Universities and Polytechnics.

Enrolled for Social and Environmental Studies degree.

Referred herself for dyslexia assessment after difficulty with examinations.

Graduated with a 2:2, and obtained part-time work with a property company.

In 2001, she was directing her own property company part-time, and planning to retire at 60. She felt the degree had given her 'a lot of confidence,' and she was reading more than she used to. Her view of dyslexia seemed to have moved to a more 'hemispherist' discourse: *'My brain is different – it's a physiological difference, not a defect'*. At school, they *'carried on teaching me the same way, even though it wasn't working'*.

Mel – age at interview: 32

Went to a small private day school in Staffordshire.

Reports mentioned paying attention and copying from boards.

Read a magazine article about dyslexia when she was 9 and identified herself with it. Reading was not a problem; enjoyed Arthur Ransome and the like.

Transferred to a Roman Catholic secondary school.

Took English and History A Levels there, and Geography at a local college.

History teacher suggested she might be dyslexic.

Began to doubt her own intelligence, so took the 'Mensa' entrance test and passed. Decided she probably was dyslexic, and went for assessment to the University of Aston.

Passed English and History A levels without extra time.

Went to London for a City & Guilds computing course.

Looked for a 'practical' higher level computing course; took HND in computer studies over two years. Also tried British Computer Society examinations, but only passed one paper out of three.

Worked for a year as a programmer in the US.

Worked for an engineering company back in the UK for three years, while studying GCSE Psychology.

Enrolled for degree in Educational Studies and Intelligent Systems, with the aim of working in adult dyslexia support.

Following this, Mel did some part-time and sessional learning support at Axbridge University, supplementing this with contract programming. She also took part in dyslexia research by taking evening primrose oil capsules. Mel is now working for a PhD.

Patrick – age at interview: 25

Had a private tutor for six years, up to O Levels.

Enjoyed art and craft at primary school; also singing, and history radio programmes.

Given extra English at secondary school.

Made friends with 'the undesirables'.

Passed four O Levels and some CSEs.

Moved to a sixth form college and enrolled for O Level English resit, OND in computer studies and A-Level computer science. Given more extra English lessons.

English teacher suggested he might be dyslexic.

Passed HND in computer programming.

Enrolled for degree in Business Information Management, but disliked economics and statistics and struggled with essay writing, so transferred to Computer Studies. Lecturer advised him to seek dyslexia assessment. Hoped this would lead to a viva after his finals, but it did not, although he disputed his examination marks and his final project.

Left with a 2:1 and enrolled for an MSc in Data Engineering.

Peggy – age at interview: 38
Started school in Edinburgh.

Frequently told she was stupid, particularly at Maths. Failed 11+.

Mother married a soldier, so she went to live in Germany when she was 12.

Went to an Army boarding school in Germany which was the equivalent of a Secondary Modern, with large classes.

Succeeded at sport, art and oral German. Passed five CSEs.

Returned to England and worked for a solicitor as a clerk.

Frequently lost files because of problems with the reference numbers.

Then worked for a demolition contractor and enjoyed co-ordinating the firm's activities.

Became an auxiliary in a hospital; wanted a qualification, but the Maths in the entrance test for SEN training looked too difficult.

Worked as an unqualified nursing auxiliary for 15 years.

Wanting a new beginning, took an Access course as a possible 'opening to further employment', but realised that she could go to university.

Access tutor suggested she might be dyslexic, but she declined to be screened.

Started degree in Geography, found essay writing very hard, and referred herself for dyslexia assessment.

EP explained the process well, and her personal tutor was very supportive.

Went on to take an MSc.

Phoebe – age at interview: 21
Born in Tanzania. Taught by a friend of her parents until she was 7, then sent to boarding school in England. Remained at the same school for 11 years.

Suffered from migraines and clashes with class teacher.

School had Phoebe assessed for dyslexia at 8.

Particular difficulty with Maths. Believed herself to be unintelligent.

Began to read at 10. Enjoyed Classics e.g. mythology.

When she was 15, her mother told her that being dyslexic had held *her* back.

Did well in lacrosse and singing in the choir.

Became House Captain. Passed 9 GCSEs, but school advised her not to try A Levels. Phoebe insisted on doing them because she wanted to go to university; took Biology, Geography, Socio-biology and Classics (after an update EP's assessment). Grades not good enough for the university she was aiming at, so went to a 'tutorial college' for a year and re-sat two subjects.

Admitted to university to read Classics.

Graduated with a 2:1 and embarked on an MA at the same university.

Rachel – age at interview: 20
Good at Maths at primary school in Lancashire, but struggled with reading and spelling. Did well at sport.

Father was dyslexic; Rachel thought that they were both unintelligent.

At secondary school, did well at public speaking competitions.

Also good at Sciences; began to think she was intelligent after all.

Dyslexia suggested by a teacher in her fourth year, but not assessed.

Passed six GCSEs. Interested in nursing, but went to a sixth form college to do BTEC Science.

Teacher there referred her to an EP. Identified as dyslexic at 16.

Did work experience at a hospital and liked the role of the occupational therapist.

Applied to University Occupational Therapy course.

Robert – age at interview: 31
Did not read 'properly' until aged 8.

Socially successful and good at sport all through his school career.

Believed himself to be unintelligent, but placed in top bands at high school 'through verbal ability'.

Told not to attend French and Maths classes in fourth year.

Reports called him 'exceptionally lazy'.

Failed all CSEs except English. Could not take Technical Drawing or Art because of the school's time-tabling policy.

Went to art college and took City & Guilds photography.

Worked for an architect's practice as a technician, seconded for BTEC in Building Studies. Interested in related law and regulations.

Dropped out of the course because of the Maths and Physics elements, but moved to another similar job and pretended he had passed the BTEC

Discovered he had a talent for painting architectural perspectives, so became a free-lance specialising in these.

Tired of chasing creditors. Decided to pursue a Law degree.

Enrolled on Access course. Tutor suggested seeking a dyslexia assessment via his GP. GP said he could not be dyslexic. Tutor told him more about indicators of dyslexia, and said he would have extra time in examinations if identified.

Parents paid for him to be assessed. Report was full of jargon which he could not understand.

Contacted University to confirm that he would be admitted to Law as a dyslexic.

Obtained a laptop and voice recognition software via the DSA.

Graduated with a 2:2. Worked for British Aerospace's building design division. Then enrolled for a Bar Vocational Course and became a barrister.

Ron – age at interview: 41
Found primary school frustrating. Given extra lessons in reading.

Very successful at sport all through his school career, but became 'deviant' at secondary school, having failed the 11+ – tried to avoid all written work.

Passed 7 CSEs and one O Level (Science).

Became an electrical apprentice with day-release training. Good at visualising wiring diagrams.

Worked as an electrician for 13 years, then as a service engineer, which involved further training.

Joined St John Ambulance 'as a hobby'.

Took City & Guilds 730 course in adult teaching, with aim of becoming a first aid trainer at work. Met a dyslexic student.

Studying learning styles made him aware of his own.

Inquired about nursing training; worked for GCSEs at evening classes for two years in order to do this.

Struggled with essay-writing and referred himself for dyslexia assessment; given extra time for GCSE examinations.

Enrolled for an Access course. Given weekly learning support tutorial.

Admitted to degree course in Adult Nursing.

Sally – age at interview: 19

Brought up in Canada. Taught entirely in French when she started school; did not speak, so moved to English instruction.

Younger brother identified as dyslexic, so Sally was also assessed at age 8 or 9.

Best school activity was ice hockey.

Moved to UK at 12 and went to a convent school. Read her first 'thick book' at age 13. RE teacher used colourful diagrams, which Sally adopted as a method for all her study.

Moved to two different state schools; second one had 'special dyslexia teachers'. Passed 8 GCSEs without extra time. Wanted to be a vet, but thought she was not good enough at science.

A Level Maths, Economics and History (with extra time, after being taken to Aston University for an updated dyslexia assessment).

Advised not to state dyslexia on UCAS form.

Admitted for degree in Accounting in Computer Science, but changed to Business Economics.

Graduated with a 3rd having 'really messed up' one of the final papers.

Began work at a stable, with the hope of one day becoming a horse breeder.

Stephen – age at interview: 22

Started life in Buckinghamshire, but lived in Australia for a year when he was 7.

Given extra reading and writing lessons in Australia.

On return to UK, taken to Dyslexia Institute for assessment. Received individual support there for three years.

Sent to a small private secondary school. Passed several GCSEs with no extra time. Took Maths, Physics and Geography A Levels at the local Grammar School. Put on report for lack of effort. Parents found him a Maths tutor. Re-assessed by the DI and had extra time for A Level examinations.

Applied to Universities for Engineering because it was his father's subject. Ticked dyslexia box on UCAS form. Admitted to foundation year in Civil Engineering, but struggled with the Maths. Transferred to Geology. Socially withdrawn.

Graduated with a 2:1. After 6 months on a research project investigating windmills in Germany, he took an MRes course at a university in London. He also volunteered to take part in dyslexia research at the Institute of Neurology, which involved having his brain scanned. In 1999, Stephen was working for the Environment Agency in Reading and taking a computer programming course in his spare time. By 2001, he had taken on a peripatetic role as a stack emission analyst. He had become less of a loner, and said he no longer thought about being dyslexic.

Susan – age at interview: 45

Described her mother as 'practically illiterate'.

Oldest of three children, she was 'weedy and very little'.

Roman Catholic primary school with many nuns on the staff.

Extra reading lessons in the cloakroom – she felt 'different'.

Felt that her parents were unconcerned about her difficulties at school because she was a girl.

Strong visual memories of her schooldays.

Failed the 11+, although by then she was enjoying reading and wanted to be a writer.

Went to a girls' secondary modern school; emphasis on 'house crafts', but enjoyed algebra and reading Buchan and Dickens.

Passed 6 CSEs. Careers teacher recommended millinery, but Susan opted for gardening and worked in a nursery.

Then became a key punch operator for several years, and tried O Levels at evening classes but failed.

Married at 19 and had two daughters. Took book-keeping and typing classes.

Worked as a secretary at her daughter's school, but resigned because of her poor spelling. Went to adult literacy class. Passed GCSE English Language at age 38, then English Literature.

Divorced. Tried A Level English but could not cope. Took several more GCSEs, then a pre-Access course at the same College. Expected to be turned down for the Access course, but completed it, and was accepted for a degree in Social Psychology.

Referred herself to Learning Support at the start of her degree course.

EP's assessment, Access Centre assessment and DSA.

Outcome of degree: 2:1. Immediately began training as a psychiatric nurse, following which she became a staff nurse at a psychogeriatric unit.

In 2001, Susan was working in a mental health day centre. She was open about dyslexia because it was 'not a problem any more'. Her view of dyslexia had changed, in that it was 'not the end of the world'. She was taking minutes in work meetings, but felt that her overall self-esteem was still not very good

Victoria – age at interview: 49

Misbehaved in class because of her poor memory for spoken language and slow written output, but remembered her reading and spelling as good.

Teachers said she would not concentrate, although she was bright.

Did well in English, Drama, Domestic Science and Scripture.

Parents sent her to a convent when she was 10 to avoid the 11+.

Then went to several different secondary schools (including convents), because her parents moved.

Passed five O Levels. Tried a short-hand and typing course and failed.

Became a nurse; passed the training with weak written tests, 'because her practical work was very good'.

Married and had five children.

Ran a successful bed and breakfast business.

Saw Susan Hampshire on television, but did not associate dyslexia with herself until she struggled with a Scottish dancing class and a friend suggested she might be dyslexic.

Friends encouraged her to go into social work, so she took Access course.

Referred herself for EP's assessment.

Offered place on Diploma in social work course through APEL.

Would have liked to work in the broadcast media or music, but felt that dyslexia had 'blocked her life'.

On completion of the Diploma, Victoria found a job in the social work department at her local general hospital.

Will – age at interview: 18

Went to a small primary school in Wales. Liked Maths, but struggled with spelling and writing. Labelled as lazy.

Mother pressed for him to be assessed for dyslexia. Seen by EP, but not identified. Mother pressed again at secondary school; he was identified at 15. Joined a private support group for dyslexic students.

Had to take French and Welsh examinations. GCSEs all C and above except these and English. Moved on to Maths, Physics and Chemistry A Level. Grades B, D and E. Admitted to Burtonforth to study Geology after some negotiation. Obtained a powerful PC via the DSA.

Made friends with international students because 'they're learning the language'. Had extra time for examinations.

Graduated with a 2:2 and decided to 'travel'.

Appendix III
Four case studies

Data presentation and analysis inevitably involve the selection and grouping of short quotations from what informants report, but do not give an overview of any single individual. These case studies provide some fuller portraits of informants.

They also illustrate ways in which the students' discourses of dyslexia affect their university experience. They provide background information for substantive chapters and recommendations. One case study is presented for each of the four discourses of dyslexia. Each interview, although broadly chronological, followed the themes suggested by the student. Consequently these portraits do not cover identical topics.

Jeremy: 'patient', 20

Jeremy was in the first year of a degree in applied biochemistry; short and dark-haired, he was wearing a sweatshirt with the badge of the university table tennis team. Jeremy soon relaxed, made frequent eye contact and spoke fluently and openly. He came from London, and remembered little about his primary school except that he had been happy there overall, but had had difficulty with spelling. He had found Maths easy and, like several other of the younger respondents, he recalled working rapidly through a scheme of workbooks. In common with 50 per cent of respondents, Jeremy had been regarded by teachers as lazy; he had early come to believe that, because he was intelligent and good at most school subjects, his disinclination to read and poor spelling must be due to laziness.

Jeremy has only one sibling, an older brother who had mental health problems. His family are Jewish and middle class; the two boys were sent to a Jewish school. Here, Jeremy had his first experience of French, and simultaneously had to start learning Hebrew; lessons in both languages involved writing and spelling, as well as reading. He soon found himself in the bottom set for both; his inability to remember parts of speech continued to be put down to 'me being lazy – my English, and not reading, and – that was always the option'. Jeremy had done well orally, particularly in English lessons, whereas in French he 'could have been – probably was – slightly disruptive'.

Jeremy had heard of dyslexia through other pupils at the school, but he did not associate it with himself. His school reports had spoken regularly of lack of reading, bad spelling and very bad handwriting, but no one seems to have mentioned dyslexia. His first comment which revealed a 'patient' discourse of dyslexia came as he spoke about the possibility of his brother's being dyslexic; Jeremy said his brother had 'a few other mental illnesses', and that his difficulties had been as-cribed to these.

GCSE brought Jeremy 8 passes, including English Language (where the teacher corrected the spelling in his course-work, having struggled in vain to help him to remember common homophones). Because of his oral ability, Jeremy mixed socially with pupils in top sets, and gained a grade one in English oral: 'I can handle myself in a talk', he said, but 'the words I speak, I can't spell or write'. (But in the course of the interview, Jeremy told me that he 'hanged around with' certain people; he also used the word 'cleansiness', and said his brother had a chemical 'disbalance' in his brain.)

Jeremy's showed self-awareness as he dissected his language difficulties. He described his inability to remember parts of speech, and the way he tended to mix tenses in essays. His self-image as a writer is summed up by his statement that 'I can't really express myself on paper'. His handwriting was very poor, but he finished examinations before the due time because he wrote very fast; he felt that his brain was 'working way ahead of what I'm writing, which is probably – accounts for half the mistakes'.

He was also quite clear about his difficulty with essay-writing, drawing a distinction between an essay which gives a series of facts – which he felt he could cope with – and one which presents arguments, which he could not manage. He had been interested in doing History A Level, but the teacher had persuaded him that the requisite essay-writing would be beyond him.

Then Jeremy described his struggles with reading comprehension. As the time to apply to University approached, Jeremy determined to try some fiction, 'just to say I'd read a book'. He chose a book he had seen the film of, hoping that this would help, but his short-term memory weakness meant it was too much for him. Turning to a simple thriller, again one where he had seen the video, Jeremy tried again:

> ... because I wanted to read a book, that was my ultimate goal. But then I thought 'I'm just reading it page after page, I can't, you can't, no one can ask, if anyone asked me a question, I've got absolutely no idea what I've just read.' So that was that for books. But I did try.

This was the only point where Jeremy expressed any envy of non-dyslexic fellow students; he went on to talk about the others 'going though novel after novel', adding wistfully that his own poor reading ability meant that: 'I just kicked it on the head, sort of thing'. However, keen to demonstrate his successful strategies, he added that nowadays he asked his girlfriend to read textbooks aloud to him.

Jeremy also knew his limitations in taking notes at lectures. Because he could not 'write down all the information and listen to it and take it in', he concentrates on writing it all down so that he could try to understand and absorb it later. When it came to writing in exams, he tried to avoid words he could not spell. His frustration about this was clear:

> I'm using loads of little short words to get to the same answer, which might take me half a page to do. ... I'll use the most appalling waffled English to try and say those words I can't spell.

This undercurrent of pride and sensitivity emerged again when Jeremy talked about his embarrassment at being asked for the loan of his lecture notes, because his handwriting was so bad. And again when he spoke of his girl-friend, who was reading psychology, telling him she thought he was dyslexic: 'I had all the, like, I don't mean symptoms, I can't think of a better word'.

At Burtonforth University, students were assessed for dyslexia by a Senior Lecturer in Psychology, who used the results for his research. Jeremy's self-knowledge was again evident when he described this assessment, made over two meetings about three months before our interview. He had been successful with a picture vocabulary test and with digit span, but overall it had been 'very very nerve-wracking', and he had had great difficulty with non-word reading and spelling, as well as with comprehension. He showed awareness of the culture-specific nature of parts of the test, mentioning a 'priest's hat' and a 'Muslim scarf' which he had been unable to identify; Jeremy also said:

> I have a slight problem with my speech, like when I say, as in 'free' the number, that's how I say it, I can't say it properly. ... My brother does it, my Mum does it ...

Talking about his assessment reminded Jeremy of a recent occasion when he was working in a rehabilitation centre. A speech therapist had shown him a picture language test 'which she would give to a head-injury patient', and he had found it very difficult: 'I didn't like that at all, I must be honest ... I really had to concentrate. I was very very nervous when I was doing it'.

Jeremy again spoke in business-like tones about his reaction to the psychologist's report: 'I took it as: 'Well that's an explanation for this, now I've got something, now I know what I've got to do to improve it.' The report did not recommend any strategies. Jeremy did not seem to have come to terms with what it did say.

Relationships with the university and tutors was the next theme of the interview. No individual learning support was available at Burtonforth at the time, and he was ineligible for the DSA because the level of his parents' income was too high. He was given extra time in examinations, but this raised the question of whether that 'concession' alone put him on a level with non-dyslexic students, or whether he should identify his work as that of a dyslexic student. Jeremy did not have a problem with finishing exams in time, but was highly conscious of the rubric he quoted: 'You will be penalised for poor spelling, grammar and handwriting'. He had been advised to identify himself as dyslexic at the top of his papers, but:

> I'm very conscious that people see it as an excuse. Now I don't want it — I want them to know I'm dyslexic and they don't mark me down for my handwriting and spelling. I don't want any special conditions, I don't want special exceptions; if I've got it wrong, I've got it wrong.

Most of the informants who spoke in these terms adopted a 'patient' discourse.

Jeremy showed contradictory attitudes to the university's efforts to support him. He did not want his peers to believe he was being given an unfair advantage, but he was also keen not to lose marks because examiners did not know he was dyslexic. He claimed to have detected inconsistency within the Faculty too. He saw the view of his department as 'being dyslexic is just a fault. It's ... a fault in your personality', although he told me 'younger lecturers actually speak to me and ask me what my problem is, so that they can learn'. He saw 'your 40-year-old teachers, they've been in the trade all their life' as the old guard.

Jeremy's coping strategies can be summed up by his response to invitations to the dyslexic students' support group: 'It's not a social thing, it's a problem I have which I'm overcoming'. Of the many informants who said they did not want to use dyslexia as an excuse for receiving special treatment or submitting sub-standard work, Jeremy was the most forceful. 'I don't like the fact that I should be writing I'm dyslexic on the top of my paper, because that to me says this is an excuse — look,

I'm writing it on my paper just to remind you'. He was using a combination of ICT ('I typed it out, I spell checked it, I grammar checked it') and human support – getting his girlfriend to proof-read his work. He summarised his approach: 'I will always ask for help. I am not one who will struggle through, bashing my head against the wall'.

His relationships with tutors concerning references for jobs and work placements were clearly important to him. He seemed fairly happy to talk to lecturers and friends about being dyslexic, but had been taken aback when his tutor said he was obliged to inform companies he was applying to for work placements: 'He said it could be an issue, because it's research'. Jeremy had succeeded in obtaining a placement with a cancer research group, but the tutor had telephoned them and said: 'You know Jeremy is dyslexic; is he going to be a problem with not getting the letters in the wrong (sic) order?' Jeremy's knowledge about dyslexia meant he knew that dyslexia is an umbrella term that covers a range of issues, and that many people have views about it which may be based on ignorance – both of which are relevant to job applications

Jeremy was obviously keen to present his dyslexia in as positive a light as possible:

> I'm probably only very mild in my – my English is only where I'm dyslexic, not verbally; it's only when I write things down. ... I'm only affected in one area.

This statement ignores the reading difficulty identified in the psychologist's assessment, where Jeremy had correctly read only 15 words out of 50 in the National Adult Reading Test. The psychologist had felt it necessary to add: 'This is considerably lower than in my sample of ordinary undergraduates, whose mean score is 36.3/50'.

However, when I asked Jeremy how he would describe dyslexia, he said:

> I probably would start by saying there are different forms of it, different types, different levels. You're not dyslexic and that's it; that's not – it's not (a) classification. I'd probably try to explain that there are different levels of dyslexia, different, um serious ca- , I mean some people are really affected, some people only slightly. And then I'd bring myself into it, what I am; because again I suppose with pride I would say there are different levels, and I'm not at the bottom of it, I'm not a very bad dyslexic, which there are. I'm only affected (in) a certain side of it.

This again is at odds with the psychologists' report, of which he received a copy. It stated: 'The problems that you have with reading and spelling are severe and reflect a significant degree of disability'. Jeremy did say that he needed help with English because it was ' a real real fault'. This is typical of one whose image of dyslexia is medical: he sees it as a biological failing. He linked his difficulty in understanding Maths questions couched as paragraphs of information with his difficulty in 'doing a neat paragraph' himself.

Twelve respondents (36 per cent) replied when I sent them transcripts and copies of the interview tape, but only six of these wrote any substantial comments. Jeremy was one of them; his letter consisted mainly of an 'update' on some of the themes from the interview. He had been for a summer holiday:

> 'During the holiday I read my first book, and I really enjoyed it, I even found it hard to put it down. The book was called *Rose Madder* by Stephen King. I found it easy to read and his language easy to understand. Unfortunately I have not read another book since'.

This success seemed to have given him courage to tackle the task of reading the background papers on the cancer research project he was joining for his placement. He described this as 'a daunting task', and said he had written notes on each paper as a comprehension aid.

To sum up: I class Jeremy as a 'patient' because of the language he uses about dyslexia. As well as the examples above, he reports that a lecturer asked him about his difficulties 'so that she knows what's wrong with me'. Jeremy's discourse of dyslexia had come to him via various routes:

- his brother's difficulties, and the family's language about him
- his own placement in remedial classes at school for handwriting, reading and spelling. When he met the other students there, he came to view dyslexia as a serious problem, but classed himself as 'shall we say higher than what the other students were'.
- his girlfriend had read about dyslexia on her psychology course and identified him from this
- the university psychologist's assessment, which referred to 'a significant degree of disability' and 'a specific impairment'.
- the speech therapist at his work placement.

Jeremy was only in the second term of his degree course when we met. He spoke of doing a PhD in due course, because 'you can't see anyone who's not a Doctor in our field'. However, when I telephoned him in April 1998, when he was in his final year, he told me he was applying for jobs as a medical representative, describing this as 'the managerial side of medical research,' and good for his 'career plan'. This was not an easy matter for him; one company had set applicants an eight page 'verbal analysis' test requiring 35 questions to be answered in half an hour, and Jeremy had 'failed'. But in November 1998 I received an email from him saying that he had graduated with a 2:1, was working for a chemical and drug company as a ' technical advisor' to customers, and had an ambition to move into sales.

At the end of 2001, Jeremy told me that he had indeed moved into sales. He had done so well that he had become the company's 'sales account manager' for London, co-ordinating a sales team, which used his 'people skills'. He said that dyslexia was 'not an obstacle' at work; he had a secretary for standard letters, and took great care with his reports. His view of dyslexia was 'I don't think about it – I just get on with it'. He had taken to listening to audio books for pleasure, and no longer regarded dyslexia as a defect.

Stephen: 'hemispherist', 22

Stephen was studying Geology. Tall, thin and pale, he was quite reserved at first. He described his reading and spelling as 'a bit of a mess' in his first years at school, and remembered having extra help with it.

Stephen's mother took him to the Dyslexia Institute for assessment when he was nine, where the EP explained that he had been 'born with it'. Overall, the label felt like 'something's wrong with me', although when reporting on Stephen's 'performance scale' (i.e. non-verbal) sub-tests, that EP had used language such as 'an extremely high level of visual thinking skills'. He had also defined Stephen's Full Scale IQ (124) as 'in the superior ability band'.

This assessment led to three years of weekly support sessions at the Institute during school hours, where Stephen was encouraged to use his strengths. On the subject of spelling, he said:

I sort of visualise it as the word written in my house. I've got a sort of picture memory.

He liked the Institute's handwriting style, which he described as 'cool'.

Although he found these sessions encouraging, Stephen had been glad that when he first started leaving his class to go to the Institute, he had a broken arm. So the other children were accustomed to his going off for medical treatment, and he did not have to 'feel like a thicky'. Also in affective terms, Stephen stressed the support his parents gave him, particularly his mother, who had made him flash-cards at home and put pressure on staff at each school he attended.

Stephen retained a view of dyslexia as developmental: 'you pop out with it, and you have to deal with it'. On the other hand, the label had its reassuring aspects:

It was nice to know you're not just – it's not just like – you have got a problem, so it's not just because you're, you can't do it.

Another recurrent affective theme in Stephen's schooldays was his dread of reading aloud in class. When he was doing his GCSE, friends began asking whether he was dyslexic when they heard him read aloud, and this was when he first 'came out' as dyslexic. He described reading aloud as 'really embarrassing and humiliating'.

He took his GCSEs at a private school. The LEA used what Stephen called the 12+ to place children at different comprehensive schools, and his parents decided that none would work for him. He enjoyed being in classes of only 15, even though 'the English teacher didn't have a clue what dyslexia was'. He remembered that the other children had not worked very hard but that he had, because his parents were paying for him to go to the school because, as qualified professionals, they set store by education. Although he had no special arrangements such as extra time, Stephen achieved good grades for his GCSEs and thought A Levels would not be difficult.

Moving to the Sixth Form at the local Grammar School for A Level Maths, Physics and Geography, Stephen was soon put in what he felt was 'the reject class' for Maths and put on a 'report card' because staff assumed he was not trying. But he had maintained his self-esteem through his enjoyment of physical Geography. He was aware that this suited his learning style, particularly on field trips:

It was easy to relate to – I could see the system working. It's like the physical properties are there. In Physics, I couldn't see the electric current.

When the school suggested that he drop an A Level, 'luckily good old Mum and Dad came in again and bollocked everybody'. Examinations remained a problem. Reading and question comprehension were issues for him: 'all the Geography exams seem to be like really poncily worded'. He returned to the Dyslexia Institute EP for a re-assessment, and was given extra time, writing 'I am a dyslexic student' on the papers. He still only managed an E for Physics and an N for Maths to go with his B for Geography and C for General Studies. Nevertheless, he achieved a place on a foundation year in Civil Engineering (his father was an engineer). Although he had indicated dyslexia on the application form, this was not mentioned at interview.

Engineering did not suit Stephen, however, and he applied for a transfer to Geology. Explaining why his Geology degree suited him led Stephen on to a more cognitive theme:

I think one of the good things about the Geology Department is they seem to structure notes so it all just builds up into a big thing at the end.

He also liked lecturers who used diagrams and flow charts. When it came to revision, Stephen used his visual memory, so that in examinations he could 'read the notes out in my head'.

Identifying himself as dyslexic on examination papers at university had a social dimension for Stephen, as it did for Jeremy. Unlike Jeremy, Stephen made a point of always identifying himself, although he doubted whether it helped him and whether 'the markers understand'. He felt that all staff should be 'educated' about dyslexia. The student-led dyslexia support group also had a social aspect. Stephen had been to a meeting, but had not felt it was useful: 'A meeting for a little chat about 'oh what subject are you doing?'

It was in the social dimension of his tutors' attitude to him that Stephen exemplified the 'hemispherist' discourse most clearly:

■ They don't seem to understand like you can't learn it that way, but you can learn it this way

■ The more diagrammatic it is, I find it easier to remember

■ I've got really good spatial and visual skills ... but the education system is just narrowed along one little line.

The major social theme that emerged from Stephen's interview was his isolation. He described himself as 'quite a big loner', and felt that dyslexia contributed to this, as he wanted to protect himself against being hurt by identifying himself as 'different'. He had enjoyed a field trip to Iceland, where he had worked on his own for eight hours a day and the tutor had told him his maps were 'absolutely brilliant'.

Stephen seemed to have developed his discourse of dyslexia from a combination of EPs' comments (when he was re-assessed at 17, the earlier conclusions were confirmed), his DI tutor's support for his cognitive strengths and his own observation of learning and teaching approaches which suited him. At one point, he remarked: 'I think my brain's a lot better than a lot of people'. But he avoided reading. He found the library catalogue difficult to use, and in any case, reading took him a frustratingly long time. Altogether, his course was 'very hard work', but he seemed to be enjoying the academic content.

After graduating with a 2:1, Stephen spent six months on a research project investigating windmills in Germany. He then took an MRes course at a London university, where he volunteered to take part in dyslexia research at the Institute of Neurology. This involved having his brain scanned. By 1999, Stephen was working for the Environment Agency in Reading and taking a computer programming course in his spare time. He had become a team leader and less of a loner.

When I spoke to him in late 2001, Stephen had a job that required him to travel the country carrying out what he called 'stack emission analysis'. He had not mentioned dyslexia when he applied for the job, but said his boss was 'OK about it'. Stephen said he still avoided reading and writing as far as possible; reports for work were easy because the vocabulary and language style were limited. He seldom thought about dyslexia but when he did, he felt proud to be dyslexic because of his 'good visual eye'. Since having his brain scanned, Stephen had come to see dyslexia as definitely a physiological matter, but one which conferred advantages.

Now 27, Stephen was unattached, and said he was still 'not good at trusting people' and 'wary of getting hurt'. He felt that dyslexia was definitely connected with this. He was now considering a PhD.

Alice: 'student,' 37

Alice was studying for an MA in education (FE). Of Irish extraction, she has curly dark hair and black eyes. She spoke in a bright, vivacious manner and made frequent eye contact. She was a rewarding subject because of her articulate self-disclosure.

What was most striking about Alice's interview was how dyslexia has affected her whole life, even though she was only formally assessed not long before we met. She felt that 'I knew I had a problem, but I didn't know what it was' and has been driven by great determination to prove that she can achieve educationally.

Perhaps because of her professional experience of interviewing in personnel work, Alice introduced both herself and her main theme within the first minute of our meeting, as well as her background:

> My parents are Irish, and Catholic, first generation English. I'm one of four. I'm the second eldest, boy girl boy girl, and we all have a slight trace of dyslexia. We get it from my father, who's extremely dyslexic, and I am probably the worst of the four children.

Shortly after that, she added:

> I pushed myself on and on to do well, and at every stage people said 'you won't go any higher', you know, 'you aren't capable, you can't expect any more'. And that would almost motivate me even more, to do more.

Alice also talked about parental support, which in her case had continued in practical ways well after she reached adulthood.

Faced with difficulties in acquiring literacy skills at primary school, many dyslexic children are inclined to give up and see themselves as failures. Their behaviour, as with all behaviour, is a result of a combination of intrinsic personality factors and experience. It would be simplistic to state that Alice's life-long drive to prove herself resulted purely from her awareness that she had a learning difficulty – she must have brought pre-existing personality traits to bear. But she certainly seems to have responded to many learning setbacks by refusing to be defeated. This is shown by her reaction when she was denied access to the 'special sort of more advanced little library' in the classroom at her primary school. Alice went to the public library, found the same books and took them out two at a time. She also made her own discovery about what the literature on learning support calls 'overlearning,' memorising spellings by persistent repetition.

Failing the 11+ was a major setback: 'There were a lot of reinforcements that I wasn't very bright that kept on coming home'. Children who were not at the grammar school were not entered for O Levels, but Alice was determined to try O Level English. Her parents supported her, although they had to pay the entry fees. Alice passed at the third attempt. A school friend had remarked on the discrepancy between her class work and her poor performance at exams. This is often found in the educational histories of dyslexic learners.

The problem with exams and the social pressure of being 'a second-class citizen' did not deter Alice from entering the sixth form. She spoke bitterly of the day she referred to a simile as a 'smiley', whereupon the teacher had made sarcastic comments about students coming from her school attempting A Levels. Accuracy of language was at times a problem for Alice. In the course of the interview, she said:

- Well I've shunned away to be honest from....
- What really spurned me on, spurted me on, was ....

Despite her persistent refusal to be denied, Alice received a setback when she decided to abandon her A Level courses. She went to a College of Further Education to do a Business Studies sandwich course, and enjoyed her work experience placement in a company personnel department, where her interpersonal skills were useful. This led to her ambition to pursue an HND in business studies, although she was discouraged:

> And she just said to me: 'I don't think you'd be able to cope with it, don't do it.' So I did it, of course.

It was for this course that Alice came to Axbridge University, as it was one of only two colleges which offered personnel as an option within the HND in Business Studies. It also meant she could live with her parents.

Living with them became significant, because she found the HND 'a real strain'. Alice was 19 when she began the course, and her parents supported her 'financially and emotionally'. But they had no experience themselves of any kind of studying, so were unable to help her when her determination to do well led her to make disproportionate efforts. For example, she chose in her 'Long Study' to review the discipline policies of twenty 'major companies', a project she now realises was far too ambitious and extensive for the course.

Alice hand-wrote all her assignments, as this was in the days before cheap word-processors and spell-checkers. She spoke angrily of being penalised for spelling, and saw this as the reason she was not awarded a distinction overall for her HND. She had never heard of Tippex, and would spend hours rewriting, making such common dyslexic mistakes as omitting words or whole lines.

This determination co-existed with fundamentally poor self-esteem: 'I thought it was a fluke that I was there'.

> I'm in the second year of an MA now, and it's only now that I'm beginning to think 'well, you know, maybe I' – I don't think clever is the word.....

Having experienced what she described as humiliation in personality tests on the 'milk round' for personnel posts, Alice was advised that she should learn to type. Here she did speak with direct pride:

> I took a post-graduate typing and shorthand course; and that, that's an achievement; I got 60 words a minute shorthand as quite a severe dyslexic.

Eventually, Alice obtained work in personnel. Her constant fear of being 'found out', that her underlying weaknesses – as she saw it – would be discovered, meant that she avoided close personal relationships and worked far too hard. She bought her own house near her parents. By trying to support her by 'taking my washing, doing my shopping', they unwittingly encouraged her to work day and night. Predictably, Alice had what she termed 'a total breakdown'.

Her treatment revealed that her stomach pains were psychosomatic, and she was referred to a psychiatrist. Once she recovered (after problems with drug treatment) and returned to work, she found that the Managing Director had decided that all senior personnel should have intelligence and personality tests. By now, Alice had heard of dyslexia and suspected that the term applied to her. The organisation brought in to test the employees told her that they did not use 'tests for dyslexics' because they did not expect top personnel to be dyslexic. This episode was too much for Alice, who had another breakdown and was back in hospital:

> I didn't come out for a month ... I just let go totally. And then that made me realise what I was doing; I couldn't keep running away.

Mental breakdown was outside the experience of Alice's parents, who were dismayed by her long periods of crying. But her mother 'knew somebody who knew somebody who'd been to a counsellor', and thus Alice was at last enabled to start feeling her anger about being dyslexic and her years of frustration. She had wanted to become a teacher while she was still at school, and now she began part-time work in FE teaching business studies. With her continuing urge to obtain qualifications, Alice soon embarked on a Cert. Ed., and this led to the MA in education which she was pursuing when we met.

Alice's developing self-confidence was evident in her interview for the MA at the end of her Cert. Ed. The tutor who interviewed her seems to have had some insight:

> Someone had written 'only an HND' across the top of my form for the entry, and he said: 'Isn't it strange what one word can do?' And he said: 'How do you feel about that?'

This had hit home, because for Alice it had 'always been 'only', and not quite enough'. She had told the tutor that she was concerned about her ability to manage the amount of reading required, because she believed she was dyslexic. The course tutor gave the common response, that this could not be true, because she had achieved so much. However, she was seen by an EP in due course, and this assessment was another trial for her:

> I was just reduced to tears when I did it. It was so emotional for me, because it was bringing back things like when you did the 11+, things that I just – they hurt me to try and do.

The psychologist gave her feedback that, on a scale of severity of dyslexia from 1 to 10, she was at about number 7, but that her coping strategies reduced this to 5. Alice could not remember his explanations of his findings, nor understand many of the technical terms in the written report. She said the assessment session had made her realise that she had been pinning her hopes on recovering from her psychosomatic stomach pains and the expectation that when they were cured, her learning difficulties 'would go away'. Now she had to come to terms with the fact that 'even if I get really well, I'm never going to be able to read any better, and I'm never going to be able to find my way'. This last remark refers to her difficulties with direction and navigation.

Alice blamed herself for being unable to talk to the EP about her fears, and blamed him for assuming that she would not be too upset by his report because she had already achieved so much. Such dilemmas of adult assessment were mentioned by many of my older respondents.

The 'student' discourse of dyslexia is not explicitly stated in EPs' reports. Regarding dyslexia as something confined to academic or literacy matters is partly a response to the label. Alice's EP used the language of IQ/attainment discrepancy, and also the 'pattern of difficulties' notion. However, like most of the psychologists who reported on these informants, he confined his discussion of the implications of his findings to academic matters. Alice seems to have made an impression on him; he ended his report by complimenting her on 'the workmanlike way in which you have managed your learning difficulties'.

Once she was formally assessed, Alice felt able to enrol for a module offered by her university specifically for dyslexic learners. Through this, she told me, she had learnt about tuning her ability to visualise, and about the use of colour and mind-mapping. She had also studied grammar and spelling, and she had come to believe that dyslexic learners 'get there in the end' by doing things their own way.

Perhaps most importantly, Alice began to realise that *'it was emotion that was pulling me down'*. She talked to her counsellor about her years of feeling *'you're not really who you think you are, you're not that bright'*, and *'you're going to get caught out, you're not really able for this'*.

Alice could at last talk to her father about dyslexia:

> And I said 'Dad, have you ever heard of something called dyslexia?' And he was sort of quiet. And I said 'you know, it's where you have problems with the type of things we have problems with'. And he said 'why do you ask?' And I said 'well, because I think I might be, and I think you might be'. And he said 'I never wanted to mention it to you'.

Her father explained that he and Alice's mother had believed that if they talked to her about dyslexia, she 'might see it as an excuse not to try'. And perhaps it would have meant that her father, and possibly her mother too, according to one statement Alice made, would have had to admit their own difficulties. Alice described her brothers as both very good at mathematical tasks but bad at literacy.

Alice's growing self-awareness was evident when she illustrated how she avoided social situations requiring her to remember people's names, as well as by her acceptance that 'when I'm tired, I haven't got the energy to get it right .... so I just let it be'. The dyslexia module at Axbridge had helped her to 'ease up, and say 'OK, so you're going to worry about it for a couple of days, but you'll get it done''.

Alice mentioned her fear of getting lost when she started secondary school, and the way she still joined fellow students rather than trying to find her way around Axbridge University on her own. She was encouraged by a television programme about a special school which employed supportive devices such as coloured arrows on the floor to guide pupils to their classrooms, and displays of labelled photographs of students and staff.

Alice's counsellor had wondered about her need to label herself, rather than simply 'deal with 'this is how I am.'' Alice commented that talking to me had 'highlighted a bit more how kind of it is in there'. She now saw dyslexia as playing an important role in making her the way she is.

Alice is a member of several sub-groups within my cohort of subjects: she failed the 11+; she has dyslexic parents; she has dyslexic siblings; she is undertaking post-graduate study; she has completed the dyslexia module at Axbridge University; she goes to a counsellor. She seemed to be achieving through a combination of innate determination, drive to prove herself, and support from other people.

Mel: 'campaigner', 32

Mel was following a modular degree course in Education Studies and Intelligent Systems. Short and slim, she smiled frequently, although often ruefully or sardonically.

Mel's learning life history contained elements of the 'campaigner' almost from the start, although initially the campaign was simply for herself. She reported trying to persuade a teacher to tell her how to spell the words she wanted to use, refusing to be kept down a year at a boarding school and persuading her parents to take her away, and reading a magazine article on dyslexia in which she recognised herself. She stored this information away for a future campaign. Mel used the language of battle frequently; she described examinations as a 'fair fight', meaning that as she saw it, all the students had equal time to demonstrate their ability unaided.

When she was in the lower sixth form, a teacher suggested to Mel that she might be dyslexic. Being forewarned by the magazine article, Mel acknowledged this, but she felt she had to prove her intellectual ability:

> Let's see: if I'm not that bright, then I've missed the point, and I can be deluding myself that I understand what's going on in class.

She therefore took the entrance test for Mensa, the high IQ society, and passed. Armed with this information, Mel asked her teachers to arrange a dyslexia assessment. Obtaining entrance to Mensa was 'preparing my case'. When the assessment at Aston University duly confirmed that she was dyslexic, Mel described this as doing 'a lot to make it easy for other people' at the school. She saw the assessment report as 'the nearest available weapon that was going to make some sort of impact'.

The English teacher's reported comment when she saw the dyslexia assessment was: 'you've got a higher IQ than I have, I can't teach you anything'. This suggests a history of conflict. Mel's language in our interview implied that she might not have been an easy student for a Convent sixth form: 'I took this a little badly', 'I annihilated their summer exams and then left', and she said about a teacher 'she was going to back off completely, throw her hands up and – brilliant!'

Mel then decided she wanted to do an HND in Computing. Again, she had her tactics worked out. She decided not to mention dyslexia at interview because it might be 'a hazard:'

> Now I view it more along the lines that everybody seems to have disabled counts, and if they can have you as a dyslexic, then their disabled stats will look good, and they're quite happy to handle you.

Working as a computer programmer in the US for a year, Mel met a family in which several of the children were dyslexic. The parents had little hope that they could be helped, but Mel's reaction was determined: 'I started getting cross about it'. Back in England, she volunteered as an Adult Basic Education tutor, which she called 'a step in the plan' for working in learning support when she was not trained as a teacher.

Mel's course at Axbridge was another step along that route. She had adopted a campaign approach to finding a course, investigating 'twenty-odd prospectuses'. Axbridge had not only strong dyslexia support but also the option of combining computer studies with an education course which did not demand teaching practice. Mel was in the process of setting up a peer support group for dyslexic students, backed up by email.

A few months before we met, Mel was re-assessed by an EP. Her earlier Aston University report had been lost, and was in any case some 15 years old. The EP's report was a model of its kind. It explained terminology such as 'standard score' and 'centile' and the significance of the various tests, and included graphical representations of many of the results. The report confirmed Mel's belief, buoyed by her Mensa test, that she had significant strengths and 'a very high level of verbal ability'. It said nothing about learning style, but it did identify her need for support with reading comprehension and spelling and note her lack of confidence about producing written work.

Her somewhat dry and occasionally sarcastic tone hid the fact that Mel occasionally had emotional 'crises'. She once had to leave a seminar because she could not cope. Although she did not say she had seen a counsellor, Mel was very self-aware. She knew that if she saw a 'blank expression' on someone's face, this might be because she had 'launch[ed] into the middle' of an idea instead of taking it step by step. But at times she was 'not so tolerant' when ' ... what I perceive as being ignored, overlooked or talked down – I get very cross very quickly, defensive I think'.

Mel sums up her hopes for the future, for which she continues to campaign, like this:

> If you're going to teach everybody, right-brained and left-brained, a sort of approach that you call on all the senses, make it multi-media, is that something that works exclusively, just for dyslexics? Or isn't it a thing which everybody does better with? So in a way, if you dealt with that, would you be making the issue of being dyslexic almost redundant?

After graduating, Mel remained at Axbridge, delivering sessional learning support to dyslexic undergraduates and administering the peer support system.

References

Albert, W (1995) What is a disability? Posting to dis-forum on Jiscmail.ac.uk (no longer available)

American Psychiatric Association (1994) *Diagnostic and statistical manual of mental disorders* (4th edition). Washington DC, American Psychiatric Association

Andersen, S (1987) The role of cultural assumptions in self-concept development. *Self and identity: psychosocial perspectives* edited by K Yardley and T Honess. Chichester, John Wiley

Anderson, PL and Meier-Hedde, R (2001) Early case reports of dyslexia in the United States and Europe. *Journal of Learning Disabilities* 34 (1): 9-21

Anon. (1980) Dyslexia is not a medical problem. *BMA News Review.* January

Arts Dyslexia Trust (2005) The home of the visual-spatial dyslexic. http://www.rmplc.co.uk/orgs/nellalex/ Accessed 6 March 2005

Atkinson, P and Coffey, A (1997) Analysing documentary realities. *Qualitative research: theory, method and practice* edited by D Silverman. London, Sage

Augur, J (1995) *The book doesn't make sens cens scens sns sense.* London, Whurr

Bakker, D (1976) *Perceptual asymmetries and reading proficiency.* Amsterdam, Paedologisch Institut

Bakker, D (1994) Dyslexia and the ecological brain. *Journal of Clinical and Experimental Neurology* 16(5): 734 – 743

Barnes, C (1996) Theories of disability and the origins of the oppression of disabled people in western society. *Disability and society: emerging issues and insights* edited by L Barton. London, Longman

Barnes, C and Mercer, G (1996) *Exploring the divide: illness and disability.* Leeds, The Disability Press

Barton, D (1991) The social nature of writing. *Writing in the community.* D. Barton and R. Ivanic. London, Sage

Barton, D (1994) *Literacy – an introduction to the ecology of written language.* Oxford, Blackwell

Barton, D and Hamilton, M (1998) *Local literacies.* London, Routledge

Barton, D and Ivanic, R (1991) *Writing in the community.* London, Sage

Barton, L (1988) *The politics of special educational needs.* Lewes, Falmer Press

Barton, L (1996) *Disability and society – emerging issues and insights.* Harlow, Longman

Barton, L and Tomlinson, S (1981) *Special education: policy, practices and social issues.* London, Harper and Row

Bat-Hayim, M (1997) Learning to learn: learning therapy in a college classroom. *Annals of Dyslexia* 47: 203-235

Battle, J (1990) *Self-esteem: the new revolution.* Edmonton, James Battle Associates

Becher, T (1989) *Academic tribes and territories.* Milton Keynes, SRHE and Open University Press

Becker, H (1963) *Outsiders.* New York, Free Press

Beacham, N and Szumko, J (2005) *DyslexSim.* University of Loughborough

Benson N, Gurney S, Harrison J, Rimmershaw R (1994) The place of academic writing in whole life writing. *Worlds of literacy* edited by D Barton, M Hamilton, R Ivanic. Clevedon, Multilingual Matters

Berlin, R (1887) *Eine besondere Art der Wortblindheit (Dyslexie).* Wiesbaden, J F Bergmann

Berne, E (1972) *What do you say after you say hello?* New York, Grove Press

Bertaux, D ed (1981) *Biography and society – the life history approach in the social sciences.* Beverley Hills, Sage

Bines, H (1988) Equality, community and individualism: the development and implementation of the 'whole school approach' to special educational needs. *The politics of special educational needs* edited by L Barton. Lewes, Falmer Press

Blackburn, S (1996).*The Oxford dictionary of philosophy.* Oxford, Oxford University Press

Bornat, J ed (1994). *Reminiscence reviewed.* Buckingham, Open University Press

Bowlby, J (1980) *Attachment and loss: loss, sadness and depression.* New York, Basic Books

Briggs, C (1986) *Learning how to ask: a sociolinguistic appraisal of the role of the interview in social science research.* Cambridge, Cambridge University Press

British Dyslexia Association (2002) Dyslexia research information. http://www.bda-dyslexia. org.uk/d07xtra/x02stats.htm Accessed 4/4/02

Brodkey, L (1987) *Academic writing as social practice.* Philadelphia, Temple University Press

Brooks, P and Weeks, S (1999) Individual styles in learning to spell: improving spelling in children with literacy difficulties and all children in mainstream schools. http://www.dfes.gov.uk/research/data/uploadfiles/RR108.doc Accessed 10/9/00

Broomfield, H and Combley, M (1997) *Overcoming dyslexia: a practical handbook for the classroom.* London, Whurr

Bruner, J (1990) *Acts of meaning.* Cambridge, Mass., Harvard University Press

Bryan, T (1986) Personality and situational factors in learning disabilities. *Dyslexia: Its neuropsychology and treatment* edited by GT Pavlidis and D Fisher. New York, John Wiley

Burka, A (1983) The emotional reality of a learning disability. *Annals of Dyslexia* 33: 289-302

Burns, R (1979) *The self-concept: theory, measurement, development and behaviour.* London, Longman

Butkowsky, I S and Willows, D M (1980) Cognitive-motivational characteristics of children varying in reading ability: evidence for learned helplessness in poor readers. *Journal of Educational Psychology* 72(3): 408 – 422

Buzan, T and Buzan, B (1995) *The mind map book.* London, BBC Books

Cairns, T and Moss, W (1995) *Students with specific learning difficulties/dyslexia in higher education.* London, Goldsmiths College, University of London

Citro, TA ed (2001) *Transitional skills for post-secondary success: reflections for high school students with learning disabilities.* Weston, MA, Learning Disabilities Association of Massachusetts

Clark, R (1992) Principles and practice of CLA in the classroom. *Critical language awareness* edited by N Fairclough. London, Longman

Clark, R and Ivanic, R (1997) *The politics of writing.* London, Routledge

Cohen, J (1986) Learning disabilities and psychological development in childhood and adolescence. *Annals of Dyslexia* 36, 287-300

Cohen, L and Manion, L (1989) *Research methods in education.* London, Routledge

Coles, GS (1987).*The learning mystique.* New York, Pantheon books

Coles, GS (1989) Excerpts from 'The learning mystique : a critical look at learning disabilities'. *Journal of Learning Disabilities* 22(5): 267 – 277

Coltheart, M, Sartori, G and Job, R eds (1987) *The cognitive neuropsychology of language.* London, Lawrence Erlbaum Associates

Congdon, P (1989) *Dyslexia: a pattern of strengths and weaknesses.* Solihull, Gifted Children's Information Centre

Coopersmith, S (1967).*The antecedents of self-esteem.* San Francisco, Freeman

Coopersmith, S (1981) *Self-esteem inventories.* New York, Consulting Psychologists' Press

Corbett, J (1998) *Special educational needs in the twentieth century.* London, Cassell

Cornwall, K, Hedderly, R and Pumfrey, P (1983) Specific Learning Difficulties: the 'specific reading difficulties' versus dyslexia controversy resolved? *British Psychological Society Occasional Papers* 7(3)

Cottrell, S (1999) *The study skills handbook.* Basingstoke, Macmillan

Cottrell, S (2001) Developing positive learning environments for dyslexic students in higher education. *Dyslexia and effective learning in secondary and tertiary education* edited by M Hunter-Carsch and M Herrington. London, Whurr

Cowan, J (1998) *On becoming an innovative university teacher.* Buckingham, SRHE and Open University Press

Cowen, S (1988) Coping strategies of university studies with learning disabilities. *Journal of Learning Disabilities* 21(3): 161-164, 188

Craib, I (1998) *Experiencing identity.* London, Sage

Creme, P and Lea, M (1997) *Writing at University: a guide for students.* Buckingham, Open University Press

Critchley, M (1970) *The dyslexic child.* London, Heinemann

Crystal, D (1997) *The Cambridge encyclopaedia of language.* Cambridge, Cambridge University Press

Dale, F (1976) If you knew Susie. *Dyslexia Review* (16): 13-15

Davis, R (1995) *The gift of dyslexia.* London, Souvenir Press

Davis, R (2001) Dyslexia the gift. http://www.dyslexia.com/ Accessed 10/6/01

Dearing, RC (1997) *Higher education in the learning society.* Report of the Committee of Inquiry into Higher Education. London, DfEE

Denzin, N (1989) *Interpretive interactionism.* London, Sage

Deurzen-Smith, E van (1988) *Existential counselling in practice.* London, Sage

DfE (1994) *Code of Practice for the identification and assessment of special educational needs.* London, Department for Education

DfES (1999) Statistics of Education – student support in England and Wales 1998/99. http://www.dfes.gov.uk/index.htm Accessed 25/10/01

DfES (2004) *Bridging the gap.* London, DfES

DfES (2002) Second Chances: Access to Higher Education Courses. http://www.dfee.gov.uk/secondchances/Chapter14_2_ba.html Accessed 1/4/02

Dockrell, J and McShane, J (1992) *Children's learning difficulties: a cognitive approach.* Oxford, Blackwell

Downey, J (1996) Psychological counselling of children and young people. *Handbook of psychological counselling* edited by R Wolfe and W Dryden London, Sage

Downing, J and Thackray, D (1972) An appraisal of reading readiness. *The reading curriculum* edited by A Melnik and J Merritt. London, University of London Press

Doyle, J (1996) *Dyslexia: an introductory guide.* London, Whurr

Dunn, R and Dunn, K (1978) *Teaching students through their individual learning styles: a practical approach.* Reston, VA, Prentice Hall

Dyslexia Institute (2005) The Dyslexia Institute. www.dyslexia-inst.org.uk/ Accessed 6/3/05

Earwaker, J (1992) *Helping and supporting students.* Milton Keynes, Open University Press

Edgar, E and Hayden, AH (1984). Who are the children special education should serve and how many children are there? *Learning Disabilities Quarterly* 7, 363-368

Edwards, B (1993) *Drawing on the right side of the brain.* London, Harper Collins

Edwards, J (1994) *The scars of dyslexia.* London, Cassell

Entwistle, N (1988) *Styles of learning and teaching.* London, David Fulton

Erikson, E (1950) *Childhood and society.* New York, WW Norton

Erikson, E (1968) *Identity – youth and crisis.* London, Faber and Faber

Evans, BJW (1997) Coloured filters and dyslexia: what's in a name? *Dyslexia Review* 9(2): 18 -19

Ewart, J (2001) Why mainstream schools may not be the answer for your dyslexic child. http://www.northeasemanor.e-sussex.sch.uk/dyslexia/provision.html Accessed 13/8/02

Fairclough, N (1989) *Language and power.* London, Longman

Fairclough, N (1992a) *Critical language awareness.* London, Longman

Fairclough, N (1992b) *Discourse and social change.* Cambridge, Polity Press

Fawcett, A and Reid, G (eds) (2004) *Dyslexia in context.* London, Whurr

Fieldhouse, R (1996) *A history of modern British adult education.* Leicester, NIACE

Fink, R (1998) Literacy development in successful men and women with dyslexia. *Annals of Dyslexia* 48: 311-346

Fish, J (1985) *Community, co-operation, co-partnership. International congress on special education,* Nottingham

Fisher, V (1974) Editorial. *Dyslexia Review*(12): 1

Fletcher, J M, Shaywitz, S E, Shankweiler, D P, Katz, L, Liberman, I Y, Stuebing, K K, Francis, D J, Fowler, A E and Shaywitz, B A (1994) Cognitive profiles of reading disability: comparisons of discrepancy and low achievement definitions. *Journal of Educational Psychology* 86 (1), 6 – 23

Fletcher, J M, Coulter, W A, Reschly, D J and Vaughn, S (2004) Alternative approaches to the definition and identification of learning disabilities: some questions and answers. *Annals of Dyslexia* 54, 2, 304-331

Foucault, M (1976) *Mental illness and psychology.* New York, Harper and Row

Franklin, A and Naidoo, S (1970) *Assessment and teaching of dyslexic children.* London, Invalid Children's Aid Association

Franklin, BM (ed) (1987) *Learning disability: dissenting essays.* Philadelphia, Falmer Press

Freud, S (1953-74) *The standard edition of the complete psychological works of Sigmund Freud.* London, Hogarth Press

Frith, U (1997) Brain, mind and behaviour in dyslexia. *Dyslexia: biology, cognition and intervention* edited by C Hulme and M Snowling. London, Whurr

Frith, U (1999) Paradoxes in the definition of dyslexia. *Dyslexia* 5(4): 192-214

Fry H, Ketteridge S and Marshall S (1999) *A handbook for teaching and learning in higher education.* London, Kogan Page

Galaburda, A (1989) Ordinary and extraordinary brain development: anatomical variation in developmental dyslexia. *Annals of Dyslexia* 39: 67-79

Galaburda, A (1999) Developmental dyslexia: a multilevel syndrome. *Dyslexia* 5(4): 183-191

Gardner, H (1987) The theory of multiple intelligences. *Annals of Dyslexia* 37: 19-35

Gardner, H (1993) *Frames of mind.* London, Fontana

Gee, JP (1990) Social linguistics and literacies: ideology in discourses. Basingstoke, Falmer. Cited in Boughey, C (2002). 'Naming' students' problems: an analysis of language-related discourses at a South African university. *Teaching in Higher Education* 7(3): 295-307

Gerber, P, Ginsberg, R and Reiff, HB (1992) Identifying alterable patterns in employment success for highly successful adults with learning disabilities. *Journal of learning disabilities* 25(8): 475-487

Gerber, P, Reiff, HB and Ginsberg, R (1996) Reframing the learning disabilities experience. *Journal of learning disabilities* 29(1): 98-101, 97

Gergen, K (1999) *An invitation to social construction.* London, Sage

Giddens, A (1991) *Modernity and self-identity.* Cambridge, Polity Press

Gillingham, A and Stillman, B (1956) *Remedial training for children with specific disability in reading, spelling and penmanship.* Published privately

Gilroy, D (1991) *Dyslexia and higher education.* Bangor, University College North Wales

Gilroy, D (1995) Stress factors in the college student. *Dyslexia and stress.* T. Miles and V. Varma. London, Whurr

Gilroy, D and Miles, T (1996) *Dyslexia at college.* London, Routledge

Given, BK and Reid, G (1999) *Learning styles: a guide for teachers and parents.* St Anne's-on-Sea, Lancashire, Red Rose Publications

Goffman, E (1959) *The presentation of self in everyday life.* Harmondsworth, Penguin

Goodwin, V (1996) *Counselling of dyslexic students in H.E.* Dyslexia in higher education – practical responses to student and institutional needs, University of Huddersfield, Skill and University of Huddersfield

Goodwin, V (1998) *Person-centred counselling for the dyslexic student.* Dyslexia in higher education: learning along the continuum, Plymouth, University of Plymouth

Goodwin, V and Thomson, B (1991) *Adult students and dyslexia.* Milton Keynes, Open University

Hales, G ed (1994) *Dyslexia matters.* London, Whurr

Hall, S. and du Gay, P (1996) *Questions of cultural identity.* London, Sage

Hamilton, M (1996) *Literacy and adult basic education. A history of modern British adult education* edited by R Fieldhouse. Leicester, NIACE

Hamilton, M, Barton, D and Ivanic, R (1994) *Worlds of literacy.* Clevedon, Multilingual Matters

Hampshire, S (1981) *Susan's story.* London, Sphere

Hannon, P (2000) *Reflecting on literacy in education.* London, Routledge/Falmer

HEFCE (1995) *Access to Higher Education: students with special needs.* Report on the 1993-1995 special initiative to encourage widening participation for students with special needs. Bristol, Higher Education Funding Council

HEQC (1996) *What are graduates? Clarifying the attributes of graduateness – a paper to stimulate discussion.* London, Higher Education Quality Council

Herrington, M and Hunter-Carsch, M (2001) A social-interactive model of specific learning difficulties, e.g. dyslexia. *Dyslexia, a psychosocial perspective* edited by M Herrington and M Hunter-Carsch. London, Whurr

Herrington, M (2001a) Dyslexia: the continuing exploration. Insights for literacy educators. *RaPAL Bulletin* 45: 10-25

Herrington, M (2001b) An approach to specialist learning support in higher education. *Dyslexia and effective learning in secondary and tertiary education* edited by M Herrington and M Hunter-Carsch. London, Whurr

HESA (Higher Education Statistics Agency) (1997) *Data Report: Students in Higher Education Institutions.* Cheltenham, HESA

Hetherington, J (1996) Approaches to the development of self-esteem in dyslexic students. *Conference Proceedings: Dyslexic Students in Higher education, Practical Responses to Student and Institutional Needs.* SKILL/University of Huddersfield (57-61)

Hickey, K (1977) *Dyslexia. A language training course for teachers and learners.* Bath, Better Books

HMSO (1970) *Chronically Sick and Disabled Persons Act.* London, HMSO

HMSO (1981) *Education Act 1981*. London, HMSO

HMSO (1992) *Further and Higher Education Act*. London, HMSO

HMSO (1993) *Education Act 1993*. London, HMSO

HMSO (1995) *Disability Discrimination Act*. London, HMSO

HMSO (1996) *Education Act 1996*. London, HMSO

HMSO (2001) *Special Educational Needs and Disability Act* (Part Four of the Disability Dis-crimination Act). London, HMSO

Hornsby, B (1984) *Overcoming dyslexia*. London, Martin Dunitz

Hornsby, B (2000) Personal communication

Hornsby, B and Shear, F (1975) *Alpha to omega – the A-Z of teaching reading, writing and spelling*. London, Heinemann

Hornsby, B and Miles, T R (1980) The effects of a dyslexia-centred teaching programme. *British Journal of Educational Psychology* 50: 236 – 242

Humphrey, N (2002) Teacher and pupil ratings of self-esteem in developmental dyslexia. *British Journal of Special Education* 29 (1): 29-35

Hunter-Carsch, M ed (2001) *Dyslexia: a psychosocial perspective*. London, Whurr

Hunter-Carsch, M and Herrington, M eds (2001) *Dyslexia and effective learning in secondary and tertiary education*. London, Whurr

Hurst, A (1996) Reflecting on researching disability and higher education. *Disability and society* edited by L Barton. London, Longman

Hynd, GW (1983) *Dyslexia: neuropsychological theory, research, and clinical differentiation*. Boston MA, Allyn and Bacon

Ivanic, R (1998) *Writing and identity*. Amsterdam, John Benjamins

Ivanic, R and Simpson, J (1992) Who's who in academic writing? *Critical language awareness* edited by N Fairclough. London, Longman

Jary, D and Parker, M eds (1998) *The new higher education*. Stoke-on-Trent, Staffordshire University Press

Jastak, JF and Jastak, S (1978) *Wide Range Achievement Test*. Wilmington, DE. Jastak Associates Inc

Kahn, M (1991) *Between therapist and client: the new relationship*. New York, W H Freeman

Kavale, KA and Forness, SR (2000) What definitions of learning disability say and don't say. *Journal of Learning Disabilities* 33(3): 239-256

Keim, J, Ryan, AG and Nolan, BF (1998) Dilemmas faced when working with learning disabilities in post-secondary education. *Annals of Dyslexia* 48: 273-292

Kelly, GA (1955) *The psychology of personal constructs*. New York, WW Norton

Kerr, H (2001) Dyslexia and adult literacy: does dyslexia disempower? *Powerful literacies* edited by J Crowther, M Hamilton, L Tett. Leicester, NIACE

Kershaw, J (1974) *People with dyslexia*. London, British Council for Rehabilitation of the Disabled

Kirschenbaum, H and Henderson, V eds (1990) *The Carl Rogers reader*. London, Constable

Klein, C (1993) *Diagnosing dyslexia*. London, ALBSU

Klein, M (1993) *Collected works Vol III: envy, gratitude and other works*. London, Karnac Books.

Krupska, M and Klein, C (1995). *Demystifying dyslexia*. London Language and Literacy Unit

Kurnoff, S (2000) *The human side of dyslexia*. Monterey, CA, London Universal Publishing

Kussmaul, A (1878) Word-deafness and word-blindness. *Cyclopaedia of the practice of medicine, Vol. 14 diseases of the nervous system and disturbances of speech* edited by H von Ziemssen. London, Sampson Row, Maston, Searle and Rivington

Lalljee, M (1996) The interpreting self: an experimentalist perspective. *Understanding the self* edited by R Stevens. London, Sage

Lamm, O and Epstein, R (1992) Specific reading impairments – are they to be associated with emotional difficulties? *Journal of Learning Disabilities* 25(9): 605-615

Lawrence, D (1996) *Enhancing self-esteem in the classroom*. London, Paul Chapman

Laycock, D (1999) DSA statistics, 1992-1997. dis-forum@mailbase.ac.uk. Accessed 6/5/99

Laycock, D (2001) Personal communication

Lea, M and Stierer, B (2000) *Student writing in higher education*. Buckingham, Open University Press

Lea, M and Street, B (2000) Student writing and staff feedback in higher education: an academic literacies approach. *Student writing in higher education* edited by M Lea and B Stierer. Buckingham, Open University Press

Linde, C (1993) *Life stories*. Oxford University Press

Little, S (1993) 'Nonverbal learning disabilities and socioemotional functioning: a review of recent literature.' *Journal of Learning Disabilities* 26(10): 653-665

Lloyd, J (2005) Learning disabilities. http://curry.edschool.virginia.edu/sped/projects/ose/categories/ld.html (accessed 22 March 2005)

Maag, J and Behrens, J (1989) Depression and cognitive self-statements of learning disabled and seriously emotionally disturbed adolescents. *Journal of Special Education* 23(1): 17-27

Markus, H and Nurius, P (1987) Possible selves: the interface between motivation and the self-concept. *Self and identity: psychosocial perspectives* edited by K Yardley and T Honess. Chichester, John Wiley

Marsh, H (1992) Content specificity of relations between academic achievement and academic self-concept. *Journal of Educational Psychology* 84(1): 35-42

Mason, J (1996) *Qualitative researching*. London, Sage

McLeod, J (1998) *An introduction to counselling*. Buckingham, Open University Press

McLoughlin, D, Fitzgibbon, G and Young, V (1994) *Adult dyslexia: assessment, counselling and training*. London, Whurr

Mcloughlin D, Leather, C and Stringer, P (2002) *The adult dyslexic: interventions and outcomes*. London, Whurr

Mead, M (1934) *Mind, self and society*. Chicago, University of Chicago Press

Meares, O (1980) Figure/ground brightness contrast and reading disabilities. *Visible Language* 14: 13-29.

Mearns, D (1994) *Developing person-centred counselling*. London, Sage

Michaels, C and Lewandowski, L (1990) Psychological adjustment and family functioning of boys with learning disabilities. *Journal of Learning Disabilities* 23(7): 446-450

Miles, M and Huberman, A (1994) *Qualitative data analysis*. London, Sage

Miles, T (1962) *A suggested method of treatment for specific dyslexia. Word blindness or specific developmental dyslexia?* St Bartholomew's Hospital, London, Pitman Medical

Miles, T (1970) *On helping the dyslexic child*. London, Methuen

Miles, T (1982) *The Bangor Dyslexia Test*. Wisbech, Learning Development Aids

Miles, T (1988) Counselling in dyslexia. *Counselling Psychology Quarterly* 1(1): 97-107

Miles, T (1993) *Dyslexia: the pattern of difficulties*. London, Whurr

Miles, T (1994) A proposed taxonomy and some consequences. *Dyslexia in children – multi-disciplinary perspectives* edited by A Fawcett and R Nicolson. London, Harvester Wheatsheaf

Miles, T and Gilroy, D (1986) *Dyslexia at college*. London, Methuen

Miles, T and Miles, E (1975) *More help for dyslexic children*. London, Methuen

Miles, T and Miles, E (1999) *Dyslexia a hundred years on (second edition)*. Buckingham, Open University Press

Miles, T and Varma, V eds (1995) *Dyslexia and stress*. London, Whurr

Morgan, E and Klein, C (2000) *The dyslexic adult in a non-dyslexic world*. London, Whurr

Morgan, E (2003) The dyslexic adult in a non-dyslexic institution: making HE more dyslexia-friendly. *Supporting the dyslexic student in HE and FE: strategies for success. Proceedings of a one-day conference* edited by D Pollak. De Montfort University and University of Hull

Morgan, W Pringle (1896) A case of congenital word blindness. *British Medical Journal* 2: 1378.

Naidoo, S (1972) *Specific dyslexia.* London, Pitman

Newton, M and Thomson, M (1974) *Dyslexia: a guide to teaching.* Birmingham, University of Aston

Nicolson, RI and Fawcett, AJ (1990) Automaticity: a new framework for dyslexia research? *Cognition* 35: 159 – 182

Nicolson, RI and Fawcett, AJ (1994) Comparison of deficits in cognitive and motor skills among children with dyslexia. *Annals of Dyslexia* 44: 147-164

Oliver, M (1988) *The social and political context of educational policy: the case of special needs. The politics of special educational needs.* L. Barton. Lewes, Falmer Press

Oliver, M (1996) A sociology of disability or a disablist sociology? *Disability and society: emerging issues and insights.* L. Barton. London, Longman

Oppenheim, AN (1992) *Questionnaire design, interviewing and attitude measurement.* London, Pinter

Orton, C (1994) The 1993 Education Act. *Dyslexia Contact* 13(2): 8-9

Orton, S (1925) Word-blindness in school-children. *Arch. neur. psych.*(14): 581-615

Orton, S (1928) Specific reading disability – strephosymbolia. *Journal of the American Medical Association* 90: 1095-1099

Osmond, J (1993) *The reality of dyslexia.* London, Cassell

Ott, P (1997) *How to detect and manage dyslexia.* Oxford, Heinemann

Parkes, C (1972) *Bereavement: studies of grief in adult life.* New York, International University Press

Pask, G (1976) Styles and strategies of learning. *British Journal of Educational Psychology* 46, 128-148

Pavlidis, GT and Fisher, DF (1986) *Dyslexia: its neuropsychology and treatment.* Chichester, John Wiley

Peelo, M (1994) *Helping students with study problems.* Milton Keynes, Open University Press

Peelo, M (2000a) Learning support in Universities: counselling or teaching? *Newsletter and Journal of the Association of University and College Counsellors*(4)

Peelo, M (2000b) Learning reality: inner and outer journeys. *Changes* 18(2): 118-127

Pillai, M (2003) Developing positive learning environments and facilitating help-seeking. *Supporting the dyslexic student in HE and FE: strategies for success. Proceedings of a one-day conference* edited by D Pollak. De Montfort University and University of Hull

Pinker, S (1997) *How the mind works.* London, Penguin

Pisha, B and Ruzic, R (2001) Learning from a learning disability: what an educational researcher has learned from his own educational experiences. *Transitional skills for post-secondary success: reflections for high school students with learning disabilities* edited by TA Citro and MA Weston. Learning Disabilities Association of Massachusetts

Plowden, B ed (1967) *Children and their primary schools.* London, HMSO

Plummer, K (1983) *Documents of life.* London, Unwin Hyman

Plummer, K (2001) *Documents of life 2: an invitation to a critical humanism.* London, Sage

Pollak, D (1975) Some aspects of dyslexia in children. Unpublished PGCE project, School of Education, University of Sussex

Pollak, D (1993) Increasing staff awareness of the effect of social and emotional factors on the learning of pupils at a special school for children with specific learning difficulties. Unpublished MA, Institute of Continuing and Professional Education, University of Sussex

Pollak, D (1999) Dyslexia and identity: some experiences of undergraduates who are dyslexic. *Dyslexic learners: a holistic approach to support* edited by D Pollak. Leicester, De Montfort University

Pollak, D (2001a) Access to higher education for the mature dyslexic student: a question of identity and a new perspective. *Dyslexia: at the dawn of the new century.* University of York, British Dyslexia Association.

Pollak, D (2001b) Students' images of their specific learning difficulties: the influence of such images on the routes to University of students labelled dyslexic. *Dyslexia: at the dawn of the new century.* University of York, British Dyslexia Association

Pollak, D (ed) (2003) *Supporting the dyslexic student in HE and FE: strategies for success.* De Montfort University and University of Hull

Pollak, D (2004) Self-esteem issues for dyslexic students in higher education. *Dyslexia: the dividends from research to policy and practice.* University of Warwick, British Dyslexia Association

Pollock, J and Waller, E (1994) *Day-to-day dyslexia in the classroom.* London, Routledge

Preece, J, Weatherald, C. and Woodrow, M (1998) *Beyond the boundaries – exploring the potential of widening participation in higher education.* Leicester, NIACE

Pumfrey, P (2001) Specific developmental dyslexia (SDD): 'Basics to back' in 2000 and beyond? *Dyslexia: a psychosocial perspective.* M. Hunter-Carsch. London, Whurr

Pumfrey, P and Reason, R (1991) *Specific learning difficulties (dyslexia) – challenges and responses.* Windsor, NFER-Nelson

Raaheim, K, Wankowski, J and Radford, J (1991) *Helping students to learn.* Buckingham, Open University Press

Radnor, Lord (2000) Personal communication

Ramsden, P and Entwistle, N (1981) Effects of academic department on students' approach to studying. *British Journal of Educational Psychology*(51): 368-383

Rana, R, Smith, E and Walkling, J (1999) *The impact of increasing levels of psychological disturbance amongst students in higher education.* London, Heads of University Counselling Services Working Group

Ravenette, T (1979) Specific reading difficulties: appearance and reality. *Association of Educational Psychologists Journal* 4(10): 1-12

Rawson, M (1988) *The many faces of dyslexia.* Towson, MD, Orton Dyslexia Society

Rawson, M (1995) *Dyslexia over the lifespan: a fifty-five year longitudinal study.* Cambridge, Mass, Educators Publishing Service, Inc

Reber, A (1985) *The Penguin dictionary of psychology.* London, Penguin

Reid, G (1996a) *A definition of dyslexia.* Edinburgh, Moray House Centre for the Study of Dyslexia

Reid, G (1996b) *The 'other side' of dyslexia. Dimensions of dyslexia Volume Two.* G. Reid (ed) Edinburgh, Moray House.

Reid, G ed (1996c) *Dimensions of dyslexia Volume One.* Edinburgh, Moray House

Reid, G and Kirk, J (2001) *Dyslexia in adults: education and employment.* Chichester, John Wiley

Reid Lyon, G (1995) Toward a definition of dyslexia. *Annals of Dyslexia* 45: 3-30

Rice, M and Brooks, G (2004) *Developmental dyslexia in adults: a research review.* London, National Research and Development Centre for adult literacy and numeracy.

Richards, T and Richards, L (1996) *NUD.IST (Non-numerical Unstructured Data Indexing Searching and Theorising) version 4.* Victoria, Australia, QSR Pty Ltd

Rickinson, B (1998) The relationship between undergraduate student counselling and successful degree completion. *Studies in Higher Education* 23(1): 95-102

Riddell, S (1996) Theorising special educational needs in a changing political climate. *Disability and Society* edited by L Barton. Harlow, Longman

Riddick, B (1995) Dyslexia: dispelling the myths. *Disability and Society* 10(4)

Riddick, B (1996) *Living with dyslexia*. London, Routledge

Riddick B, Farmer M and Sterling C (1997) *Students and dyslexia: growing up with a specific learning difficulty*. London, Whurr

Riding, R and Rayner, S (1998) *Cognitive styles and learning strategies*. London, David Fulton

Robson, C (1993) *Real world research*. Oxford, Blackwell

Rodis P, Garrod A and Boscardin ML (2001) *Learning disabilities and life stories*. Boston, MA, Allyn and Bacon

Rogers, C (1951) *Client centred therapy*. Boston, Houghton Mifflin

Rourke, BP (1988) Socio-emotional disturbances of learning disabled children. *Journal of Consulting and Clinical Psychology* 56(6): 801-810

Rourke, BP, Young, GC and Leenaars, AA (1989) A childhood learning disability that predisposes those afflicted to adolescent and adult depression and suicide risk. *Journal of Learning Disabilities* 22(3): 169-175

Sagmiller, G (2002) Dyslexia, my life. http://www.dyslexiamylife.org/wb_dyslexia.htm Accessed 4/4/02

Salzberger-Wittenberg, I, Henry, G and Osborne, E (1983) *The emotional experience of learning and teaching*. London, Routledge and Kegan Paul

Sanderson, A and Pillai, M (2001) *The lottery of learning support in higher education*. BDA 5th International Conference, University of York, BDA

Sartre, J.-P (1948) *Existentialism and humanism*. London, Methuen

Saunders, W and Barker, M (1972) Dyslexia as a cause of psychiatric disorder in adults. *British Medical Journal* 4: 759-761

Schunk, D (1990) Self-concept and school achievement. *The social psychology of the primary school* edited by C Rogers and P Kutnick. London, Routledge

Scott, A (1991) *1966-1991*. Reading, British Dyslexia Association

Seymour, P (1986). *Cognitive analysis of dyslexia*. London, Routledge and Kegan Paul

Sigmon, SN (1989) Reaction to the excerpts from 'The Learning Mystique:' a rational appeal for change. *Journal of Learning Disabilities* 22(5): 298 – 300, 327

Simpson, E (1981) *Reversals*. London, Gollancz

Singer, J (1993) Experimental studies of ongoing conscious experience. *Experimental and theoretical studies of consciousness* edited by G Bock and J Marsh. Chichester, John Wiley

Singleton, C ed (1999) *Dyslexia in higher education: policy, provision and practice*. Report of the National Working Party on Dyslexia in Higher Education. University of Hull

Singleton, C (2000) Recent developments in the identification of dyslexia. Lecture, De Montfort University, 15 September

Singleton, C and Aisbitt, J (2001) A follow-up of the National Working Party survey of dyslexia provision in UK universities. Fifth BDA International Conference, University of York, BDA

Singleton C, Pumfrey P, Stacey G and Gibberd D (2001) Dyslexia in Higher Education: a review of progress in the UK. Fifth BDA International Conference, University of York

Snowling, M (1985) *Children's written language difficulties*. Windsor, NFER-Nelson

Snowling, M (2000) *Dyslexia*. Oxford, Blackwell

Springer, SP and Deutsch, G (1998) *Left brain, right brain*. New York, WH Freeman

Stacey, G (1994) My brain is wired differently. *Dyslexia Contact* 13(2): 18-19

Stanovich, KE (1982) Individual differences in the cognitive processes of reading. *Journal of Learning Disabilities* 15: 435-493

Stanovich, KE (1986) Matthew effects in reading: some consequences of individual differences in the acquisition of literacy. *Reading Research Quarterly* 21(4): 360 – 407

Stanovich, KE (1991) The theoretical and practical consequences of discrepancy definitions of dyslexia. *Dyslexia: integrating theory and practice* edited by M Snowling and M Thomson. London, Whurr

Stanovich, KE and Stanovich, PJ (1997) Further thoughts on aptitude/achievement discrepancy. *Educational Psychology in Practice* 13(1): 3 – 8

Stein, J (2000) The physical causes of dyslexia. *Teaching and supporting students with dyslexia in FE colleges*. Birmingham, Network Training

Stephens, C (1996) *Dyslexic Students in Higher Education: practical responses to student and institutional needs*. Huddersfield, University of Huddersfield

Stevens, R ed (1996a) *Understanding the self*. London, Sage

Stevens, R (1996b) The reflexive self: an experiential perspective. *Understanding the self* edited by R Stevens. London, Sage

Stewart, I and Joines, V (1987) *T.A. today*. Kegworth, Lifespace

Street, B (1984) *Literacy in theory and practice*. Cambridge, Cambridge University Press

Street, J and Street, B (1991) The schooling of literacy. *Writing in the community*. D. Barton and R. Ivanic. London, Sage

Strydom, J and du Plessis, S (2000) The right to read. http://www.audiblox2000.com/book.htm (accessed 22/3/2005)

Stuart, M and Thomson, A eds (1995) *Engaging with difference: the 'other' in education*. Leicester, NIACE

Summerfield, P (1998) *Reconstructing women's wartime lives*. Manchester, Manchester University Press

Summerfield, P (1999) The production and performance of memory. Lecture, University of Lancaster, 15th June

Swanson, HL and Trahan, M (1996) Learning disabled and average readers' working memory and comprehension: does metacognition play a role? *British Journal of Educational Psychology* 66, 333-355

Temple, C (1993) *The brain*. London, Penguin

Thomas, K (1996) The defensive self: a psychodynamic perspective. *Understanding the self* edited by R Stevens. London, Sage

Thomson, A (1994) *Anzac memories*. Melbourne, Oxford University Press

Thomson, M (2001) *The psychology of dyslexia*. London, Whurr

Tizard, J ed (1972) *Children with specific reading difficulties* (Report of the Advisory Committee on Handicapped Children). London, HMSO

Toates, F (1996) The embodied self: a biological perspective. *Understanding the self* edited by R Stevens. London, Sage

Tomlinson, S (1982) *A sociology of special education*. London, Routledge and Kegan Paul

Tropp, A (1974) The dyslexia controversy. *Dyslexia Review* (11): 5 – 9

Turner, M (1997) *Psychological assessment of dyslexia*. London, Whurr

Vail, P (2001) Treating the whole person: emotion, denial, disguises, language and connectedness. A Fawcett, *Dyslexia: theory and good practice*. London, Whurr

Vernon, M (1975) The Bullock Report. *Dyslexia Review* (13): 8 – 11

Vinegrad, M (1994) A revised adult dyslexia checklist. *Educare* (48): 21-23

Vygotsky, L (1962) *Thought and language*. Cambridge, Mass., MIT Press and Wiley

Wales, A (1982) Dyslexia: a miswiring of the actual basic structure of the brain? *Current research into specific learning difficulties: neurological aspects*. Reading, Berkshire and Oxfordshire Dyslexia Associations

Warnock, HM (1978) *Special Educational Needs*. London, Dept of Education and Science

Warnock, Baroness M (2000) Personal communication

Waterfield, J ed (1996) *Dyslexia in higher education: Learning along the continuum*. Dartington, University of Plymouth

Webster, R (1995) *Why Freud was wrong*. London, Harper Collins

Wechsler, D (1981) *Wechsler Adult Intelligence Scale – Revised*. New York, Harcourt Brace Jovanovich/Psychological Corporation

West, L (1994) Whose story, whose terms? Some problems of reflectivity in life history research. *Life Histories and Learning*. University of Sussex

West, T (1991) *In the mind's eye*. New York, Prometheus Books

West, T (2nd ed. 1997) *In the mind's eye*. New York, Prometheus Books

Wetherell, M and Maybin, J (1996) The distributed self: a social constructionist perspective. *Understanding the self* edited by R Stevens. London, Sage

Williams, L (1983) *Teaching for the two-sided mind*. New York, Simon and Schuster, Inc

Williams, K (1989) *Study Skills*. Basingstoke, Macmillan

Wilson, A (1999) Reading a library – writing a book: the significance of literacies for the prison community. Unpublished PhD thesis, University of Lancaster

Winter, D (1992) *Personal construct psychology in clinical practice*. London, Routledge

Winter, R (2000) Orchestrate cerebral cells. *Times Higher Education Supplement* 24th November, 30-31

Withers, R and Lee, J (1988) Power in disguise. *The politics of special educational needs* edited by L Barton. Lewes, Falmer Press

Wolf, E (1987) Some comments on the selfobject concept. *Self and identity: psychosocial perspectives* edited by K Yardley and T Honess. Chichester, John Wiley

World Federation of Neurology (1968) *Report of Research Group on Dyslexia and World Illiteracy*. Dallas, TX, WFN

Wright-Strawderman, C and Watson, B (1992) The prevalence of depressive symptoms in children with learning disabilities. *Journal of Learning Disabilities* 25(4): 258-264

Yow, V (1994) *Recording oral history*. Thousand Oaks, Sage

Zigmond, N and Thornton, HS (1988) The future of learning disabilities. *Learning disabilities: state of the art and practice* edited by KA Kavale. Boston, MA, College-Hill Press

Index